THE ROVING WRINKLY

THE ROVING WRINKLY

Mary Edmonds

Book Guild Publishing
Sussex, England

First published in Great Britain in 2010 by
The Book Guild Ltd
Pavilion View
19 New Road Brighton,
BN1 1UF

Typesetting in Garamond by Ellipsis Books Ltd, Glasgow

Printed in Great Britain by CPI Antony Rowe

A catalogue record for this book is available from The British Library.

ISBN 978 1 84624 470 4

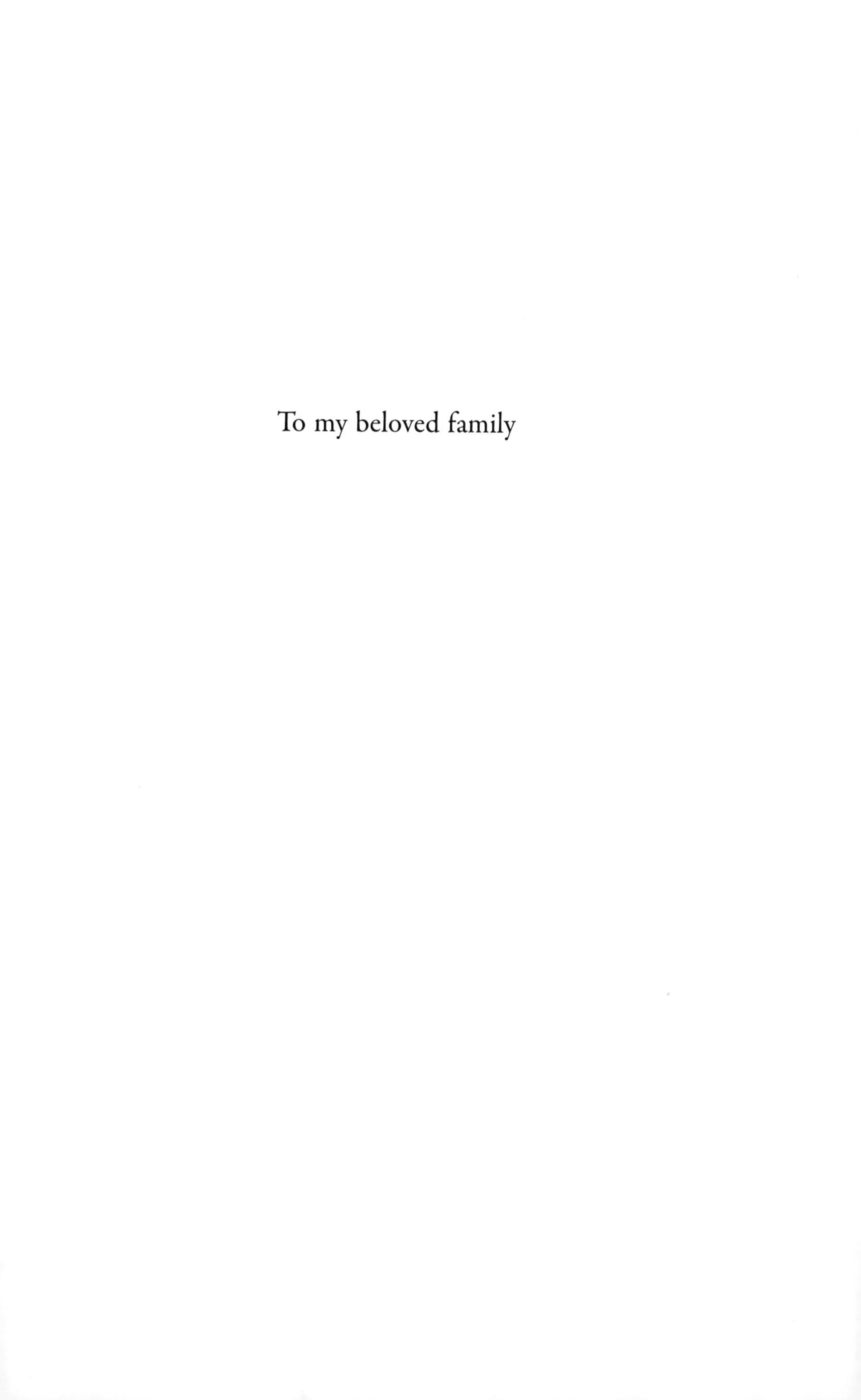

To my beloved family

ACKNOWLEDGEMENTS

A big thank you to those dear friends who encouraged and supported me throughout the long haul of writing this book.

Many thanks to John Deighton and Caspar Hodgson for their initial work on the book cover.

To Book Guild Publishing for making it happen.

INTRODUCTION

In foreign lands everything is delightfully out of doors; in Britain, happiness and comfort are within. The one dazzles the imagination, the other roots itself in every fibre of one's heart.

Mary Eyre, *A Lady Walks the South of France* (1865)

It would not be surprising if an element of unease stirs in the sturdy breasts of potential women travellers as they read of the death of yet another female adventurer. The tragic and horrific list of killings and kidnapping that have befallen British women abroad in recent years – in Africa, India, Southeast Asia and Australasia, as well as now the very real threat of terrorism – would be enough, you would suppose, to deter even the most indomitable women from travelling alone in search of adventure.

The fact is though, that it will not. But why do they do it? Are they all thoughtlessly hell-bent on traipsing an unknown highway of recklessness as far as possible from the comfort and security of their own backyards? I think not. The disincentives for independent female travel – sexual harassment, assault, sickness and, not least the loneliness – will always haunt those without a champion at their side to cheer them on and protect them. But what many women travellers have is a flair for accomplishment, for dealing with the unexpected and for sidestepping the dangerous with particular determination and resilience. The desperately unlucky women who have suffered at the hands of vicious criminals have been the victims of circumstances that could have applied on their own home patch; brutality is not predominantly confined to foreign parts.

There is nothing new about women travelling alone; there are precious few corners of the world that if explored at all, have not been explored by women. Whilst they are aware of dangerous situations, fear of them has not in the past, and will not in the future, extinguish their urge to seek adventure. Women have fought long and hard for recognition of their worth and the right to make choices for themselves. They know they can avoid the trappings of early marriage, cast off the constraints of sheltered family restrictions and put off the commitment to a long and perhaps boring working life, at least for the time being. In the meantime, these resourceful and enterprising travellers concern themselves with the experience of exploring the world and thus exploring the limits of their minds and bodies as they establish an identity and forge their independence.

The Victorian age was the golden time of women travellers. The difference for those brave and feisty ladies was that not only did they have the courage to tackle the globe, they had to defy convention to do it. There was at that time a prevailing notion which implied that you could not be both a real lady and a real traveller, but the evidence of women who travelled alone over 200 years ago and since, dispels that myth.

Reputation has played a large part in the history of travelling women. Travelling alone meant impropriety – being alone with guides and occasionally being obliged to hitch up one's skirt. Sweatiness and hard boots were not the general forte of 'drawing room ladies', but they did it in spite of disagreeable travelling conditions and heavy luggage, and without the benefit of modern medicine and facilities to buffer the exasperation and frustration of moving about in strange lands.

Some of these travels resulted in scenes that few European women of refined and civilised habits ever risked. Ana Jameson, a lady of quality and literary talent if ever there was one, wrote in 1883 that 'it was hard to be elegant and amusing when faced, point blank, with a human and horribly feminine scalp dangling from the belt of a savage'. All the same, the women of the middle nineteenth century were radical souls and many were accomplished travellers, but they were not the first.

Even in earlier times, young women would set out with little more than the proverbial shoestring, looking for ways to travel the wide world which at that time was almost unknown to the majority of people. Some travelled far afield as pilgrims. Their good name was protected by the worthy cause, if not in this world then at least, hopefully, in the next. Others, through family service to the Commonwealth, were less altruistic. The motives of the 'moneyed' ladies of the 17th and 18th centuries were to ostentatiously display their wealth and nobility. They could not be too outlandish however, for fear of tarnishing rather than polishing 'one's quality'. Others travelled precisely to flout social pressures, caring not a fig for reputation. They preferred notoriety to anonymity: anyone could tour, but to *travel* –!

Travelling ensured that feminists of those earlier times could achieve the kudos men enjoyed – the daring, the brave and, for that era, the bizarre. But where should a girl go for her travels? For many intrepid women travelling for the sake of it, Africa was a good place to go. Great chunks of it were comfortably pink on the globe. Once there, their activities ranged, according to Lady Mary Barker in 1877, 'from taking tea with a Kaffir princess to killing a snake in the baby's nursery'.

Mary Ann Parker, widow of a sea captain, travelled to Australasia in the wake of the First Fleet around 1852, three years into the penal settlement in New South Wales. She wrote 'a dreadful mortality had taken place on board most of the transports which had been sent to that country; the poor miserable objects that were landed died in great numbers so that they were soon reduced to at least one-third of those who had quitted England'.

Young Elisa Bradley was shipwrecked and captured by Barbary Arabs in 1818, and Fanny Parker wrote in 1850 that 'roaming about with a good tent and a good Arab one might be happy for ever in India'. The good Arab in Fanny's case was a horse. 'Hunting her food and sleeping wherever she found herself at night' was enough to satisfy Florence Dixie, travelling across Patagonia in 1880.

Neither ill health, deprivation nor foul weather was enough to quench the spirit of these pioneers who demonstrated strength and willpower in their quest for independence and adventure.

Today's women, travelling in their easy-care clothes, would be amused at the advice given to their Victorian sisters. 'Wear as few petticoats as possible, dark woollen stockings in winter and cotton in summer. Shoes, never boots and your gown made neatly and plainly of flannel, without ends or loose drapery, to be ordinary ankle length and a close fitted jacket. Dark grey is suitable, but whatever, should not show mud or dust and also preserve the colour . . . Stays should be worn, not elastic but light ones with few steels . . . If the clothes are at all damp from perspiration they should be carefully turned inside out and dried . . . A broad brimmed hat to relieve the encumbrance of a parasol. Flowers, ribbons and feathers are in the worst possible taste and should be avoided.' Mary Kingsley, who travelled to West Africa around 1897, wrote that 'you have no right to go about in Africa in things you would be ashamed to be seen in at home'. For her, clothes of impeccable propriety were tantamount. Wherever she went on her travels, she presented her neat trim figure in stiff, stayed black silk, black button boots and a black astrakhan hat.

In our new millennium, female travellers are not to be so encumbered, but have been endowed with all the glamour and mettle of their undaunted sisters of the past. An Englishwoman's reputation abroad is still intact. On the whole she is regarded with respect and esteem wherever she goes, and in my own experience, it seems that the older you are the more respect and esteem you are afforded. Even now, although travel is a capricious business, delicious to some and difficult for others, the same unquenchable optimism that has carried women travellers throughout time leads them from one adventure to the next, and there is always a convincing case that the journey must be done.

Part 1

MOLDOVA 1994

1

It seemed to me at the time, back in early 1994, that mine was a convincing case all right. Recently retired, and more dramatically recently widowed, over the months since these events, I had allowed myself to become a miserable mess. Hung up and hungover for much of the time, I was not dealing with my situation very well at all. I needed to get away.

To do alone what we had planned to do as a couple was a daunting prospect even if I had the heart for it at all at the time. To take a joyride round the world for as long as we could afford had been our dream, and there was precious little joy in me after the premature and calamitous end to that venture. In high spirits we had actually started out on our journey, but by the time we reached our halfway destination in Sydney, it was becoming increasingly obvious that all was not well. It was there, in Australia, that our dream ended.

So – what to do? Perhaps I could travel abroad and do something useful as well? Why not? I approached Voluntary Services Overseas, that very prestigious organisation that sends worthy people of any age up to 70 years old to put their various talents and skills to good use in places where they are most needed. Feeling that I could teach English to a brick wall after so many years teaching in English schools, I offered my services. However, they very gently informed me of their policy not to engage the newly bereaved. They were quite right of course.

Bereavement is a horrible state to be in. The desolation and despair of grief generate a flicker of awkwardness all around; it isolates, it is also a perpetual twisting of the guts, and it shows. Familiar sights and sounds become a minefield and the newly bereaved are, of course, particularly sensitive to actual or even imagined slights and feel victims of circumstances beyond their control.

Maybe I did become uncharacteristically brittle for a while. I felt people were moving towards and away from me. I resented what I saw as token gestures, people ringing up to see if it was 'all right' to come round. Of course it was bloody all right! But when they did come, I felt they were only checking progress, and that they wanted with a clear conscience to resume the regularity of their own lives. I bristled at their well-intentioned advice – you are drinking too much, snap out of it, move on, move house, *get normal!* They seemed to be rushing me through the process of grief, and they had no idea. All I wanted was time, however much it would take to adjust, to learn to navigate my own way through uncharted seas of distress. All the same, having made an initial move to do something, I was seriously determined to get away.

I was aware at the time, but admittedly not particularly concerned about the political upheaval taking place in Eastern European countries that had formerly been part of the Soviet bloc. Only when the tragedies of the Romanian orphanage children emerged was the conscience of people raised, and then there was a general call for aid for these luckless kids incarcerated in uncaring places not fit for pigs.

It was around this time also that I heard of an organisation that undertook to escort groups of people prepared to go to Eastern Europe to teach English in previously Russian-dominated schools. I applied to go and was accepted.

I was told I would have to be flexible and adaptable; that I might have to do without life's little luxuries. Conditions would sometimes be quite basic, but I would be housed with a family charged to take good care of me and to keep me fed and watered. OK. Fine. I would do that.

My family were appalled. Knowing my penchant for saying the right thing at the wrong time, or the wrong thing at any time, it took little to convince them that the entire family resources would have to be spent to extricate me from my shackles, anchored to the wall of some prison I was bound to be held in sooner or later.

'I'm teaching,' I patiently explained, 'in a school, with other English people, in Moldova.' 'Moldova? Where's that?' 'I dunno.'

Within a month or so I was on my way. Clutching vast bags of various teaching resources, warm jumpers, clothes I considered at the time to be suitable for anywhere near Russia, I presented myself at the appointed departure point at more or less the appointed time. The Information Sheet informed me that the first stage of the journey would be an interesting and relaxing drive to Lviv, the capital city of Ukraine, taking approximately twenty-four hours, with plenty of comfort stops, a night stop, and then on to Moldova by train. Well, that was all right then. I had no idea where either of these places were; on my somewhat out-of-date map of Europe, Moldova was not even shown, but I thought maybe it was somewhere between Poland and Russia.

Victoria Coach Station on that Sunday evening stank of diesel fuel and gentlemen's lavatories as usual, but it buzzed with so many travellers milling around. Evidently, some were only going to Eastbourne by the look of it. Eastern Europe sounded much more exciting to me.

We found the coach; the Romanian driver looked harassed and irritable, and it took ages to stuff all the luggage into the hold. My beloved family, reluctantly foregoing the thrills of the FA Cup Final to see me off, hovered around the bus, their faces etched with anxiety; they checked my stuff was on board, and waved limply as we finally left, an hour late.

It was a warm night, and less than fifteen minutes into the journey I realised my first mistake. I had chosen my seat carefully, next to a window and near the front. I was joined, however, by a young lady whose overly generous proportions threatened to become an unwelcome invasion of my body space. She was already very hot, and we had a long way to go. She unloaded piles of magazines, tissues, sweets, talcum power and throat spray into the pocket in front of her and another bag of supplies into the locker above. A coat, her slippers and her book went under the seat. She then promptly got started on her sandwiches.

Munching away, she launched into her inquisition. 'Where are you going?' I told her that like everyone else on this trip I was bound for Moldova on a voluntary mission to teach English. She craned her neck to get a closer look into the poor light. 'Are you retired?' 'Yes, I am.' I resisted the temptation to tell her how fit, able and qualified I was, even if she did think I looked well and truly past it.

Until now I had not really taken stock of my travelling companions, wedged as I was between the flesh and the metal, but at the ferry port in the early hours I was somewhat mortified to observe that I was indeed the only wrinkly aboard. None of my other travelling companions looked a day over twenty.

We were held up boarding the boat because the driver had mislaid his paperwork. We therefore missed our slot and waited half the night to get the next one.

Francesca, a beautiful, buxom young graduate from Leeds University, had, towards the end of the coach ride to the port, reduced everyone to a giggling heap. Having inspected the bus toilet facilities and found them wanting, she had rummaged in her holdall and produced a rag and disinfectant. This was not something I would have thought to travel with, but Francesca disappeared down the steps into the toilet again, and after much banging about in such confined quarters, she finally emerged looking very cross indeed and informed us all, in no uncertain terms, that the toilet was now as clean as it was ever likely to be and more or less fit for human occupation, and THAT was how she expected to find it in the unlikely event of having to use it again.

Now, within minutes of boarding the ferry, her bright green eyes glittered as she surveyed the bar where the commercial lorry drivers were gathered for a quick bevvy before dossing down for a couple of hours in their own usual quarters. Francesca was obviously well informed regarding sleeping accommodation on ferries, which of course we had not been allocated. She cheerfully engaged a couple of likely lads, had a drink with them, and off she went.

She reappeared five minutes before we docked at Ostend looking infinitely more refreshed than any of the rest of us felt, happily acknowledging that she had done some sort of deal with one of the better-looking guys, who really did not mind sharing his bunk! Well, well, – Francesca's credulity clearly went up several notches within the group, including mine.

Throughout the following day and well into the night, it was an endless drive through Belgium before getting lost in Berlin and then again in Poland. The driver could not, or would not, understand that we really did need a comfort break. He adamantly refused to stop and to emphasise the point, he would relinquish his hands from the wheel, shoot both arms forward, stab his watch and vigorously shake his head, thus demonstrating that we must continue on account of the fact that we had lost so much time already. Thanks, mate. No chance to buy food, and sick of drinking Fantas, I decided to make a start on the duty-free brandy. My direst need, however, was for a cigarette.

In spite of the fetid heat emanating from my very close companion, I managed to doze fitfully during those long dark hours, with my arms pinned across my chest. Towards dawn I awoke to an almost imperceptible waft of tobacco smoke drifting my way. In your dreams love, I thought – but no, somebody was definitely smoking.

The driver was blissfully puffing away at the wheel with one of the girls sitting beside him in the well of the driving area, and she was also enjoying a cigarette. Well, I'll be blowed! I hastily clambered over the vast thighs of my snoring seat-mate, anxious to join this highly unexpected activity of smoking on a strictly non-smoking vehicle. What's good for the goose is good for the gander chum – try stopping me now! Liz, my newly-found-smoking-best-friend, obligingly moved over to let me sit in her place. Boldly, I lit up, and looked the driver straight in the eye. He responded with a sly, conspirator's leer.

International buses have, like large lorries, a plethora of gears to cope with their weight on the various gradients of road. The price apparently, for having an illicit cigarette was to allow this seedy Romanian to slide his dirty, oil-stained mitts over and up the thigh of any luckless, desperate-for-a-fag soul sitting next to him every time he changed gear. Now I knew why Liz was so happy to move.

I was not about to spare this horrible little toad from the embarrassment of rejection. 'Fok off,' I said sweetly. In spite of the shortcomings of his grasp of the English language, he got my drift all right and I was able to smoke the first of several lifesavers right down to the butt, without further fumbling.

At daybreak, a total mutiny was avoided only by the boys insisting that the driver stopped at the very next roadside cafe. He knew they meant it: he clocked the size and muscle of these lovely lads and pulled up within ten minutes at a concrete shack, partly obscured by tall trees, just off the main road.

We could smell the chips and the lavatory; several of us, in fact most of us, mindful that it might be healthier, peed behind the trees and on the bushes behind this primitive building. The proprietor was totally out of his depth at the enormity of providing something hot, or even enough cold food for fifty-odd people, and it didn't help him to be harassed by the driver jumping up and down stabbing at his watch.

The proprietor's wife appeared and between them they made a brave attempt to feed us, until finally we told them to shove everything cooked

– bread, anything edible – onto two large platters and we would all have a pick. Those delightful, if slightly bemused, Poles rose well to the occasion. Not every day did they have a horde of foreigners anxious to partake of their amenities. Were we interested in Gnomes? There were dozens of them, gaudy, grinning gnomes of all shapes and sizes, cast in cement, thickly painted and arranged enticingly on a scrubby patch of grass to one side of their establishment. We murmured our appreciation of such fine art, but no, we really couldn't buy any, we'd just stick with the chips, but thank you all the same. He and his wife beamed at us, appeared grateful for the odd collection of currency we gave them, and waved frantically at the back end of the bus as we got under way again.

It had taken us two hours to get through Polish customs, where we were required to remove all our baggage from the hold and our belongings from inside the bus, walk 50 yards or so across to the Ukrainian border, reload our stuff, and wait another hour before being allowed to proceed. We eventually arrived in Lviv, the capital city of Ukraine, fourteen hours late, for a night stop.

The hotel in the centre of the city was ancient, once a splendid venue for the rich and famous, but now sadly neglected. There were crumbling walls inside and out, peeling paintwork, hand-crafted ornate cornices and coving damaged by damp; proud oak floors that once gleamed were now scratched and splintered, covered by the occasional threadbare carpet. The corridor that was ours for the night sported three toilets, two working and one best avoided, two cold-water showers for fifty-two people and we were obliged to sleep six or seven to a room in this vast baronial building. The toilets and showers were guarded by very cross-looking ladies wearing slippers and headscarves, handbags clutched to their bosoms and treating everyone still queuing for some sort of ablutions to very hard stares indeed. There was no soap, no loo rolls, nothing to pinch, and we had no valid currency to make up for the fact that we were there at all.

We were starving. We enquired in vain for some sort of organiser to give us even the vaguest idea of where it was possible to eat. There seemed to be no restaurants, no bars, but finally an elderly gentleman staying at the hotel, glad to exercise his limited command of English, pointed a group of us to an out-of-town dump where we had our first proper meal for forty-five hours. It was good, it was wholesome, washed down with generous refills of neat vodka in tiny cups and accompanied by balalaika music; we all felt much, much better. On hard, narrow horsehair mattresses, we slept like logs.

Breakfast was interesting. Nobody knew what to do with it. Salted semolina, oiled gherkins and tomatoes, thinly sliced cheese and little black things I dared not eat, all in separate bowls, and a minuscule cup of very black coffee. No bread. We were waited on by sullen, po-faced boys and smiling, blushing girls falling over themselves to attend to all the needs of our young men. They obviously could hardly believe their luck. Unfortunately, time was at a premium.

The group was then ushered into a rather formidable reception area with huge columns supporting high ceilings, unlit chandeliers replaced by fluorescent strip lighting to grace what space was left between the cobwebs and sagging beams. The hotel staff stood around in military-style uniforms eyeing us suspiciously, which I supposed was meant to be intimidating in case we were about to organise a coup in this wretched place. There we were weeded out by a very agitated and short-tempered chappie by the name of Richard, based apparently in Lviv and employed as our Organisers' Representative. Some of us were detailed to go to Kiev apparently, while others were going somewhere else. The organisational skills of whoever dreamt up this trip in the first place were pathetic – no one knew what was happening, I just followed the herd.

The Kiev crowd were taken off. The rest of us had a lovely time in the capital. For a whole day we were at leisure to take in our surroundings. Lviv is a beautiful city, with its ornate eighteenth-century architecture, much of it sadly neglected, though the churches were now open again and used for worship. The markets were chaotic, with plenty of seasonal soft fruit and vegetables, locally produced, as was the meat laid out neatly on slabs in full sun and covered in flies. Still no bread, and the grocery shops were practically empty. We managed to collect survival food for the next leg of the journey by train to Chisinau.

In blistering sun, it was a long wait sitting on the pavement outside the mainline train station whilst our 'representative' found out about which platform we should be on. Tea money had obviously exchanged hands to get tickets at all, since they had not been booked in advance . . . for thirty-two people?

Suddenly, there was an almighty panic. 'Grab your bags and run for it.'

'Run? You must be joking!' Our gallant Representative, detailed to escort us to Moldova on the overnight train, eyes bulging with the effort of heaving his own luggage, led us up and down steps, through tunnels, and finally to the very end of the furthest platform. The last of us were still scrambling on as the train moved. I depended heavily on a leg-up to the high steps of the carriage. Our bags were lobbed up after us and we were all safely away, just!

I was reliably informed that the Russians have a thing about punctuality, I heartily wished at the time that they would also worry about safety and hygiene. The solitary toilet was obscene (and the whole train must have heard Francesca's lurid commentary about that!) and we had twenty-four hours to go. The carriages were like filthy cattle trucks and the Russians would not move an inch to make space for us. My new young friends though, were indomitable. Nothing daunted them, nothing impaired their gritty sense of humour, and there was no ageism either, especially when I shared the last of my plasters, bananas, and remaining dregs of brandy with them. Some of us had to share bunks, but no matter, we sat up most of the night anyway, getting to know each other.

I found I was developing a real fondness for these young people I was sharing that long, uncomfortable night with. We all realised by now that we were embarked on a somewhat thorny, unpredictable experience together, and the survival of it was going to depend very heavily on the tenuous thread of friendship already forged during the past few days. They were determined to have fun, and to their great credit, seemed able to have the capacity to take simple concentrated pleasure from ordinary things.

The following morning we were still on that damn train; the windows would not open and the smell was becoming horrendous. The mice and ants had eaten the remains of our biscuits and cake during the night, so our survival supplies were down to a bottle of very still water and Polo mints. By now, I was seriously considering that at the end of this stint, I would not be going home the pretty way.

At the Moldovan border the carriage was unhitched and shunted into a siding. We were relieved of our documents by armed guards. Eventually, a Very Important-Looking Person, also armed, appeared from the back of the carriage clutching a single passport. Mine. 'Was I in charge?' 'No, I am not.' 'You come.'

I was then obliged to follow this grim-looking fellow and pick my way across enumerable railway lines, dragging all my belongings as best I could, sincerely hoping there would be no other trains using these very same lines at this very same moment. In a dark, dingy guardroom they cross-examined me, turning the pages of my precious passport over and over. 'Had I got any money?' 'No, only traveller's cheques.' They fondled my cassette player lovingly and wanted me to leave it behind. Definitely not. I was now beginning to get very rattled indeed, but finally and very reluctantly, I gave them my beloved Beatles tape and I was allowed to find my way back across the tracks to the carriage, and to my very anxious mates.

We reached Chisinau, the capital city of Moldova, at last. The train station there was not inspiring and we were in no mood to do the conducted tour, but rumour had it that several of us were to be based in schools in and around this area. In the event there remained 15 of us who were detailed to leave for the last leg south to Bălți. After another long, miserable wait, we were finally given directions to a ramshackle tin-hut cafe, where, we were assured, we would be given a hot meal. In the meantime our overstretched, exhausted organiser was to arrange ongoing transport. Again, I was beginning to feel like a gorilla, my arms practically hanging out of their sockets in the attempt to keep me and my luggage together.

The food was almost worth it: cold soup, warm chunky bread, a rissole thing and brown rice, washed down with a warm lemonade drink served out of buckets.

Six girls, including me, and nine boys traipsed off to the bus station. Our transport was a very battered local bus complete with locals and their children and animals, and still another formidable mileage to our final destination. We were all too hot, too tired and too utterly pissed off to speak.

Almost exactly four days after leaving London, we arrived outside a large, incredibly ugly school building. All schools were apparently numbered from 1 to 16, this was number one. It was 9.30 p.m. and our host families were there to greet us. They must have been aghast as they stood silently watching us get off the bus. A more tired, motley lot would have been hard to find, and not in the least what they were probably expecting as English teachers.

No one was allocated to the families; instead, they chose from us. I, I am mortified to admit, was chosen last. After everyone else was sorted out it appeared I was to accompany Natalie, a very attractive girl, heavily made-up, her dark eyes weighted with mascara, her mouth generously applied with vermilion lipstick, and dressed very flash in a short, tight little black and gold number. She was a bizarre contrast to the other women waiting to escort us to their homes, dressed – albeit in their best clothes – but still reflecting the peasantry in their style. The younger teachers looked very apprehensive at this situation since most of the families were headed by swarthy, unsmiling men clad in singlets, camouflage trousers and heavy boots. I was by now at the point where I expected the worst, and anything else would be a bonus.

My 'home' for the next three months was my worst nightmare realised: a dreary grid of anonymous half-finished tenement apartments, surrounded by an old village. I learnt later that most post-war buildings were incomplete because the authorities regularly pulled the plug on financing such enterprises as building homes, or anything else that would improve the standard of living for its citizens.

Three floors up and through the front door, I was accompanied by Natalie and a very depressed taxi driver, elderly and with obvious cardiac problems who looked fit to drop after dragging my bags up the stairs.

The apartment was clean and quite exotically furnished; a massive dog of indeterminate breed opened its huge mouth to have a jolly good old bark, licked my filthy boots and there I was – arrived. I had quite a nice room, overlooking the gardens and sheds of the old village. The sofa bed had seen better days and took a bit of imagination to get it to look remotely like something to sleep on. A small desk, no hanging or drawer space, carpets on the wall, well-worn lino on the floor, and an Anglepoise lamp.

Forget about a shower. The bathroom was primitive and the family anxious to please. I was soon presented with a plug and a bucket of hot water. This I tipped into the bath, cleaned my teeth, washed my hair and sat in all two inches of it. Bliss!

My supper was ready. Three fried eggs, a tomato and a gherkin soaked in oil, half a Russian pancake and tea, complete with plenty of big green tea leaves and no milk. Oh, for a very large Gin and Tonic!

It had been yet another very long day: conversation was difficult and I was happy to go to bed. With no evidence of a light switch, I tried the Anglepoise. It went on but not off. Judging by the sniffing at the door, I felt uncomfortably sure that I had got the dog's bed space. I slept fitfully;

how will I get back to the school tomorrow? Must get up early – classes – we had been told, begin at 9 a.m. sharp.

I walked the mile or so to school with Natalie and I was allocated my class, simply observing for the morning and then taking over from Laura who was leaving for home the following week. She was a charming, elderly languages graduate from Stroud, doing her twopenn'orth for humanity like the rest of us and spoke at rate of knots in her wonderful plummy shires accent.

The class was made up of three third-year medical students, two graduate engineers, a group of four students learning English at the local college and three teachers from the school, and all a mix of Russians, Romanians and Moldovans. No one appeared to understand a word Laura was saying and they sat, unsmiling, in rows.

Moldova was once one of fifteen sovereign republic states forming the USSR. To emphasise their new independence, the Moldovans had demonstrated in favour of official recognition of their own language and the use of the Latin alphabet rather than the Cyrillic. Official guide books tell us that sixty-five per cent of the population is Moldovan, obscuring the fact that the majority of the inhabitants of Moldova are culturally and ethnically Romanian.

Furthermore, a good percentage are Russian, born and bred in Moldova and speaking their own language. So, with all this confusion of languages, I was quite glad really that I hadn't bothered to learn any of it.

The class was attentive; they stared, motionless and unblinking at Laura, who blithely prattled on, seemingly oblivious to their incomprehension. The morning was split into four forty-minute periods. First break five minutes. I sniffed out the coffee – couldn't drink it – too black, too thick and syrupy. Second break – water? Warm and drinkable if you were desperate. I was. Third break half an hour. I made my own coffee with the warm water and found my English colleagues. We frantically gathered in the yard to smoke a fistful of cigarettes and commiserate. We forgot the time and also which floor each of us was working on.

Back to the classroom. I took over from Laura, who had been trying to discuss 'work' situations with these adult students. They thought she was talking about WALK. I realised this and physically demonstrated 'work' by scrubbing at the classroom floor with the board duster on my hands and knees. WORK, I wrote on the brown, peeling and squeaky chalkboard. I got two of my highly educated medical students to join me on the floor to work. WE ARE WORKING, I scratched out. Good. A demonstration of walking, arm in arm. WE ARE WALKING, OK? A couple of spins around the desk. Now WE ARE DANCING. Brilliant! Everyone by now was convinced that they had a complete nutcase on their hands, – including Laura – and I was very relieved to see that these bemused students could actually laugh.

There was a pitiful attempt at a Seminar after school with our 'coordinators'. They wanted to tell us about the programme. We wanted to know about the bank, the Post Office, currency, transport. What about a MAP? It turned out that the main thing was to locate the Flamingo bar, the regular watering hole for the English contingent. It was here, apparently, where a vast supply of unreliable information could be counted upon.

My host family, charged with the responsibility of feeding, accommodating and looking after me, were Natalie and her husband Ehab, a twenty-three-year-old Arab who thankfully spoke excellent English. They shared a two-bedroom apartment with Natalie's Russian mother and her younger sister, who spoke nor understood any English at all.

Ehab and I talked late into the night. He was there illegally, but was reasonably safe while married to Natalie, although he could not work. The patriarchal figure of this household was, according to Ehab, abroad for the time being, but where abroad and why, he was not prepared to elaborate. It was no concern of mine, but I suspected that they must have had considerable financial support from somewhere if their expensive clothes and jewellery were anything to go by.

All domestic services at that time were still controlled by the Russian authorities. We were allowed hot water through the tap every other week, cold water most of the time, but periodically no water at all and it was against the law to conserve water in the house. My ever-ready handy golf ball sits into most plug holes and I was therefore able to collect whatever water dripped from the tap overnight into the sink basin in the bathroom, thus avoiding a personal and unwelcome early-morning trip to the public well, one hundred yards up the road.

New bread was baked on Sundays; by Saturday we were eating the last of the week's supply. Very dry and often mouldy, depending on the weather, it was accompanied by the dreaded oiled gherkins and flash-fried potatoes. I must, I considered grimly, try to remember to keep up with the vitamin tablets!

I was taken by Ehab and Natalie on a tour of the town, my arms firmly clasped by both of them to avoid the spectacle of their charge falling over in a most undignified manner amongst the rubble surrounding the building, in front of their neighbours. The consummate ugliness of the place was depressing, and I was hurried past gawping kids, their mums, and macho men.

At the top of the road was a wooden shack; with its corrugated asbestos sheets serving as a roof, sagging gutters, it was one of many in the village and home to innumerable children, pigs, goats, geese and dogs. Children and animals communed naturally, roaming free on the verges of weeds and wild flowers whiskering through the broken asphalt of the road. They all looked dirty, but seemed happy and healthy enough. These were Moldovan families and obviously seriously underprivileged compared with the Romanians and Russians.

Everywhere there were street vendors, dispirited-looking women, all selling the same – tomatoes and gherkins from buckets, cigarettes one at a time, and warm beer, Coke and pink champagne. The town was typically Russian, albeit with Lenin removed: it had the perfunctory Square, Lake and Fountain which only worked on Fridays, or on high days and holidays. The Co-operative was a huge departmental store with nothing in it, save the last consignment of lard, sardines, cheap shoes and boring fabrics imported from Romania. There was a scrubby park with broken swings, a derelict theatre with no theatre company, and a University campus, all badly run down since the Communists no longer reigned supreme. I concluded that Bălți was monumentally dull.

I was invited by the family to visit friends and to be shown off. As an English visitor to their modest home, with half the street in attendance, I was feted, clasped to their bosoms and force-fed. Neat vodka was diluted with liqueur and served at the beginning, throughout the meal and after it. I was assured that it would be considered extremely rude to refuse. Dancing began at the end of the first course, and continued with great enthusiasm until the early hours.

I don't mind telling you, by the end of that evening I think those delightful and generous people were mighty impressed with *my* rendering of Russian folk dance!

The following morning I woke feeling frail, hungover and decidedly ill at ease. It was Saturday, but all the same, I had to make an early start to get a grip on lesson plans for the following week. No books, no photocopier, only my tapes, cassette player and thankfully plenty of pens, paper and a few books and worksheets I had had the wit to bring with me.

As the family had at that point not yet surfaced, I was obliged to open the front door to the insistent clanging of the doorbell. I was not a pretty sight, dressed only in crumpled T-shirt and knickers and large fluffy slippers belonging to my host 'mother'. Standing there on the outside landing was an elderly lady from the nearby village calling to present me with a big jug of fresh milk from her own cow. 'Far be it from me to complain,' I had implied by way of exaggerated gagging signs a few days earlier, 'but your sour milk is not really to my taste.' The dear soul beamed as I fell on her neck in gratitude – fresh milk! What better cure for a hangover?

She had also come to tell me that the children from the village and from these ghastly tenement apartments were having a concert in my honour that evening, outside in the yard.

I was in no mood that morning to deal with the endless struggle to converse with Natalie's mother and her ever-present little sister. I had to escape for an hour or two on my own. In the burning heat of the day, my shoes stuck to the melting tarmac on the road, it was a long walk to the town, but I finally met up with my mates at the Flamingo. We enjoyed the release of a giggle and speaking English at normal speed and for me at least, the 'hair of the dog' drink. There was a wonderful generosity of spirit between us. We had nearly all been indisposed one way or another as a result of climatic and dietary changes and we had all been quite hungry. All the same, none of us was really miserable; the raw humour of these young Brits was exquisite, and we all mucked in sharing money, food and medication.

The girls in the group pointedly ignored the overtures of the local mafia (who controlled the police and therefore the town). Pity, they said, about the smell and the abundance of gold teeth. Everyone it seemed, had gold teeth to a greater or lesser degree. It was no status symbol either. There was also an unusual number of amputees in the area, and we suspected that they treated limbs very much the same as they treated teeth – removed at the first sign of trouble – except that teeth were very evidently replaceable with cheap gold molars.

I dressed up in my best to go to the concert. A dangerously wobbly platform had been erected and decorated in all manner of paper drapes, to accommodate the Master of Ceremonies and the 'orchestra'. A handful of elderly gentlemen, who had taken time over their appearance for such an important occasion, gingerly perched on spindly chairs and fussed over their instruments: a bassoon, a cello, a fiddle or two, castanets and miraculously, an electronic organ.

The proud owner of this highly prized equipment ostentatiously adjusted the various knobs and buttons for sound and tested the swell pedal for volume – and it did indeed do a fine job of drowning out the renderings of the other musicians.

The children were scrubbed, beribboned, hair curled and crimped, beautifully decked out in elaborate home-made dresses, shirts and bow ties.

The mating game begins very early in the lives of Moldovans. No expense is spared, up to the limits of the family's meagre financial resources, to dress up the little girls in fancy clothes. At a very young age they are taught the art of captivation, so that by the time they are fifteen or sixteen they can be seen promenading around the main town square, tight miniskirts, brightly coloured blouses, high-heeled shoes and generous applications of cheap cosmetics – vivid lipstick, rouge and eye shadow – and firmly clutching the arm of some luckless lad doomed to an early union. Heaven help the contender who challenges this situation. I saw many a catfight ensue, usually between the mothers, who were keeping a watchful eye on their little darlings from a distance.

In the evening sun, the concert progressed. The children sang, danced and acted out their nursery rhymes, and I was enthralled.

I was entreated to 'do' something. I was not about to subject them to my singing, or dancing come to that, so reluctantly I contributed 'The Owl and the Pussycat who went to sea, in a beautiful pea green boat' . . . not that they understood a word of it, but it was enough, particularly for the parents, to hear our language spoken at length, a language so different from their own. My performance of 'Fly Me to the Moon' on the old boy's electronic organ brought the house down and undoubtedly convinced the owner of that shaky machine that I really had come off the moon.

The children and their parents clamoured to have their photos taken. Fathers shuffled in front of the children with arms folded across their chest, mouthfuls of gold teeth flashing back at my camera. Brightly coloured cakes and sweets appeared from nowhere and were reverently handed round. The innocuous pink champagne was dished up with a ladle into mugs and the men surreptitously passed round the brandy.

At last it was dusk. The yard looked dingier than ever as the children said goodnight in English and were taken off to their beds, and I retired to mine. The dog determinedly accompanied me to my room and lay like a plank across the bottom of the bed.

2

We had now completed five or six weeks of teaching at School No. 1, and some of us were beginning to feel the strain. Even in English schools we would have had the chance to gather our wits and look forward to taking a break at half-term, but not here in Bălți, apparently. Most of us had a long walk to and from the school every day, which meant a very early start and a late finish, leaving very little time to relax or, more importantly, to take stock of what we were doing.

The work was made much more difficult by the total lack of resources – no photocopier, typewriters, or suitable books or consumables other than those we had brought with us; the books had done the rounds and the paper and pens, and even the chalk, were fast running out. Although my young colleagues were very intelligent and imaginative, they had no formal teacher training and for them it was even more challenging to keep their classes interested without the introduction of new ideas.

We decided to get together for a bit of brainstorming. But where? We couldn't use our lodgings; the school chucked us out the minute classes were over (and every door was firmly locked with a big black key!); the Flamingo bar was unsuitable and anyway, the mafia lurking about would have assumed that at the very least we were planning a dastardly coup; so after school we went en masse to the park.

Sitting under a wide sycamore tree, it was pleasant there in the shade armed with bottles of water and a few tasteless biscuits, and the first thing we unanimously decided upon was that we needed some time off. Teaching at the best of times – in familiar surroundings and with everyone speaking the same language – is hard work, but in that prison-like school there in Moldova, with precious few facilities and no common means of communication, it was exhausting.

We planned a rota between us so that we could put two classes together for an hour or two each week, thus giving us time and space to prepare new work on a regular basis. It was no good telling our 'organiser' – he could never be found. We would have to appeal directly to the school administrator to agree to this.

So far, as a group, much of the work we had prepared was passed around between us as most of the classes (except mine) were composed of children between the ages of eight and eleven. Individual worksheets were out of the question (no photocopier). Everything had to be done by hand (no typewriter); very time consuming and frustrating. Someone thought his host family had a portable typewriter we might borrow, and two of our girls were taking Art degrees and were brilliant illustrators, and their talents were to prove very much in demand in the following weeks.

It was decided then that it would be much easier if each of us planned a Scheme of Work for the next six weeks, of which all of us were to have a copy so that we all knew what each of us was doing. We would rotate the work between the classes, helping each other and sharing our ideas more effectively.

Two of the boys were detailed to go to Chisinau to locate a photocopier (there *must* be one there for God's sake, it *is* the capital of Moldova), and I was delegated the task of approaching the school administrator, through the services of his translator.

Between us we prepared a list of our requests, explaining in detail the viability of the programme for the next few weeks and our proposed plans, albeit with a little time off, for the successful outcome of his 'Summer School'.

However, it also turned out quite late on during our discussion in the park that our students were *paying* for their classes and that they and the staff understood that these fees covered our 'wages'! This revelation was in direct contravention of the conditions under which we went to Moldova in the first place, and was very disturbing news indeed. It had only come to light because one of our party was actually lodging with a Russian English-speaking teacher from the school who also served as their main translator.

We had in fact paid out of our own pockets to come on this trip, an amount generous enough to more than cover the cost of our transport and our keep to our host families, and we certainly were not paid for our teaching services. Nor, according to the literature we were provided with before we left the UK, were our students expected to pay for this voluntary service.

On the strength of this information, I was determined to buttonhole our organiser and insist that he attended the interview with the administrator to add what little clout he could muster to the proceedings. The translator was also to be invited.

Our list of requests now became more a catechism of demands – the most important being that we *needed* a photocopier, a typewriter, and an ongoing supply of reasonable-quality paper. Also, would he please see his way clear – urgently – to arrange the hire of the equipment, and the purchase of art paper, exercise books, proper folders for the children plus pens, pencils and paint, etc. – which I felt sure would be no problem, given that he had the funds available generated from the students fees? I handed him my shopping list.

The administrator, looking like a pantomime Baron Hardup in his olive green uniform, complete with epaulettes and brass buttons, was a big, flat-faced, portly man and obviously not accustomed to being told to do anything, least of all by a woman less than half his size, and an Englishwoman at that. He did not take kindly to the situation at all.

All the same, within three days, after much huffing and puffing, a photocopier was lugged in by four porters, and two typewriters appeared in the office for our use. A big box of assorted paper, another of pencils, pens, paints and crayons and lots of very useful consumables, all previously provided by the children themselves – if they could afford it – were magically placed in my classroom. Blimey, what a result! Someone had a mighty guilty conscience!

With great deliberation, and lengthy exhortations from old flat-face about how very inconvenient it was bound to be, we had been granted a long weekend off. Little groups of us went away in different directions to take a closer look at this country we found ourselves in. Some of the boys went to Chisinau to find a bit of life outside our depressing little outpost where we were working. I went with a group of girls to visit Rezina and Tipova, 60 kilometres east of Bălți on the western banks of the Dniester River. We knew from our research of the area that we should have little trouble finding accommodation for a couple of nights and that there were interesting places to see within easy reach of the small town of Rezina.

We found a 1960s boarding establishment – it could hardly be called a hotel, but at least it was somewhere we could put our heads down in slightly more comfortable surroundings that we were experiencing in Bălți and it was near – we could hardly believe it – a restaurant, complete with bar, casino and discotheque!

Alice, Joanne, Karen and Francesca, all in their twenties, were delighted and looked forward to a rare night out. I was ecstatic at the prospect of a decent meal and a good night's sleep on a bed that didn't sag in the middle and didn't include the company of a big, hairy dog lying across my feet.

Those girls were such fun. Po-faced Alice, her pretty strawberry blonde hair tied severely back with elastic bands, always wearing an oversized T-shirt over her skinny frame, had an incredible knack of making a joke out of any situation; her dry observations turned hilarious, and uttered from her unsmiling face, they always had the effect of really making us laugh.

Joanne, beautifully spoken, and coming from a highly professional musical family, had every kind of complaint she could think of and never had any money. Always on the cadge, she borrowed from everyone; sooner or later though, every penny of it was paid back, just in time for her to borrow some more! Always generous with her time, we had very good reason in the weeks to come to enjoy and be grateful for Joanne's musical talents.

Cool, elegant, intellectual Karen, the eldest and quietest of the four, looking forward to getting married at the end of her postgraduate teaching course, was a joy to talk to in our quieter moments. The children adored her, they clamoured for her attention and she found time and space for them all. It was she who had done the research for our excursion, and happily took all the stick when things didn't pan out as planned.

And then there was the big, bold and beautiful Francesca. Oozing sensuality, drawing attention from every red-blooded man within fifty yards, she knew what she had and how to flaunt it, and saw the whole thing as a huge joke. Just when the situation was getting too close for comfort, she would tuck up with the rest of us, link arms, and off we would go with me visibly reprimanding her like a mother hen. This tactic had been very useful on several occasions in Bălți, when the mafia boys, in black singlets, tight jeans and gold medallions prominently displayed on hairy chests, thought they were on to a winner with this lovely English girl. They could not have been more wrong. Francesca couldn't stand them. 'Their gold teeth make my eyes go funny,' she would say and the boys of our party never left her alone with any of them.

Moldova is a landlocked country most western Europeans have hardly heard of or have any idea of where it is. Vague reports, if emerging at all, would highlight extreme poverty, illegal organ trading, human trafficking, civil war and Communism. Such reports about this rarely visited country could not possibly conjure up images of the sunflower fields, enormous watermelons, bucolic pastoral lands, and remote monasteries cut into limestone cliffs. Moldova's rural countryside lacks dramatic scenery – no mountains, just gentle rolling plains; no raging rivers, only the tiny Prut and Dniester. Yet there is a quiet rhythm to the place; warm-hearted villagers offer an unbridled welcome to visitors and will take you to their homes for fresh peaches, sweet almonds, and a taste of their home-made wine, the delicious *palinka* made from apples and pears.

We were invited by one family to join them at All Souls' Day, which, as in all Catholic countries, is a celebration of the dead. The families visit each grave, most of them monuments to exquisite masonry, to give their blessings; hundreds of candles light up the graveyard and the verdant park that surrounds the cemetery; Mass is conducted here, followed by a picnic shared with anyone who cares to join in. For me it was an impressive and warm experience.

Chatting as best we could with these country people, it seemed that they didn't miss the Communist regime, even though many of its controls and regulations were still in place in those early days of independence, but they were suffering from serious unemployment, and what pensions they had been able to look forward to were no longer to be relied upon. They were a philosophical people; poverty and the hard life was no stranger to them, and we came away chastened by their fortitude.

We knew that from the small town of Rezina on the western banks of the Dniester River we could find our way to the Orthodox Saharna Monastery. Founded in 1495, the church presently used dates from the 19th century and sits in a small valley. There are walking trails all around, some offering stunning views of the entire monastery complex, and one leading to the Virgin Mary's footprint in rock, protected by a glass covering. Near a lovely waterfall tumbling off an overhanging cliff, we stopped to eat our picnic. From a tiny market in the town we had managed to buy fresh bread rings, cheese, tomatoes on the vine and ripe velvety peaches. Water and a bottle of home-produced wine completed our feast. It was so quiet, save for the sound of the waterfall, and we lay back after our meal on the tufty meadow grass and as one, promptly fell asleep.

An hour or more must have passed before we were rudely woken by Joanne, hysterically shouting, 'Go away, go away!' She was sitting up staring into the face of a big, brown, long-haired billy goat, who was far too interested in us to go anywhere. These animals in this remote place had no reason to fear people, and although his horns look intimidating, he seemed unlikely to use them. Deciding he had seen enough, he eventually wandered off, but not before he left his mark in no uncertain terms right in the middle of Joanne's backpack!

The following day we found our way by bus to Soroca, the Roma capital of Moldova. The large Roma population, even in Soviet times, was renowned for its much higher standard of living than that of most Moldovans, and this was probably the main reason for the palpable prejudice that existed against them. There are still stately mansions that the richer Roma people built for themselves on a hilltop facing the river with Ukraine over the other side.

We had come to see the Soroca fortress, where visitors can imagine medieval times while wandering around the grounds of what is part of a military chain of fortresses built by Moldavan princes between the 14th and 15th centuries to defend Moldava's boundaries. We visited the fantastic museum on the site, with its thousands of archaeological exhibits – far too much to see in one go – and we decided that this would be a good place to bring some of the children for an outing (at Baron Hardup's expense) to learn a little about their own heritage.

Back at the school, the break had lifted our spirits enormously, and with the availability of our newly acquired equipment and resources, we were on a roll. Videos, books and face paints that Andrew's parents had sent out to us finally arrived and all of it was to do with animals – *The Lion King* in particular – giving us the wild idea of putting on a pantomime. The more we thought about it the more feasible it became, and in no time our enthusiasm took hold and the entire curriculum was quickly adjusted to the Lion King theme.

Finding a video player was nearly a major hiccup until a member of my class 'borrowed' one from the hospital where he worked, and then the entire school was invited to see the film. From then on we had the cooperation of everyone; my adult students, the teachers and the administrative staff who theoretically were on holiday, all joined forces for the production. That video was played over and over again in the ensuing weeks.

The parents were wonderful. We needed costumes for our creatures of the jungle. They came up with ragged and not-so-ragged fur coats for the lions, tigers and leopards; candlewick bedspreads and floral curtains were dyed black and brown for the monkeys; we had a tall, golden giraffe with a long skinny neck and ears constructed of papier mâché; a baby elephant appeared in grey leather, fashioned from a jacket belonging to the child's father; twin girls turned up as plumped-up bumble bees sporting striped yellow-and-black knitted outfits, complete with fairy wings; and we had two Tarzans and a Jane. It was incredible what imaginative work was done in such a short time, and the children were so excited.

It was a terrific time. We forgot about taking breaks, everyone was so involved. There always seemed to be someone who could get something we needed, from where nobody ever asked; it was all for a good cause.

A stage was erected in the main hall, held up by scaffolding (the mind boggled as to where *that* came from), and miraculously stage lighting appeared and fixed up by a couple of medical students from my class; and all the time they were all progressing in learning to speak and read the English language. As many of the children as we could fit in had a few lines each, to either learn by heart or read from the page, it didn't matter which, as they learnt how to come in on cue. Others were learning to sing to Joanne's specially composed words and music. Elsewhere, little groups were making trees and butterflies from polystyrene and cardboard, and painting backcloths on old sheets for the stage set .

In a little over five hectic weeks, and a week or so before we were due to leave Moldova, we were as prepared as we were ever likely to be for the Grand Performance.

On Saturday at 5 p.m. the show would go on. By 3.30 p.m. the cast were assembled; costumes had to be adjusted, clever face painting by our own Art students was applied and brought to life the illusion of our creatures of the jungle. Last-minute nerves were dealt with by lots of encouragement and a big bag of boiled sweets. We were ready.

The invited Dignitaries of the town were seated in the front row, having been greeted by the school administrator, his normally dusty uniform freshly brushed and pressed. Usually behaving like some sort of peacock trapped in the seams of the lower echelons of society, he now bowed and scraped, happily accepting congratulations for his 'fine work' with a complacent smirk. What a two-faced miserable little git he really was!

The place was packed. The main lights were switched off and the stage lights came on and transformed that inhospitable hall into an auditorium of hushed anticipation. The children entered from the back of the hall in pairs, some standing up and some on all fours, but all singing loud and clear: 'The Animals Came in Two-by-Two, Hurrah, Hurrah!' One little creature clambered up onto the stage alone. 'Where has that donkey come from?' I whispered to Karen. 'Beats me,' she said, checking her cast list. 'There are no donkeys on here.' 'No, and there should be no bloody donkeys in the jungle either,' I muttered.

The audience clapped and whistled with unabated enthusiasm and the children played their parts (and waved to their mums), hardly missing a cue. Joanne's music on a piano that badly needed tuning, accompanied by two guitars, a harmonica, a flute and Bongo Drums belonging to the owner of the Flamingo bar, provided drama and atmosphere to the scenes unfolding before our eyes.

During the interval, the children needing a drink and the stage managers needing a stiff warm pink champagne, a short, sharp scuffle broke out at the back of the hall. We reckoned that someone may have recognised his scaffolding; or perhaps the mutilated grey leather jacket now transforming someone's child into an elephant may have caused a domestic quarrel; we didn't know, and it didn't last, and it seemed there were no hard feelings.

The second half was performed with aplomb and confidence, and we all, kids and staff, acknowledged the applause at the end of the performance with big, silly grins on our faces; we were so proud of all our students and pleased with ourselves that everything had gone so well. And then the audience of parents, the school staff, and the people from the town who had supported us, along with their Dignitaries, stood and sang their national anthem, and our little band of English teachers, standing to one side, wept with fatigue and pride. The children were at last gathered up and taken home, still in their costumes and smudged face paint. The donkey just disappeared into the night.

3

We had ten days before we were due to leave, and nobody seemed to have any idea what arrangements, if any, had been made to get us away from Bălți and home.

Three of the group had already gone. Jennifer had been really unwell from the start, pathetically homesick, and totally out of her depth in the classroom, so within a matter of a week or two her parents had paid for her to fly home. Peter got fed up and left, apparently to seek fresher fields somewhere in the direction of Greece, and poor Alan had fallen down a hole where there should have been a manhole cover and badly damaged his leg. Not trusting anything the local hospital could do, he harangued his insurance company until he was flown home too.

So that left twelve of us in Bălți and another thirteen in Chisinau; presumably there were others in Lviv and Kiev. The Bălți crowd, myself included, were adamant that there was no way we were going home the really ridiculously difficult and exhausting way we had come. I had seriously toyed with the idea of making my own way to Bucharest and going home independently from there, but we were by now a closely knit bunch and I felt I should see it out to the bitter end with them.

First though, we had to retrieve our passports. A Very Officious Person had arrived at the school in the middle of our work on the pantomime, accompanied by the administrator, and with Richard our 'organiser' hovering in the background, demanding that we produce our passports. After a cursory glance at each one he finally informed us in a Very Important Tone that none of us was registered. As one we stared at Richard. 'What does he mean we are not registered?' Looking decidedly ill at ease, he regretted to say that apparently we should have been re-registered after six weeks as visitors to Moldova. 'Also, your permits to work are out of date.' *WHAT?*

Properly advised, we would have known to renew our permits and re-

register with the police in Chisinau, a simple (as things go in Moldova!) formality when done in time, but now we were illegal. 'So why were we not told?' He didn't know. 'So what do we do now?' He didn't know that either. The heat of the situation cooled only slightly on the arrival of the English translator.

Nevertheless, the Very Officious Person insisted on relieving us of our passports, saying that he would instigate the preparation of new permits. Each of us would then be obliged to present ourselves to the Chisinau police station to re-register and only then would we get our passports back. 'How long is that going to take,' I wanted to know, 'bearing in mind that according to International Law, passports may not be withheld for more than three days – unless there is criminal involvement?' I wished I hadn't added that last bit, thinking it might sow an unwelcome seed into his big fat head. Without another word, he strode off.

In the meantime, according to the administrator – unable to resist sticking his oar in – we were to sign in at the school on a daily basis (as if we didn't do that already!) and were not to leave the town under any circumstances!

Two weeks later we still had no confirmation that our permits had been issued, and by now it was imperative that we were in possession of our passports and any other documents we needed to get *out* of the country.

There was an official Agency based in Chisinau that theoretically was the authority between us and the UK outfit that organised this trip in the first place. We were all frustrated by the lack of communication or cooperation within the school to regulate our situation, so en bloc, we cancelled all classes and in contravention of Official Orders we left Bălți and made our way to the capital, 150 kilometres away by bus, to pay a visit to the Agency. Richard was dragged along with us, complete with whatever paperwork he had – enough, we hoped, to at least prove who we were.

We arrived at lunchtime just five minutes before the Agency closed. All of us together virtually filled that rather smart-looking office, and we crowded around the counter where a very perplexed-looking woman sat on a high stool. 'What is your problem?' We told her. She knew nothing about it. 'Then you must find out,' we told her. 'You have a responsibility for us for which you are being paid, and therefore you must make all necessary enquiries to see to it that we have the correct documentation for us to leave this country and for us to be in possession of our passports – *today*.'

The poor woman, ashen faced and visibly shaken, went off to find a colleague. 'We are closed for the day,' announced a wimpish young man with an indeterminate accent. 'We will deal with your problem tomorrow.' Yeah, yeah. 'Sorry mate, we will wait here in your office – all night if we have to – so we suggest you reopen this establishment and make a start now.' Richard made a move to go. 'Oh no you don't, you stay here with us as our hostage.'

Our host families knew a bit about what was going on and that we didn't know how long we would be in Chisinau. Some had packed food for us, and we had bought fruit and water at the halfway stop from Bălți. Spread out over a few chairs, with the rest of us sitting on the floor of that office, we cleared brochures from the low table set in the middle of the room and ate our lunch while the Agency staff looked on aghast, and Richard looked very embarrassed. All the while, the telephones were ringing, the Fax machine clattered occasionally, and whispered consultations were held behind the counter.

It was hot in that airless place; a ceiling fan turned slowly and ineffectually and we, although we tried not to show it, were equally as fed up as the staff, deprived of their afternoon off. We waited. It was nearly four hours before anyone spoke to us. Eventually, we were asked to print our names in full alongside our normal signatures, and to state our place of birth, all this on a long sheet of paper. 'Have you located our passports?' No answer.

At 7.54 p.m. two burly police officers arrived at the Agency doors complete with pistols and handcuffs ready to hand in their heavy leather hip belts, and automatic rifles slung over their shoulders. We all stood up, not at all sure about this turn of events. It appeared they were to escort us to the police station to collect permits and register our presence in this country, a country I have to say we were all increasingly anxious to get out of. 'What about our passports?' We were to collect those from the Consulate in the morning. There was precious little we could do but be marched by the police, feeling very conspicuous, through the streets to their station. We left Richard at the office to fend for himself, but not before we told him that since we seemed obliged to stay in Chisinau overnight, we would expect him to have made the necessary *firm* arrangements for our journey home, not all the way by bus the way we came, but as far as possible by train, with properly reserved seats. We would be back, we assured him, in the morning after we had been to the Consulate.

Pictures of Chisinau, where there were any in the middle nineties, would have shown sprawling concrete esplanades smartly bookended by concrete apartment buildings, and although it was the capital of one of Europe's poorest countries at that time, it was the cosiest of all Soviet-style cities rebuilt after World War II. An earthquake in 1940 and almost total destruction by bombardment during the war left very little remaining of its historic heart, but some of the old buildings of the 17th and 18th centuries were still there, evidence that Chisinau was once graced with pride and beautiful architecture. It is still a very pleasant place to wander about in. Just a block away from the main drag the concrete gives way to the lush foliage of the parks and lakes that surround and hold the city in a seemingly fond embrace.

We booked in for the night at the Hotel Meridian, where two or three of our boys had been before on their various excursions into the city. 'Handy,' they had said, 'for the nightlife.' Low budget, it faced the bus station and seemed nearly engulfed by the sprawling central market filling the streets all around. It was far from being a peaceful place, but at least it was clean and comfortable inside and the staff were very accommodating, finding us towels and soap and giving the bathrooms a good wipe round before we used them.

The market was huge; porters scurried about with trolleys; cars honked crazily as they tried to squeeze through the bustling crowds; women spat out sunflower seeds as they sold their wares; and old men huddled in groups on the pavement as they placed their bets on the local lottery.

Guided by the boys, we made our way through to a street nearby where there were kiosks and small cafes, and we found one big enough to accommodate all of us, where we were served delicious mystery-meat-filled pasties and fresh vegetables, fruit, and as much beer and as many vodka shots as we could manage. Forgotten were the aggravations of the day, the utter tedium of that office, the intimidation of the police, *and* the fact that they had confiscated Andrew's camera because he had taken photos of soldiers in the park – all that for the moment was of no consequence, and we could wait until tomorrow to worry about getting home. Moldova that night, after a good meal and more than enough to drink, suddenly didn't seem so bad.

The children and their parents, our host families and many of the staff from the school were sad to see us leave Bălți. It was a strange mix of tears and excitement with so many of them gathered at the bus station. 'Please come again,' they cried. We knew we wouldn't but we promised we would all the same. The administrator was there, looking shamefaced and emotional as he shook hands with us one by one. 'We hope we can continue your wonderful work,' he said. Mind you, he had no excuse now – he had the equipment, and we had left most of our own behind, my cassette player, Joanne tape recorder, and others had left videos, books and all manner of useful stuff for the children. 'My best salutations to your people,' he said. 'Tell them about us kindly.' Well, well, who would have thought this rough, tough man could have a tear in his eye? We were going home, we could forgive anything!

From Chisinau it was twelve hours on the fast train to Lviv, an overnight stop in reasonable comfort, and then all the way to Brussels with only one change in Warsaw, on good trains, reserved seats, and with suitable provision for passengers on international journeys. Richard had done us proud.

It was strange going home with these people, people I hadn't known three months before but now felt bonded to by respect and genuine affection. Stroked by the kindness of strangers, I felt enriched by the experience we had shared and I knew it had helped me to reconcile myself to the fact that now I would always be out there to manage on my own, a fact I had struggled with but been given precious little time to think about in Bălți.

By now it was a little over a year since my husband had died, a year when it had in turns been excruciatingly long and terrifyingly short, and a time when I had been running my life on mental tramlines, leaving no room for diversion. But there were still mornings when I woke after a fitful night and his death hit me with as much pain as it did a year ago and I longed not to wake up at all. I wanted desperately to get past all that, to be released from grief, to somehow move forward, and I felt now that I had taken a step or two in the right direction.

Going home was another step – to go back into that house we had shared and where its walls had contained our lives for so long. Could I now look at his books without remembering him reading, lying close to me in our bed? Could I play his music without weeping? Would the spirits still be in my eucalyptus tree?

Part 2

THAILAND AND VIETNAM 1995

4

BANGKOK

Early one morning we passed the sandbank (south of Packnam)
and as the sun rose, shining over the flat plain, we steamed upstream,
along numerous curves in the river passing under the shadow of the
large golden pagoda and reached the outskirts of the city.

There it lay, spread out on both banks of the river, this oriental
capital, which has never had to bow to a white conqueror;
an extensive, wide area of brown bamboo houses, a mass of interwoven
mats and leaves – architecture in the style of a vegetable garden grown
out of the brown muddy earth.

Bangkok is also a city of canals. On both banks of the yellow waters
of the Menam, which is as wide as the Rhine at Mainz as it surges onwards
to The Gulf of Siam, an intricate labyrinth of canals criss-cross
the fifteen Square miles of lowland on which, circled by white walls
inset with towers, Bangkok lies.

It is, so to speak, two cities, one on top of the other. First the city of
the river and the canals with thousands and thousands of floating
houses and a storey higher on the mainland, towers a second city of
stone And wooden houses.

It is all flat alluvial land, the work of the great Menam, which here,
like the Nile in Egypt, waters the land and occasionally floods large
areas. So the people who live here have become sort of amphibians
Those who live on the mainland spend half their lives on or in the water,
those who live in the water spend all their lives there . . .

Joseph Conrad, *Shadowline* (1906)

Much has changed in Bangkok since Joseph Conrad wrote his observations in 1906. The headlong pace and flawed modernity of the city today match few people's visions of the capital of the old exotic country of Siam, now known as Thailand. Spiked with high-rise blocks of concrete and glass, it is a vast flatness which holds a population of six million and feels even bigger. But under the shadow of the skyscrapers, you will find a heady mix of chaos and refinement, of frenetic markets and hushed golden palaces, and of dispiritingly shameful zombie-like sex shows. You will either love or loathe the place. If the challenge of slogging through traffic jams made up of top-of-the-range cars, buses and tuk-tuks, and the consequential fug of pollution and noise, gets to you, as it most certainly will, you can always get away from it all and spend time in the quiet, spiritual atmosphere of the many temples in the city.

Bangkok is a relatively young capital, established in 1782, after the Burmese sacked Aytthaya, the former capital. A temporary base was set up on the western bank of the Chao Phraya River, in what is now Thonburi, before work started on the more defensible east bank, where the French had built a grand, but shortlived, fort in the 1600s. The first roads were built on European lines, and under King Rama V (1868–1910), a new residential palace in Dusit was built, and it was he who laid out the areas of grand boulevards.

Since World War II, and especially since the 1960s, Bangkok has seen an explosion of modernisation, which has blown away earlier attempts at orderly planning and has now left the city without an obvious centre. Most of the canals have been filled in and replaced by endless rows of concrete shophouses. These drab piles of boxes are now the capital's most prominent architectural feature.

In London the winter months of 1994–1995 were long and dreary, perpetually damp, grey and depressing. A blanket of cloud had hung low from the sky for weeks on end and I was becoming more and more lethargic, stale and dull. I seemed to have lost the will or initiative I had drummed up earlier in the year to go to Moldova, an experience that had forced me to live less within myself and simply concentrate and deal with each new day as it came.

Now I was beginning to feel unnerved by the endless quiet, the huge solitude that prevailed in the house now that I was alone in it. I knew though, that somehow I had to retrieve the will and energy to push my thoughts outward again if I was to avoid a seriously depressed state.

Out of the blue, the matter was taken out of my hands when a dear friend and colleague from my working days in school rang me late one evening. 'There's a job you might be interested in – how do you fancy Thailand?' Always good for a laugh, I thought she was joking. 'Thailand,' she repeated. 'Go for it!'

It was a long flight from London, giving me plenty of time to fret and to consider the wisdom of taking on a job after such scanty briefing, and to wonder why I had not taken the precaution of having at least some point of connection in Bangkok should the worst happen and nobody turn up to meet me on arrival. By the time I finally arrived at Don Muang Airport, I was decidedly fraught.

As I yanked my excessive luggage from the carousel, the handle of my holdall broke. Stuffing the damn thing under my arm along with bits and pieces of hand luggage, and trying to haul a huge suitcase at the same time as best I could, I must have looked a very sorry sight indeed to Duangchai, resplendent in purple Thai silk who I immediately recognised from my interview in London. She was there bless her, with her handsome uniformed chauffeur hovering in the background. My relief at the sight of her was immense.

I was gathered up, whisked away through the fairy-lit streets of the city, and dumped off in a small, stark, but what appeared to be a reasonably comfortable apartment. I had no idea where I was in relation to the rest of Bangkok, but the obsequious, bowing and scraping Japanese landlord who greeted us assured me and Duangchai that I was most welcome, yes, yes, most welcome. (When I later calculated the rent for this place, I was not at all surprised that I was most, most welcome!) The guards, he said, would take very good care of me. The *GUARDS*? Blimey!

My new employer was obviously very anxious to get back to the comfort of her bed. 'You will find whatever you need – sleep well,' she said. 'Sangpong will pick you up in the morning at nine.' On that happy note, she and Sangpong shut my new front door and cleared off.

It suddenly struck hard to me at that moment that although I had been getting used to being alone, this time I was really on my own and very far from everyone I loved. I felt endangered and incomplete. I had deliberately removed myself from my support system in the risky, groping business of trying to stand on my own two feet again and getting on with the rest of my life.

Yeah, well, get on with it then I thought, as I wearily appraised my new pad. Huge fridge with several big bottles of water, no gin, no tonic, no nothing apart from the water. Was I meant to wash in it? Vast double bed, covered in a violent orange-coloured overlay of terry towelling. Plenty of wardrobe space, minimal lighting, a table, a wicker chair and a small balcony.

Miserable and desperate to sleep, but aware of a persistent irritating background noise which I eventually realised was the over-zealous air-conditioning. Floundering around, gradually removing my travelling clothes, I finally located a batch of switches anchored to the wall. I tried one and the lights went out; tried another, got it – the noise stopped. I opened the glass doors to the balcony and sniffed the fetid night air. It had been twenty-two hours since I had left home. I showered under a warm but reluctant pressure of water; no towels, so I dried myself on the innocuous-looking bedcover. Satisfied that I was not overlooked from that part of the apartment, I wandered about, searching my luggage for a book to send me off to sleep, fearing that in the absence of anything to eat and no nightcap, I would lie awake all night contemplating my fate until it was time to get up to meet Sangpong.

Another horrible noise – mozzies! Why do they always buzz around the head of any luckless soul trying to sleep? I leapt to my feet to close the balcony doors; only by stretching tall I could reach the lock, and in the process, I exposed my total nakedness to the entire city of Bangkok. Oh well. Back in the relative safety of my bed I covered myself completely with the now very damp, tasteless orange bedcover and made a mental shopping list: forty-four cans of Mosi-guard, 3 bottles of gin, tonic, and chocolate biscuits for emergency sustenance – and a new bedcover.

I was woken by the birds twittering and singing to each other. The sun was trying to shine through the hazy city fug. What's the time then? My watch was still set at Greenwich Mean Time. I vaguely tried to calculate what it must be in Thailand, gave it up, got up, and pondered over what to wear. It was warm enough for a cotton dress that had certainly seen better days, but I hoped it would see me comfortably through the day. My well-worn sandals completed the outfit.

I tentatively let myself out and went down the staircase to find someone who would tell me the time. No one. OK. I ventured further out of the building. I discovered that the gates to the street were locked. *I AM LOCKED IN!* A young man appeared, immaculate in white shirt, black tie and trousers (I was to discover that all young men working in towns and cities in Thailand wear white shirts and black trousers, unless they are monks), and flip-flops. A guard! He understood a squiddum of English, which did not extend to the time, but after much poking at my watch, he pointed to the time on his own watch. 'Ah, thank you. What is your name?' 'Buck.' 'Pardon?' 'Buck.' It was 5.27 a.m. precisely, Bangkok time.

I was picked up at nine as promised, on the dot. Bleary, bitten and jetlagged, I presented myself to Sangpong. In daylight he was more handsome – probably in his mid-thirties, and entirely of gorgeous Thai origin. Unusually tall, well-built, high cheekbones, golden skin and well-cut jet-black hair. I had no objection whatsoever to him being my driver, my guard, or whatever! He smiled sympathetically at the bites on my face and hands and proceeded to practise his very limited English. 'You are Ben Mairee?' 'No, Ben is a boy's name, I am just Mary.' 'Ben', it turned out, is a courtesy title for mature ladies of indeterminate age. Oh well, Ben Mairee it is then, and it was the name I answered to throughout my stay in Thailand.

After a series of interviews, character testimonials, confirmation of my qualifications and a stringent health check, I had finally been selected by a firm of Consultants in London, employed by the Thai embassy to select a suitable candidate to set up a new private school in Bangkok. The job itself seemed, even at the time, vaguely obscure but important enough for the Principal, Duangchai, to come to London to see for herself who it was the Consultants had finally drummed up to do the job.

My brief was, apparently, as 'Educational Consultant', to oversee the foundation of a new private school dreamt up and to be financed by Duangchai, whose husband incidentally, was, or had been, the Thai Ambassador to Austria, and had many connections in diplomatic circles. The school was to be funded by her and their rich Chinese-Thai cronies. Most of the serious wealth in Thailand is in the hands of the Chinese Thais, and these people had their fair share of it, judging by the way money was so casually and extravagantly spent in the ensuing weeks.

The concept of the school was primarily to offer crash courses in the English language and also to arrange and supervise 6-week trips to England for the students, in order that they would in that time acquire good English manners and appropriate social behaviour. The ultimate aim, evidently, was to prepare their little darlings and others who could afford it to gain entry to the prestigious International British School in Bangkok, or, if all else failed, to the International American School.

All the money in the world could not buy the Thai children entry to these schools unless they could demonstrate an ability to achieve a level of English speaking, understanding and reading, in order that they would be able to cope well in mainstream classes in subjects across the curriculum. That, apparently, was where I came in.

The Thai government, incidentally, had recently ruled (and when they rule they usually mean it, unless it suits them not to) that all teachers of English must hold an appropriate University degree. A bit short-sighted in a way, because there were many good language teachers in the city, well able to teach but who had not necessarily specialised in English. On the other hand there were also many, many Australian, American and European travellers passing through who thought that because they could speak English, albeit with their various accents, they could also teach it, earning a quick buck in the process, and moving on after a month or so to other far-flung places of exotica. Not much help to the kids trying to get a grip on a new language.

5

The 'school', to my amazement, was a grand, solidly built and fairly modern two-storey house, set well back from the road and secured by ornate, spear-tipped wrought-iron railings and gates. Passing through the gates, the house was reached by a long, elegant driveway hedged with exotic blooms and shrubs. Guards, gardeners dedicated to cutting lawns, pruning, planting and endless watering, were all there beavering away to maintain what looked to me to be already the perfect garden.

Duangchai floated out from the wide entrance to greet me on that first day. I was stunned at the sight of her. She was slender and fine-boned, her thick black hair coiffed high on her head. She wore an embroidered green and white silk *ao dai*, a traditional tunic over silk pantaloons. The pale pink polish on her long, tapered nails matched her lipstick, and round her neck hung pearls matching the series of bracelets around both wrists. Crikey, I thought, and felt decidedly frumpy. She had nothing, however, on her feet. First rule: all footwear is deposited on the verandah before entering the house. I was glad that at least my feet were clean.

Duangchai immediately gave me a conducted tour of the house. Polished teak floors and staircases that turned and led to wide landings and panelled doors, leading to endless airy rooms with high ceilings and casement windows. Naked nymphs and cherubs graced the covings around the ceilings. There were shower rooms and bathrooms, all exquisitely tiled, a massive kitchen with every conceivable culinary device, and everywhere was immaculately clean. A house? It was a mansion.

The whole place was surrounded by verandahs, greenery, flowering shrubs and trees, some I now have names for, and I could see a white-painted very pretty Victorian folly, taking pride of place in the middle of the extensive lawns and back gardens. But no desks, chairs or equipment, certainly no pupils, nothing to indicate that this was deemed to be regarded as a school, private or otherwise.

After the tour of the house I was introduced to Peter, a young Englishman who was apparently the school's General Manager. He was sitting in an otherwise empty room on the ground floor, at a big important-looking desk, which as far as I could tell was the only piece of furniture in the whole house. He looked up briefly, arched his eyebrows, nodded at my presence, fiddled with his pen and resumed giving his undivided attention to a single sheet of A4 paper in front of him, without uttering a word. Do we have a little problem here? I asked myself.

I trailed after Duangchai as she strode barefoot through to the far side of this lovely house and arrived at wide doors leading to the most exotic conservatory I have ever seen. The flank wall was covered in a mature flowering vine, entwined with climbing pelargonium in rich magenta and vivid pinks; sweet-scented jasmine, its fine tendrils carefully tied and trained onto a dainty wooden trellis. I spared a thought for my neglected plants in my piddling little greenhouse at home.

Innumerable hand-crafted and hand-painted terracotta pots, in all shapes and sizes, contained pink-tipped rubber plants bursting with life, ferns, geraniums and great shiny fan leaves. There were tufted, bulbous trunks showing the promise of more splendid additions to the plant life in this amazing indoor garden. Every corner of this magnificent appendage to the house was embraced with greenery and was enhanced by a small fountain, spraying fine jets of water over a bronze cherub, with his arrow pointing straight at my head.

This was Duangchai's domain – her office – and here there was indeed furniture: A desk, boardroom size, exquisitely carved in fine Siamese teak, and a huge leather swivelling contraption which my new boss collapsed into, looking like a diminutive doll with her bare feet hanging at least six inches from the floor. There was a chiffonier, entirely picked out in parquetry and mother-of-pearl, almost smothered by the plants, and I was invited to sit on a low, hard wooden bench.

The telephone rang, and Duangchai rummaged through her paperwork to find it. The desk, large as it was, almost sagged under the weight of the piles of catalogues and brochures, together with lists, coloured files, endless pots of pens, highlighters, and a wire basket full of paint samples. A beautiful bronze lamp with an elaborately fringed and beaded lampshade illuminated this chaotic mess.

Between constant interruptions by kitchen staff wanting to know about food and gardeners wanting to know about gardens, as well as repeated telephone calls, I was able to roughly determine from a very disjointed conversation what my appointment would involve.

I gathered I was being instructed to employ supporting staff, and to equip the school with appropriate books, suitable furniture, consumables, sports equipment and T-shirts, and these to be emblazoned 'The Little Professors'. 'The little *WHAT*?' 'Professors.' 'Oh, right.' Each time she drew breath, I was handed another pile of leaflets, catalogues and so on, rifled from the pile on her desk.

Also, I was informed, I would be relied upon to create English language courses at Elementary, Intermediate and Advanced level, based in part on activity work – namely, Playing and Doing, Art and Crafts, Cookery, Business Studies, Sport, and Social Skills. Is that all? Politely, I asked about the ages of these potential pupils. 'Oh, anything from three to sixteen' my Principal said airily, 'and some may only have anything from three weeks to three months to complete the courses.' As much as that! Goodness me. 'How soon do you expect to actually open the school?' I ventured. 'I have invited prospective parents to an Open Day in two weeks; we should have something to show them by then,' she replied. 'We shall discuss all that later and also the trips.' The *TRIPS*, of course!

Duangchai was now attempting to concentrate her mind on yet another series of phone calls, and I was dismissed with a wave of the well-manicured hand. I wandered off, thinking I had better have another look at this Peter and maybe glean a little more about the set-up here.

I found him, still seated where I left him, smoking a thin, reedy-looking cigar. A silver coffee pot, a steaming jug of milk and a sugar bowl all placed on a silver tray now adorned the desk alongside his piece of paper. I knocked and was treated to an openly hostile stare as I entered the room. 'General Manager?' I enquired sweetly. 'So what is it exactly, that you generally manage?'

After several utterly frustrating days, I set about interviewing people who had been short listed by Duangchai, one of whom was to be appointed as Head of the Nursery Department. I cannot be bothered to go into how dim the first four were; suffice it is to say that they had no idea, no imagination whatsoever (and that was a priority under the present circumstances), and one incredibly lethargic nineteen-year-old chappie, dressed in layers of vests and waistcoats, and with a baseball cap firmly welded to his head, didn't even know what a curriculum was.

After lunch there was one more interview. Pauline. Big, lumpy, pasty-faced and unsmiling, she presented herself in clothes that, although not following the dictates of fashion, were tasteful, clean and tidy. She spoke in clear, modulated tones and was direct and to the point. In her mid-thirties, she had spent much of her teaching career in foreign parts, most recently in Egypt. Her credentials proved that she was well-educated and well qualified in nursery teaching. She had also taken the trouble to learn a little of written and spoken Thai. Now I was impressed! In spite of her somewhat abrasive manner, I warmed to her, told her that I too was pretty vague about what her duties would be, but would she be supportive and prepared to run the nursery end of this somewhat obscure outfit that I had been contracted to.

Duangchai was a past master at changing her mind, but from what I could gather so far, allowing for many incidental changes of policy on the way, the school was to be divided into three main parts: a Youth club, a Nursery Department, and Trips.

The Youth Club, like everything else at that time, was without any youths. This was to be 'managed' by Peter, who, it appeared to me, was on some sort of gravy train, since he had survived in Thailand for four years with no qualifications whatsoever but had obviously established a few Connections. He was, however, without doubt, the most qualified know-all I had ever met, totally lacking in manners or finesse and at twenty-five years old, he had the self-assurance of a man twice his age who really did know it all. He had also engaged the services of three of his mates, without consultation with either me or Duangchai, to assist him in the running of this Youth Club without any youths.

I decided in my wisdom as educational consultant (note the absence of initial capitals) that job descriptions needed to be at least vaguely determined, and that mutual cooperation also had to be generated, if that was at all possible in the present climate, before anything at all could be achieved. 'Wouldn't it be a good idea,' I suggested brightly after several days of biting my tongue, 'if we had a staff meeting?' Ignoring the exaggerated raised eyebrows from the entire Youth Department, I went on. 'We should be deciding what resources we require, delegation of duties, and, most importantly, what ideas we have regarding Schemes of Work.' 'Schemes of what?' chortled one of Peter's newly engaged nerds. My patience was wearing very thin. 'Unless you have a *plan* for at least half of the first term, you won't know what equipment you will need, will you?' After a poke in the ribs from Pauline, I continued. 'Furthermore, I would like to have regular staff meetings at least once a week to provide a forum for an exchange of ideas, *and* to monitor progress.' The silence was palpable. Peter rallied, eventually. 'Yerse, so, OK, you wanna meeting.'

Pauline had taken very positive steps to set up a NURSERY DEPARTMENT, the second prong of the school. She knew exactly what she wanted and where to get all the stuff to provide a suitably equipped space to teach these little children who had not yet been enrolled, or even born so far as I could see! 'I need art paper, paints, chalk, crayons, books, little tables and chairs for little bums, cupboards for storage, music equipment, and leave it to me and I will get it,' she said.

She had also produced a generous budget. She grinned enigmatically at me, and I was encouraged by her support and confidence. Later, over a beer (of indeterminate origin since it was supplied in a five-litre plastic bottle), Pauline told me that she knew these people, they would cough up any amount of money to prove they were superior in any situation, materialism providing a kind of security of status, it seemed. 'This time it's going to be the most superior nursery in town,' she assured me. Wow!

It looked to me by now that, apart from creating language courses across the entire curriculum, monitoring and employing staff, and in between times teaching on a one-to-one basis (not a problem as yet, since I had no one to teach), my duties would also include organising the TRIPS, the third and, hopefully, the last department of this dream machine.

No, the children did not go to the UK in order to be educated at public schools, which had been my first impression. What they were to do was to spend six weeks posted in various areas of England – the Lake District, Ashtead in Surrey, Torquay, and Edinburgh, staying with host families in middle-class homes with the space and patience to feed and accommodate them, show them the sights, and generally induct them into the The English Way of Life. On a daily basis they would also attend language classes, given by luckless volunteers drawn from the local community, and held in church halls, various municipal buildings and perhaps on fine days, in someone's back garden.

This travel aspect of the school was not, of course, spelled out in detail in Duangchai's carefully prepared and expensively produced glossy brochure for the benefit of prospective parents, who, it appeared, in spite of the immense cost, were falling over themselves to send their children as young as eight years old to the UK to stay in a totally alien environment, with very minimal supervision other than from Duangchai herself and these virtually unknown families. The families, as far as I could determine, would be paid peanuts for their trouble.

I, apparently, was to coordinate these trips, write to the various agents in the UK in my very best English, and prepare these as yet non-existent trippers by way of language, English social behaviour and customs, how to hold a knife and fork and whatever else they could expect when they got there! My mind absolutely boggled.

My apartment in the prestigious Vilarma Suites was light, airy, adequate for my needs, and above all, private. From my minute balcony, I overlooked from the third floor the posh end of the Sukhumvit Road, the main thoroughfare of the city, which, if you drive, cycle or walk on it long enough, will take you all the way to Cambodia. However, from my bedroom window at the back I also overlooked a building site in the initial stages of pile-driving the perpendicular supports for a new 3-storey hotel.

I had been watching the clearing of this site when the young Thai workers arrived just after dawn each day, and before they began the pile-driving they had established temporary homes for themselves and their families. Home for the time being was a ramshackle hut, little more than a shed built from odd planks of wood, no windows and a metal roof, all tied to the boundary wire that separated the new site from our apartments next door. In the dense, humid warmth that permeated the city at night, it must have been very uncomfortable accommodation for the wives and children of the workers.

All, in their turn, did their ablutions in oil drums filled with water pumped from the bowels of the accumulated rubble. It was an engaging sight in the mornings, I can tell you, to see these virile young men dunking first themselves and then their children in these grubby oil drums. The best bit was watching them get out!

Once work really got started the families arrived, and men, women and children all threw their weight behind the project and lived on the site until it was finished.

They worked hard, together they began in the early hours of the morning. In between digging and the removal of rubble, they also helped the drivers of the clapped-out, resentful and resisting bulldozer, and also the pile-driver contraption which operated in tangent with the bulldozer, offered the heavy base thump to the bulldozer's wheezy whine. Since so many workers and their children were only too anxious to have a go on these ear-splitting machines, there was no relief from the intensity or offensiveness of the noise. My very next priority, I concluded, was to move!

There was a law in Bangkok at the time prohibiting lorries from using the streets during the daytime, thus avoiding adding to the general mayhem of congestion, so their only alternative was to deliver goods and materials at night. Great. The Building Site required many, many metal poles, thousands of the bleeding things, delivered over a period of several nights, to form the main initial structure of this brand new hotel.

My sleep pattern by now was not merely hugely disturbed, it was practically non-existent. At three o'clock one morning I was so utterly pissed off with trying to get enough sleep to see me through the next day that I got up, went downstairs in somewhat scanty night attire, and demanded of the guard on duty that he get his boss out of his pit to see me, NOW.

My landlord lived in a bungalow at the other side of the apartments, well away from the racket I was subjected to night after night. Finally he appeared. During the day this diminutive Japanese gentleman was always immaculate, oily black hair lathered down, collar, tie, crisp white shirt, the inevitable black trousers and highly polished shoes. In the middle of the night, however, he was a pitiful sight. His hair stood up on end like a flue brush, huge tortoiseshell spectacles perched precariously on the end of his nose, and his fearful buck teeth gleamed fretfully in the subdued light of the reception area. He hugged a vast black-and-white-striped kimono around himself and looked like a sagging tent.

'I cannot stand another night of this noise,' I cried, waving my arms dramatically in the general direction of the building site. 'Either you find me another apartment on your side of the Vilarma Suites or I leave – tomorrow.' It turned out that his son, for whom the hotel was being built by way of an investment for him, had an apartment just exactly where I wanted to be. 'Good,' I said, 'I will change places with him and *HE* can watch and hear his investment grow.' My little landlord was beside himself with cooperation. 'Ah so, it will be done.' It certainly bloody better be, I thought as I tottered irritably back to my bed.

And it was. Without warning I was moved, lock, stock and barrel, that very weekend by a small army of guards, the girls who did the washing, ironing and cleaning, and Mr Kimono himself. I expressed my humble gratitude and found myself in a larger, well-appointed apartment, artwork on the walls and spanking-clean polished wood floors. This is more like it, I thought gleefully.

There was, however, a rather embarrassing twist to this move. I was not allowed to lift a thing or given time to pack. 'No, no Ben Mairee, we do it, no wucking furries,' said a small, dainty Thai girl solemnly. Forthwith, my entire belongings, my lingerie, and everything else a girl thinks of as private were bundled up and carted off to my new abode.

Among all this stuff was a small wicker basket I was too late to retrieve, containing odds and ends – pencils, pens, nail file, odd earrings, things dumped there in passing. Also in this basket, I am reluctant to admit, was a collection of syringes and condoms.

Before, dear reader, you jump to conclusions, I will explain. Before I left the UK my doctor advised me that in view of the rampant AIDS situation in Thailand generally, it might be prudent to carry my own hermetically sealed syringes should I, for any reason, need an injection. Sound advice – hence the syringes.

The condoms were supplied courtesy of the Cabbages and Condoms restaurant, owned by a couple of Australian wits, and situated very near the Non-Scalpel Vasectomy Clinic in Soi 12 off the Sukhumvit Road. Instead of the usual miniature chocolate bars, these little complimentary packets of condoms, two at a time, would be placed in the saucer of your coffee cup at the end of a meal. The food was excellent, so I ate there with friends quite frequently. Not wishing to appear ungrateful for this thoughtful but, in my case, quite unnecessary little extra, I would deposit said condoms in my handbag and finally they became stockpiled in my wicker basket. So that, I would have hoped, would have cleared that up if only I had been able to explain it to the delightful Thai staff, who now, it seemed in my imagination, began to look at me in a whole new light.

In spite of my resolution to remove myself from raw scenes of grief and sadness at home, a grief which overtook all of us as a family so suddenly, tiredness and homesickness could account, I suppose, for occasional bouts of near-depression. However, my new pad cheered me up enormously and I began to buy pictures and plants to tart the place up more to my taste. I had already treated myself to a new, rather luxurious bedcover. The view from the new balcony was a treat. I now overlooked not a building site, but a pretty, traditional old Thai house. Its gabled roof with tilted eaves was almost entirely smothered in magenta bougainvillea. Fan palms, jacarandas and frangipani trees fought for space around it, and pink and blue wisteria grew from an old gnarled tree trunk, providing seeds and a nesting place for the birds. I was now buying bird seed and nuts for the squirrels, who soon began visiting me on the balcony for their morning treat.

At twilight the intoxicating smells of sandalwood and spices would waft up to my rooms, and this was the time the occupants of the house would eat outside out of bowls with chopsticks, the children sitting on reed mats on the dusty courtyard and their parents on tired rattan chairs. An older woman, presumably a grandmother, as these people were not prosperous enough to engage a nanny, would be seated in a cloth and cane swing, suspended from the rafters of the verandah, rocking an infant child to sleep. That's what I should be doing, I mused. In those moments particularly, I missed my own young grandchildren. All the same, this was a pleasant time of day for me; sitting on the balcony, plastered in Mosi-guard, I could still work a bit and listen to the high, tinkling voices of what seemed to me to be a very happy and contented family below.

I had been putting in long hours at the school, trying to pull together a coherent programme of priorities. I attended a very useful meeting with a departmental head at the British International School, who advised me to slow my speed by half, delegate to the point of total confusion, and wait. This apparently was the ethos of Thailand. It took some getting used to.

In the meantime I had been pointed in the right direction to buy books and consumables, and I spent several satisfying days being driven about by Sangpong in the Mercedes all over the city and beyond to choose suitable textbooks and innumerable books for the library. Although some of these were not entirely suitable for the purpose intended, I was looking forward to a jolly good read myself when I found the time. Funds were obviously not a problem – I was being given fistfuls of baht daily to spend, and I did.

Pauline accompanied me to a warehouse, a virtual Aladdin's cave of wonderful goodies for the 'Arts and Crafts' Duangchai was so paranoid about, and we had a lovely time spending someone else's money.

I could empathise with Duangchai's enthusiasm for creating a new place of learning in the city, apart from the fact that it was a very prestigious exercise in the eyes of her particular community.

Even rich kids at other private establishments would sit in overcrowded, ill-equipped, gloomy classrooms, with nothing on the walls to distract, learning by rote from outdated, uninspiring textbooks. Their teachers were Thai of course, and this was to be expected until it came to teaching English. The teachers had been taught by other Thai teachers who had learnt to speak, write and pronounce English very badly – it was painful to listen to and quite hard to understand at times.

Poor children in Thailand were only obliged to attend school until they were twelve years old, and the families were expected to pay; although what appeared to be a nominal sum, it was almost prohibitive if they had several offspring. The primary occupation of their parents was farming, and many had no guaranteed income.

Government attitudes towards schools were varied in 1995. There was a move at the time by the National Education Commission to create a loan system which would, in theory, expand the opportunities for pupils to stay on at school to improve their social mobility and ability to compete in the workplace. Some educationalists agreed with this policy and some did not, for a variety of reasons.

There were those who worried that families in rural areas would lose what little land they owned, and therefore also their livelihood, in an effort to pay back the loans. Then there were those, who in their wisdom, suggested that formal education was a waste of time anyway (yeah, on the poor!). These bright sparks, who had themselves enjoyed at least a half-decent education, declared: 'The more people learn in the school system, the more they lose their confidence. They need only to learn that which responds to their needs. People in the mountains should have knowledge that will help them sustain their lives, those who live near the sea should know the nature of the sea.' *Bangkok Post*, 1995. 'Learning,' they maintained, 'will not solve the problem of the human "green harvest".' The human 'green harvest' was a complex problem evidently, not solved by chucking more money at learning to prevent child prostitution and the iniquities of the commercial sex business. The roots of this vile aspect of Bangkok's low life spring almost entirely from the dire poverty of rural families, who are unable to discourage their girls – often very young – from coming to the city to earn money, however that manifests itself.

Pauline was proving to be a godsend. She lived nearby and had already introduced me to the local supermarket and beer garden, run by charming Indians (originally hailing from Birmingham), and we were all on first-name terms in no time.

The family supermarket supplied everything I could get in my local Spar at home, including gin and the specially ordered batch of tonic water. I could also eat there. The well-intentioned, kindly matriarch of this family cooked the most amazing selection of Indian food, and would pile up a plate of it for me because she thought I looked too thin. Compared with her well-upholstered frame, I suppose I did. I was also very grateful that, because I often had no currency, they allowed me a 'slate'.

It was time, though, for me to venture alone beyond the immediate vicinity of where I lived. Needing a change from Indian food and my good old standbys of cheese and biscuits, I went out at dusk one evening in search of somewhere else and something to eat. I walked alone along the Sukhumvit Road, over the bridge and down the other side, mentally registering that I had turned left, and then right. So far, so good.

This main thoroughfare, like the other streets in the city, abounds with stalls and little shops selling cheap ready-mades, tie-dyed T-shirts, ethnic clothes, imported fake designer goods, watches, jewellery – anything and everything to attract tourists and people like me, new to Bangkok, looking for a bargain and something cool to wear. The whole atmosphere drew me like a magnet, but I was hungry and there seemed little in the way of restaurants in the immediate vicinity. What I didn't know at the time was that most restaurants and the inevitable girlie bars have smoked-glass windows, providing their clientele with an element of privacy. I was not about to chance going through the wrong door. Darkness descended in minutes, and I was beginning to feel uncomfortable wandering about on my own, so I decided to get back onto more familiar territory.

I located the bridge to wend my way back. A different bridge. I had no idea that there were so many bridges crossing that main road, and I had forgotten to notice exactly where it was I had turned off. I had wandered further than I thought. Now there were no Europeans about, and when I came to think about it, I was not entirely sure of my address either, even if I could have conveyed it to a Thai taxi driver. Just as desperation was about to set in – *alors!* My friends from the supermarket spotted me from across the road, and never have I been so grateful to see a familiar face. '*What*,' they wanted to know, 'are you doing here?'

The entire Indian family were eating away from their own watering hole, in a smart French bistro that looked like a dental surgery from the outside, and they, bless them, insisted I should join them. I did magnificent justice to a delicious medium-rare steak and French fries and was driven home in style – side-saddle – my new tie-dyed ethnic skirt flying in my face on the back of a very large, high-powered motorbike. I felt as though I was on a magic steed!

There was a notice in the *Bangkok Post* which merrily pronounced that 'footpaths will be turned into roads where necessary to ease traffic congestion'. The locals, not easily roused to anger, were very cross about it. Some gentleman in authority who claimed to know about all things transport seemed to have come to the conclusion that it must be pedestrians who were to blame for Bangkok's troubled traffic jams. The total disaster caused by the lack of movement on the city roads, he decided in his bureaucratic way, was the fault of the poor blighters who could not afford a car, or any other mode of transport, and who had the nerve to walk on the footpath as they trudged about their daily business, thus depriving long-suffering Mercedes-Benz drivers and their ilk of precious driving space.

The cynical had spotted a few holes in the official announcement, not to mention in the footpaths in question. 'What footpaths?' Bangkok has probably got fewer footpaths/sidewalks/pavements per ambulatory citizen than any other city in the world. No one needed reminding that the few apologies for pavements that did exist were little more than pedestrian death traps, designed to send any unwary biped to the nearest hospital forthwith.

That latest move to solve the traffic problem also greatly irritated those for whom it was claimed the footpaths were intended in the first place – street vendors and motorcyclists.

A further claim of deprivation caused by the potential disappearance of walking space came from the hole diggers from the Electricity and Water

Departments. It had, it was claimed, been a long tradition with these auspicious authorities to take turns at digging vast holes in the footpaths for no apparent reason, at regular intervals. They were polite about it though. Each department waited patiently for one lot of hole fillers to finish their job before the next brigade of diggers came, to spend months over new excavations in any given place, sometimes in the same place. Once their task was completed, in came the others from a different department to repeat the process; all this to a bemused, stoical Bangkok citizenry. At least, they said, people were being employed. All very civilised, but it was no small worry that soon there would be no more footpaths to dig up!

Most people would agree though, that there can be no worse place to drive than in Bangkok. It often surprised me that in spite of the Thais' generally gentle demeanour as they go about their daily business, the Thai driver, whatever he is driving – Merc, tuk-tuk, taxi, bus or motorbike – is little short of a maniac. Simple things – signal before you turn, overtake from the right, and basic rudimentary practices of driving, such as 'slow down and look before you zoom through an intersection' – elementary rules designed for the protection of the driver and his passengers, and pedestrians, – are totally ignored. Drivers on those roads had little regard or respect for life, limb or other people's bumpers.

They have a manic antipathy towards anyone who is a second late restarting their engine in a traffic jam. Thai men are usually very polite, but behind their status symbol on wheels they are not. They have a self-righteous chauvinistic aversion towards female drivers, and female drivers are correspondingly callous towards male drivers' feelings or their rear lights. There was also a definite pecking order among drivers. I was able to make these observations by way of occupying my time sitting next to Sangpong on our various forays into the city. I concluded that if you happened to be a woman, even if you were driving the old man's limo, you were definitely at the bottom of the pile.

At the top of the social driving ladder are the public buses. Basically, these are often driven by hypertensive idiots who care not a fig about their bus because they don't own it, and who will drive on whatever side of the road they please, stop when and where they feel like it, disgorging passengers at irregular intervals, seldom waiting long enough for the last one to get off or on. It doesn't help either, that many pedestrians walk in the road because the roads are in marginally better condition than footpaths, and the risk from falling masonry dropping from the endless demolition/building work that has been going on in the city for years, is less.

I had a very unpleasant experience on one of these buses. The Number 11 air-conditioned bus was my lifeline to most of the places I wanted to go to in the city. It was always standing room only, if you can squeeze in, until I found to my surprise one day that in spite of the crowd there was a vacant seat. I sat in it. Within seconds I was being shouted at and severely whacked about the shoulders with the metal ticket and coin container held by the female conductor as she went about her business collecting fares. That container, shaped like a baton and applied across my back with a very heavy hand, really shocked me and only with barely contained restraint did I resist smacking her across the mouth. What could have been a very ugly situation was saved by a European gentleman explaining to me that I had committed the crime of sitting next to a *MONK*! Evidently, it is tantamount to a criminal offence for a woman to even touch the clothes of a monk, let alone sit next to him! I have to say it was quite a while before I used the Number 11 air-conditioned bus again.

By now I thought I had exhausted the various modes of transport in what was often a futile attempt to move around the city on my own, and because I had very little time to myself after the endless demands of Duangchai, it was imperative that I spent no more time sitting in or on vehicles than I was obliged to.

Taxis were a rip-off – the drivers never understood anyway where I wanted to go unless my destination was written in the Thai language, and that was only ever achieved by nailing a Thai colleague to the floor while he or she tried to follow my finger across the map of Bangkok. Many of the cities' inhabitants know very little about any other location in that heaving metropolis besides the one in which they themselves actually live.

The three-wheeled tuk-tuk was cheap and all right if you could stand the terror of the ride and the pollution from the back end of everything else on the road. Another law, laid down by those senile bureaucrats who frequently laid down laws and then forgot about them, was that *no vehicle* was allowed to emit poisonous carbon dioxide exhaust fumes, at any time or in any place, and this was punishable by instant and heavy fines if they did.

Well, the biggest and most unremitting offenders of these offensive emissions were the buses, and *they* were owned by the authority who instigated the law in the first place! Many people wore masks on the streets to protect themselves from the filthy, stultified air, and those who didn't could expect premature expiration from disease of the lungs. Including me.

If you are really in a hurry there is always the motorbike. Clapped-out machines driven by young dolts of fourteen or so who will, for a mere handful of coins, whizz you to your destination. Riding side-saddle, hanging on for dear life, grasping the scrawny boy round his middle with one arm till surely he cannot breath, clutching a purse and holding down a billowing skirt, it was not my first choice of transport.

However, seeing me arrive at my post back at the ranch with trembling knees and a dirty face after yet another such hair-raising experience, Pauline, once she had stopped grinning, decided it was high time I was introduced to the river bus.

Bangkok was built as an amphibious city around a network of canals, and the first streets were constructed in the second half of the 19th century. Most of the canals have been turned into roads on the Bangkok side, but the Chao Phraya River is still a major transport route for residents and non-residents alike, forming more of a link than a barrier between the two halves of the city.

There are several different kinds of boats that use the river: the Express, the ferries shuttling to and fro between the banks, and the Longtail. These Longtail boats do not necessarily stop at every landing – they will only pull in if anyone wants to get on or off, which is not always very helpful if you don't know where you are at any given point on the river. Nevertheless, they are probably the quickest and most interesting way of getting across town, if you can stand the stench of the water.

The very next Saturday, Pauline and I organised ourselves so that we could have a full day out together. Up and away early, we made our way towards the river, where the pier was located at the back of several side streets. The houses looked less and less salubrious as we threaded our way through a teaming tunnel of life, brightly coloured awnings made of paper, toy-tiny stalls selling soup and barbecued chicken, and even live chickens, patiently waiting to have their necks wrung. We finally reached the Chao Phraya River, where shacks of thatch and bamboo raised on stilts crowded the banks. A rickety wooden platform stretched forward to accommodate passengers getting on and off the river craft. The prow of the boat was raised and the sides had rolled-up faded tarpaulin sheets, tied back by ragged ropes, unlikely to have been untied for a very long time.

'Oh, this is nice,' I commented to Pauline, 'once I can get my leg over without doing permanent damage.' No sooner had I steadied myself to sit on the planks that served as a seat, than we were off. This battered-looking craft suddenly revved up and literally whizzed away almost immediately at tremendous speed; the river sprayed up and over everyone on the bank, and completely soaked the passengers. Pauline was agog with merriment. 'Thanks, mate.' In my sopping wet Thai-style trousers I mentally observed how much prettier she looked when she smiled. 'The trick, dear,' she advised me belatedly, 'is to keep your nose and mouth covered. One drop of that river water in your innards and you are dead!'

We alighted at Damrong Rak Road, the nearest stop to Chinatown. The Chinese have been a dominant force in the shaping of Thailand, and commerce is the foundation of their success. Chinese merchants first gained a toehold in the mid-fourteenth century, when they contributed so much to the prosperity of the city-state of Ayutthaya that they were the only foreign community allowed to live within the city walls. Soon their compatriots were established all over the country and when the capital was eventually moved to Bangkok, it was to an already flourishing Chinese trading post. By the end of the 19th century, the Chinese dominated Thailand's commercial and urban sector, while the Thais remained in firm control of the political domain, an arrangement that apparently satisfied both parties. As an old Chinese proverb goes, 'We don't mind who holds the head of the cow, providing we can milk it.'

Pauline led me firmly by the arm towards the markets, through a sprawl of narrow, busy alleyways, shophouses, open-fronted warehouses and remnants of colonial-style architecture. We walked past Hua Lamphong Railway Station to a wedge of land solely occupied by a single temple. Outwardly unprepossessing, Wat Thai Temple boasts an absolutely stunning interior feature – the world's largest solid gold Buddha is housed there. Over three metres tall and weighing more than five tons, the Golden Buddha gleams as if coated in liquid metal, seated on a high plinth, placed amid massed candles and surrounded by offerings of lotus buds and incense.

I stood entranced for a while, barefoot, almost immobilised by the sheer splendour of this massive effigy, and wondered whether I too could make my contribution to the massed candles all around me. Pauline indicated that I could, and as I fished in my bag for coins, I realised that my trousers were steaming. Plumes of soft mistiness rose from my clothes, still damp from the dousing on the boat. 'I think,' my friend and colleague whispered solemnly, 'you are getting a bit atmospheric.'

She hauled me outside to dry, and it was only the rough terrain that reminded me that my sandals were still on the steps of the temple. No they weren't. Someone had decided that my footwear was in better condition than theirs and had thoughtfully left their battered soles in recompense.

I limped along, an alien thong digging in between my toes, darkly inspecting other people's feet for the short time it took to arrive in Sampeng Lane. Stretching about one kilometre, Sampeng Lane, with its history of opium dens, gambling houses and brothels, makes an interesting introduction to commercial Chinatown, but another street which crosses it about halfway along promised to be a more sensual experience.

Packed with people from dawn till dusk, this dark alleyway is where you go in search of ginseng roots – apparently absolutely essential for good health – as well as still-quivering fish heads, cubes of cockroach-killer chalk, and pungent piles of cinnamon sticks. There were ancient Chinese grandfathers, enigmatically watching their descendents plying their trade, traditional pharmacists concocting bizarre potions to order, and alleys branching off in all directions to gaudy Chinese temples and more market squares.

In an open area of the market, there were fish and toads floundering around in half an inch of smelly water in big metal pans. Barbecued chicken blazed away next to the clothes stall, the languid street vendors seemingly oblivious to the smoke while they sold bright, silky ethnic clothes and sarongs among rudely emblazoned T-shirts.

Pandemonium reigned, with noise coming from competing vendors selling their idea of the latest pop music, and shouting across to each other in good-natured banter. Near-naked tiny children happily ran around, unencumbered by reprimand, bar a sharp slap round the head if they got too near the numerous fires. Groups of women were clustered around innumerable small covered barrows, providing a primitive kitchen for the preparation and cooking of what seem to me an impossible variety of dishes. Rice, noodles, vegetables, meat and fish, and what one barrow didn't provide another one did, and nobody minded if you selected something from each.

I was starving, so was Pauline, and at the first sign that we were about to partake of their tempting food, we were immediately provided with a couple of plastic chairs and a wobbly table covered in oilcloth. We were able to eat our food there and then, armed with chopsticks and paper plates.

Pauline admitted later that she had never been in that district before, but at the time she mustered the aplomb of a matriarch doing her weekly shopping. She bought cinnamon sticks; I nervously bought ginseng in a small polythene bag, and we found our way to another street, where there were more holes in the ancient walls, now specialising in paper funeral art. Believing that the deceased should be well provided for in their afterlife, the Chinese buy miniature paper replicas of necessities to be burned with the body. Especially popular are paper houses, cars, suits of clothing and, of course, money.

A hundred metres or so on, with me still in extremely uncomfortable footwear, there was an odd assortment of shops in the square known as Nakhon Kasem – the Thieves Market, once full of illicit goods but now stocked high with a vast range of metal wares, from antique gongs to modern musical instruments and machine parts.

Before Sampeng Lane finally fizzled out, another street led us down and back towards the river. On the way, there was Wat Chakrawat, home to several long-suffering crocodiles, not to mention monkeys, dogs and chess-playing locals. Crocodiles have apparently lived in the tiny pond behind this place for about fifty years, ever since one was taken there after being hauled out of the Chao Phraya River, where it had been endangering the life and limbs of residents of the stilt houses built on either side of the river. These people expected to perform their daily toilet arrangements in and around their own patch of water without fear of interference from dangerous carnivores. This original crocodile, now stuffed, sits in a glass case overlooking the current generation in the pond.

Across the other side of the Wat compound is a grotto, housing two unusual Buddhist relics. The first is a black silhouette on the wall, decorated with squares of gold leaf and believed to be the Buddha's shadow. Nearby, the statue of a fat monk looks on. The story goes that this monk was so good-looking that he was forever being tempted by the attentions of women, and the only way he could deter them was to make himself ugly, which he did by gorging himself into obesity.

6

It took several weeks of working seven days a week from 8.00 a.m. till late evening before I felt that maybe now I could think of myself as a true Educational Consultant, with initial capitals, although I was reluctant to confide that to Peter.

I didn't mind the long hours, since my social life was pretty limited at that time, – apart from the various orientation trips and a late drink of an evening with Pauline at our Indian friends' beer garden at the top of the road. The work at the 'school' (hopefully to become a school if our efforts to make it so were ever to pay off) was challenging and absorbing.

Peter had reluctantly taken on some of the responsibility to research appropriate furniture and equipment and, if it was approved by the Powers That Be, to organise delivery, all part of his General Managing. It had also been tartly suggested to him once again that it might be an idea if he were to sort out his little band of merrymakers to knuckle down and actually plan what they intended to do, so that if and when they ever got any youths to try out their brilliant expertise, they would be prepared for it.

There now seemed a preponderance of staff employed at considerable expense when weighed against the fact that there was little or no money coming in, and plenty of it still going out. In addition to Peter there were now Dave, Paul and Martin in the Youth Department. I had engaged the services of Joanne, a charming English girl, qualified in English as a Foreign Language and for the time being, content to plan coursework so that when the boys got fed up kicking a football around (Learning by Doing), their students could actually study the blunt end of the English language, thus providing the learning bit.

Duangchai had also invited Una, a crony of a friend of a friend of hers, to be Office Administrator. She was a most glamorous 50-year-old Eurasian widow, and she was joined by Superin, at 21 a graduate in classical Thai dance who also had a very good command of English. Superin had been working in the National Museum giving free guided tours to visitors, compensated by free meals in the Museum cafeteria. She seemed very happy to be doing quite menial office tasks, and between us all we gradually established a measure of cooperation that would have been beyond my hopes a few weeks earlier.

Much of this conspiring together was developed through a mutual frustration and wry amusement at Duangchai's constant changes of mind. Policies changed every day, sometimes twice, and a little suggestion would sow a seed until it became a Number One Priority in no time.

There was the day I happened to comment on how attractive the gardens looked early in the morning – and they did. Tamarind, banyans and rain trees filtered the light, the heady smell of jasmine permeated the air, and glossy leaves of exotic plants were all freshly watered; green lawns lovingly tended and trimmed by Duangchai's army of young Thai gardeners. Everything grew by the yard, and there was shade just where it was needed at all times of the day, provided by mature fan palms. There was a pond, but this so sadly neglected. 'What a shame,' says I, 'what that pond needs is some fish to swim around in it, and some ducks.' Hardly a second ticked by.

I knew, I already just knew, I should have kept my mouth shut. 'What a marvellous idea,' gushed Duangchai, her imagination captured immediately. 'I shall take care of the fish but you must drop everything,' she said, visibly warming to her subject. 'Go right now, go and get some ducks, Sangpong will take you.'

I should have realised by now that Chinese Thais, or any other Thais come to that, are not known for their sense of humour, and my protestations that I was only joking fell on stony ground.

There and then, much to the delight of my staff (also not yet known for their loyalty), with me dressed in an ankle-length cream skirt and new Thai silk shirt, open sandals and painted toenails, and Sangpong complete with chauffeur's cap and light grey, well-pressed suit, we were dispatched to paddle through muck, slime and rotting vegetables in Klong Toey Market, in search of ducks.

We undoubtedly stood out like a couple of lighthouses amongst the stinking fish, newly slaughtered meat and the general squalor that is the lot of these lowly Thai market workers. They smiled a lot, at least those who were not drugged to the eyeballs or lying comatose on an old sack; mostly they were grinning, but not without reason, as they were amused to see me and my bodyguard haggling over the price of four dingy feathered ducks, who – we were assured – would be producing ducklings at any minute. Oh yeah? I thought it very unlikely indeed after having their feet firmly tied together, stuffed into a polythene bag and lobbed into the boot of the car, albeit the jolly old BMW, for the journey back to the school.

Amazingly, they quickly recovered once they were fed and shoved into the dank pond in the garden.

We were promptly coerced to make a very reluctant return trip to the market to buy terrapins and turtles for that damn pond and then, unbelievably, Peter, beginning to fancy himself as the wit of the outfit, piped up to say, 'We only need a goat – the children [still non-existent] would *love* a goat!'

The following morning, carried away with the success of the new inhabitants in the pond, Duangchai greeted me at the door before I had a chance to even remove my shoes, clutching a handful of high denominations of baht – for the Goat!

'Duangchai,' I said vehemently, 'I will do almost anything to further the prestige and success of your school, but I will not stuff a goat into the boot of the car, nor will I have it sit next to me *IN* the car, and I certainly will not walk it all the way back from Klong Toey Market!' They allow elephants to walk the streets of Bangkok, but a goat? Not with me, sunshine! 'Ask Peter,' I suggested malevolently, anxious to get my own back. 'He likes managing things.'

The school, now optimistically registered as 'The Little Professors', was by now looking a little more like an educational establishment. Peter had used his arrogant airs and graces to good cause, demanding deliveries on time of desks and chairs, and a variety of designer sports equipment – enough, I thought, to entertain the youths of the entire city of Bangkok should they ever be enrolled. Quality cupboards and shelves for the library arrived, and suitably scaled down but no less expensive furniture for the Nursery Department. The nursery was of no interest whatsoever to Peter, but, jostled by the formidable Pauline, even he did not see the point in wasting time arguing, and anyway, as he pointed out to excuse his submission to her demands for everything she was likely to need, it wasn't his money. Quite right.

Books, materials, staffroom suitably kitted out with filing cabinets, copiers, and computers – all things pertinent to accommodate our workload more or less – were in place. For a moment, I cast my mind back to the days in Moldova, and remembered how difficult it had been to acquire even a modicum of learning aids for those hard-working kids in Eastern Europe.

Peter had also treated himself to a new desk, expansive enough to mirror his own vision of power. He condescendingly granted that I could have his old one. 'How very kind,' I murmured.

Duangchai had spent a further small fortune on strategically placed house plants to enhance the entrance hall and staircase, and after her evening inspection when the entire staff were clearly exhausted with placing all this stuff to its best advantage, she announced that we were ready (as ready as we were ever likely to be) for the prospective Parents Open Day.

'Would you,' Duangchai enquired silkily of me, 'prepare some of those proper little cucumber and fish-paste sandwiches like they have for tea in England? I think the Queen has them at about four in the afternoon.' I gaped. Far be it for me to question the point, and I didn't, but where, pray, was I to get fish paste in Bangkok?

The bone china tea sets, silver trays and teapots were delivered from goodness knows where by phantom van drivers and probably at mind-boggling expense, and masses of delectable tiny cakes arranged prettily in little flowered baskets arrived, complete with napkins, proudly embossed 'The Little Professors' in what looked to me like pure gold. Millions of my finger sandwiches, stretched to four different fillings (no fish paste), were arranged seductively on Top-of-the-Range sandwich plates.

'Marvellous,' they said, 'so English, and you are so warm.' You can say that again, I thought grumpily as I fumbled to separate my knickers from my sweating skin.

The boys wore their new designer T-shirts, bright red and emblazoned with the school logo, designed by Paul and Martin after a few jars in the bar up the road. After a few abortive attempts, mainly of rude children doing rude things, all of which Pauline and I were invited to admire, they had finally produced a gross image of a small child wearing a tasselled mortar board and waving the Thai flag. It was meant as a laugh but instantly captured Duangchai's imagination. '*Perfect*,' she trilled happily, clapping her hands together. 'You lovely boys are so-ooo talented,' And she planted a very conservative lipsticked kiss on both their cheeks. Neither of these two jokers even had the grace to blush. 'Told ya,' smirked Peter aside to me. 'I know how to pick 'em.' He certainly did.

Pauline, Joanne and I did our best to subserve and placate, and gave generously of our time, murmuring evasive but convincing answers to the enquiries and concerns regarding the education of the Illustrious Connections' offspring, who, very soon, it would appear, would be descending on us at the school in droves, if Duangchai was to be believed.

It was a surprisingly good turnout of prospective parents, who, judging by their lovely clothes and fine jewellery and expensive limos lining the drive, were all pretty well-heeled, and all certainly seemed to be having a good time visiting their investment.

I wearily concluded later that evening, sitting down at last with a well-deserved, generously poured G & T, that this gathering of the clans had been as much an exercise in social jockeying as a concern to find a good school for their children.

Probably as a direct result of the Parents' Day, Pauline and I were invited by Duangchai to a diplomatic do at the prestigious Oriental Hotel the following Friday evening.

Any function of any importance is almost inevitably held in one or other of the swanky hotels in the city. Very rarely is anyone invited to the homes of the rich Thai families – in fact, I could not even say where Duangchai lived, let alone profess ever to have been invited to her house the whole time I was in Bangkok.

However, this do apparently was going to be a posh occasion and the Oriental was a very posh hotel. Pauline and I had a giggly afternoon trying to buy something to wear – she really was a big girl and not easy to kit out in something glamorous, and I was not as young as I would like to be, so we shared an almost insoluble problem, except that I was more interested in clothes and was determined to do at least some justice to myself and the occasion. Pauline, on the other hand, dolefully assured me that as long as she could find something to fit her, she would wear it. Well, we had to do better than that!

We did. She looked lovely in a silk tie-dyed jade green outfit of trousers and tunic, which she sulkily tried on and then surprised me and herself by wanting earrings and bracelets to match. I sorted myself out with a nice little black lace number costing me a small fortune, but I thought it worth it under the circumstances. I also bought black silk stockings, which, in spite of the sheer denier, might in conjunction with the Mosi-guard, keep off at least some of the mosquitoes that lurk on lawns after dark. How right I was!

On the morning of the grand do, I was greeted at the school by Duangchai asking whether I was thinking of having my hair done. No, I wasn't. I do my own hair, I wash it most days, and on special occasions I might slap a bit more conditioner on it to keep it down, but generally speaking I am satisfied to know that my hair – unruly though it may be – is regularly cut and always clean.

'No, no,' expostulated Duangchai, 'you must come with me to *my* salon, get your hair *properly* attended to, and anyway, the President will be there this morning!' Oh well then, in that case of course I will have my hair done. The President no less, did he have his hair cut in a ladies' salon? I was impressed and, not being one for missing out on a new experience, off I went with Duangchai to get 'properly attended to' and to meet the President.

I was immediately enveloped in a voluminous black gown, which was tied at the back, and then I was slapped onto a black leather trestle table, lying totally horizontal with my neck stretched backwards over a black sink with elaborate gold taps.

My hair was washed vigorously – very vigorously, long fingernails scraping my scalp, in freezing cold water. I loathe cold water on my head and I was already beginning to get into a bad mood. Where was the President? Was *he* going to be subjected to this ruthless treatment?

I was eventually swathed in a multitude of towels and led to a swivel chair in line with other women being given various treatments. Some were having a manicure, a pedicure, or a face mask, and some were also having tin foil wrapped around tiny strands of hair; most had a tray of coffee at their elbow. A tray of massive rollers appeared at the side of my seat.

The young male stylist was not encouraging. With his hands on his hips and his mouth pursed into a disapproving moue, he moved around me contemplating my short, curly mop. 'This won't do, this won't do at all,' he said, flapping his hands about. 'Very well,' he sighed, and promptly attacked me. My hair was stretched and pulled and fixed tightly into dozens of pink plastic rollers until my head really ached. I was planted under a noisy dryer. And then the President arrived.

Duangchai, getting the whole works, with nails, feet and face being attended to simultaneously, loftily introduced me to Sebastian, who, it turned out, was the *esteemed* representative of Toni & Guy salons in London, doing his rounds, checking up that all was well with the salons in this neck of the woods.

He spoke with a distinctive Brummie accent. 'What are you doing here?' he enquired of me. 'Some President,' I said, disagreeably patting my pink rollers. 'Get me out of here!' I left that horrible place looking like Edna Everage in her most outrageous wig; no way was I going back to school looking like that. I made my excuses, went back to my pad, washed my hair and prepared for the evening jamboree in my own way.

The Oriental Hotel, as luck would have it, was within easy walking distance from where Pauline and I lived, so, tarted up in all our posh gear, we stopped for a quick bevvy at the top of the road – much to the delight of our Indian friends – before wending our way into the fray, so to speak.

Hotels in Thailand bear comparison with those anywhere in the world, and some are among the very best. Bangkok's famous Oriental is something of a legend, having for many years been voted the world's top hotel by visitors travelling on business. This, the first and oldest of Bangkok's hotels, which, from the day of its opening in 1887 came up to European standards and expectations, was actually known for decades as 'The New Oriental', since it took the name, location and most of the clientele, from an earlier seamen's lodging house. Since then it has welcomed countless crowned heads, heads of state, and many other famous people – Somerset Maugham still has a suite there dedicated to his name – and has kept all its glamour. Anyone can go there, paying guests or not, to at least soak up the atmosphere evoked by the fame of the place and take afternoon tea in the Old Lobby or enjoy a 'sundowner' on the famous terrace overlooking the elegant gardens and the river.

It was here we were introduced to the Austrian Ambassador to Thailand and the Thai Ambassador to Austria and their wives, and to others whose names we couldn't even begin to pronounce, let alone remember. So there we were, relieving them of their delicious canapés and doing polite justice to fine French wines that were constantly being circulated among the guests by busy waiters. We were having a very good time of it indeed.

During light, easy conversations, I detected a note of admiration for

Duangchai, who had, it would seem, earned a lot of brownie points for having gained the services of real live, qualified teachers brought all the way from England. 'They speak so well, so precise,' they said, 'so informed, such charming English accents.' Where we came from in London, in the unlikely event that we would even be invited to such a function with comparable upper circles there, we would have found these remarks extremely patronising, but there, among all those really nice people, they simply sounded genuine and reassuring.

Pauline slid off to go home, to nurse the mozzie bites she was collecting in spite of her trousers and generous dousing of Mosi-guard, but I was happy to stay a while longer to enjoy the moment and the music from the orchestra, assembled out there on the lawns and under the stars.

I felt mellow, tanked up by – for me – copious amounts of wine. The musicians, having exhausted their repertoire of scores from the musicals, now played on with haunting, nostalgic Irish ballads.

Probably in an effort to account for my whimsical nature as a child, I was reliably informed by my maternal and somewhat reproachful grandmother that out of the average eight pints of blood in the human frame, unfortunately at least four pints of mine were Irish. I hardly knew my father, he being conspicuous by his absence most of the time. In my ignorance, I had assumed that he, in common with half the male population of Ireland in those days, was digging up the Great South West Road, and at weekends was creating havoc in many of the pubs in West London. I have since learned that he was doing no such thing: apparently he had other fish to fry.

Feeling an emotional and patriotic stirring of my four pints of Irishness, I began to sing. Very quietly, to myself. 'O Danny boy . . .' Carried away I was, what with the midnight sky and the stars and everything. '. . . I long to hear you . . .' I was totally unaware that anyone was within yards of the sanctuary of my leaning post behind the potted plants, until a voice murmured, 'Lovely, lovely.' I nearly jumped out of my skin, aghast that I had been overheard. My horror at being heard 'singing' can only be explained by the fact that I really, really cannot sing. In my time I have been chucked out of the school choir and the church choir, and was never allowed to go carol singing with other kids in case I put them off.

I turned to see a very handsome gentleman; he had sidled up to me with his left hand cupped to his ear, and close to my head. I was deeply embarrassed. The band was still on its wretched Irish theme. 'Shall we sing together?' he invited me. Clearly he was an Irishman. 'If you ever go across the sea to Ireland,' he crooned in a light, soft lilt, 'maybe at the closing of your day . . .' My knees were weak, my voice a croak. '. . . you will see . . .' The French wine was coursing freely through my veins. We sang together, with me sounding like a nutmeg grater, tipsily adding some ghastly resonance to his tenor.

He was delighted, and so were the fifteen or so fellow guests gathered nearer to hear us. We sang on – if he couldn't remember the words then I did, and so we filled in the gaps between us.

I dared not drink another drop, nor eat another morsel. I made my excuses to leave. I bade goodnight to my hosts and humbly accepted their thanks for the spontaneous 'entertainment with your gentleman friend', who had now blatantly cleared off.

He was standing by the revolving doors leading out of the hotel, with a limo parked in the drive. Wordlessly, he indicated for me to get in. I did. 'Where to?' he said, grinning. He had beautiful teeth. 'Vilarma Suites.' I really was feeling an absolute idiot by now. 'Somewhere off the Sukhumvit Road.' Oh dear.

'Connor,' he said, holding out his hand. 'Connor from Boston, Dublin, County Cork, Boston, and now Bangkok.' He added, 'My parents were Irish, my father was in the Diplomatic Service. And you?' 'Mary, no fixed abode, and Bangkok, if we can find where I live. My father was an Irishman too, but I don't remember much about him.' At this he hooted. 'C'mon, let's go and have a nightcap somewhere.' I needed another drink like a hole in the head. 'No thank you.' Now I was firm. 'I really can't, I have to be up early tomorrow, and anyway, I think I have blotted my copybook quite enough for one night.'

He didn't insist, but chattered happily on about all things Irish all the way home. 'Goodnight Mary,' he said gallantly as the guards swung open the gates to let me in.

7

The school had now enrolled a number of students, but only eight were attending during the week. These were younger children, mostly the responsibility of Pauline. Others who were attending their own schools during the week, only showed up at weekends, giving the boys from the Youth Department something to do at last.

Physical exercise for children seemed not to be high on the agenda amongst the upper echelons of Thai society, but some parents were beginning to see the sense of our plans for including exercise and outdoor activities in the curriculum. Paul, Peter and Martin were good at encouraging participation in football, tennis and miniature golf, and took the teenagers swimming and ice skating, and soon we were inundated with applications to join the school for the weekend sessions.

With the exception of European-style winter sports, virtually every form of modern sport can be enjoyed in and around Bangkok; there are clubs, grounds and tennis courts all open to everyone for a modest fee. The ice rink and swimming pools, comparatively new amenities in the city, were underused, with rich kids too lazy to go, and being unaffordable for poor families whose children were often expected to work.

The better-off Thai children do very little with their free time at home. They had every conceivable kind of toy, musical instrument and technological appliance, but were easily bored, and there was never enough to keep them amused for very long. Most weekends they would go shopping – again – and be indulged with more CDs, videos, and designer clothes. The highlight of the outing – invariably with a nanny – would be to eat in McDonald's. With its cheap junk food, although expensive compared with the usual rice-based diet common to most Thais, McDonald's was considered a real treat and the place was always crowded.

Street kids, however, when they were not working, could often be seen kicking a ball about, and everywhere is deserted when there is international football on television. Girls as well as boys know the names of all the famous players.

A better atmosphere of cooperation had developed between me and the Youth Department. They gradually saw the point of following up their activities on the field with language worksheets, and since I prepared most of these and they didn't have to do the work themselves, they became quite keen to use them. They were also behaving more like the young men I was used to, my sons and their friends, and began to talk about their families and girlfriends and almost everything else under the sun.

They were delighted one day to find a Bangkok Yellow Pages, printed in English. 'Now we can find out where all the action is,' they said, 'like where all the girlie bars are' (those they didn't already know). Some of the advertisements were full page and very explicit indeed. 'Can we use these as worksheets?' 'No you cannot!'

All three of the boys had long-standing relationships with lovely Thai girls, so it really was all talk. When I reminded them that I was the only one in present company who was actually free to consider the flavours of the Orient, they promptly found an advertisement for me. 'You could do with a good rub down,' they informed me, scrutinising the claims of some of the more dubious massage parlours, and decided between them it was high time I improved my education and took a visit to the seamier side of Bangkok.

They took me to watch an international rugby match, played in my home town in West London and shown on television in a very disreputable bar in Soi Cowboy, very decadent and not at all a place for a nice girl like me. It was packed full of European men, flirting outrageously with very young Thai girls and their mothers, and I had a whale of a time chatting up the barmen.

Now of course, we were all very much more relaxed in each other's company and the boys took it as their cue to use common expletives in times of stress or even just to enhance their normal conversation. Pauline was doing the same when she really wanted to make a point, and coming from her it just made me laugh. But it was catching.

Duangchai was forever admiring the boys for their athleticism on the field. 'You are so fit, so handsome in your shorts,' she exclaimed regularly, and she hung on to their every word. Every weekend we would see them, the boys in their ever-shorter shorts, urging their students to kick, run and tackle on the field using very ripe terminology indeed, while Duangchai clapped and cheered on the sidelines.

'Fuck it,' Duangchai announced one afternoon, 'that bollocks fax machine has bloody broken down again!' She really didn't see anything out of order in her choice of words, and although I wanted to laugh as the others were, collectively collapsing in a hysterical heap, I felt sure that such language would not be approved of by the Illustrious Connections.

At the next staff meeting a new policy was firmly put in place: 'No Swearing Inside the Precincts of the School'. It didn't last, of course.

I was beginning to think it was time to get a pattern of regular time off, not only for me but for all the teaching staff. Snatching a day off now and then was not good enough for any of us.

At one of our (now regular) staff meetings, we agreed on an arrangement of ten days on and four days off. Pauline, Joanne and I were committed to one-to-one language lessons at weekends and the boys were at their busiest at this time as well. Since weekends were pretty much the same as any other day, we worked out that with a bit of shuffling, we could have two of us off at the same time during the week.

Now all I had to do was to tell Duangchai of our decision. The trouble with the Chinese Thais is that when they employ you they think they have bought you lock, stock and barrel. '*FOUR DAYS?*' 'Yes, but we work long hours for ten.' I also told her that our teaching commitments should finish at 4 o'clock during the week and at 3 o'clock on Sundays. 'But what do you want to do if you are not here in school?' 'Get a life!' I said.

Our plan worked well. We took it in turns to finish at 3 o'clock on Sundays, which gave us a better opportunity to travel further afield on our days off. We came back refreshed by clean air and a change of scenery. We would exchange experiences of where we had been and how we got there. Thanks to Pauline, I discovered Hua Hin.

Hua Hin is on the west coast of the Gulf of Thailand and is Thailand's oldest beach resort, dating back to when it used to be little more than a fishing village, with one exceptionally grand hotel. Around the turn of the century, members of royalty were Hua Hin's main visitors, but the place became more popular in the 1920s when the Bangkok–Malaysia railways made short excursions to the beach much more viable. The Victorian-style Railway Hotel was built shortly afterwards to cater for the leisured classes, and in 1926 King Rama VII had his own summer palace erected at the northern end of the beach. The royals still go there for breaks, and everyone knows when they are in town because the streets are decked out with enormous billboard portraits of the King and Queen and the little shops hang out the national flag.

When I was there in 1995 there were very few five-star hotels, but many others, unfortunately, were in the process of being built. The old Railway Hotel remained a classic of colonial-style architecture, with cool, high ceilings, polished wood panelling and wide sea-view balconies. All was much the same as it was 70 years ago, but the cost of staying there was well beyond my means.

I stayed instead at one of the pretty wooden guest houses squashed in the back sois (side streets) behind the seafront. It was great to go there when it was my turn to finish early and get away on a Sunday. I could leave the school just in time to catch the late-afternoon bus for the two-and-a-half-hour trip, armed with a cossie, a book, and basic needs for a 3-day break stuffed into my backpack.

My room in the Bird Cage Guest House was clean and simple, with shower and toilet facilities crudely sectioned off in one corner. A hose poking through the wall served as the shower, and the water that trickled out of it was infinitely colder than the sea.

There was a beach vendor cooking barbecued shellfish, shrimps and sardines, and since sometimes I would be the only person on the beach I became, when I was there, his favoured customer. In the evenings I would wander to the night market along Sa Song Road, to eat at little restaurants on the old pier that served fish, chicken and vegetables, often all mixed up together in a very tasty soup. The proprietor of the Guest House would serve steaming coffee and warm croissants in the morning for breakfast on the wooden verandah. I loved that time of the day, sometimes with other visitors to chat to, sometimes on my own. Either way, it was very relaxing.

At other times on my days off, I would go 90 kilometres south of Hua Hin on the train to Prachuap Khiri Khan, providing another bolt-hole. I could stay for less than £2 a night at the Yutichai Hotel, near the station, and marginally more upmarket than the Bird Cage.

The streets there were vibrant with bougainvillea and vivid hibiscus blossoms around quaint wooden houses painted in bright colours. This place too, had a busy night market near an otherwise dismal beach.

Prachuap is only 12 kilometres east of the Burmese border, and I could see the mountains by climbing 417 steps up the monkey-infested Khao Chong Krajok at the far end of the town. Less than halfway up, I heartily wished I had never started smoking in the first place, and threw the current pack to the monkeys.

Peter and Martin came back from one of their excursions rhapsodising about Ko Samet. 'Idyllic, matey,' they said, 'but you need to knock off early to get there before dark.'

Well, I couldn't knock off early and I did get there after dark. I missed the 4 o'clock bus from the Eastern Terminal for the 3-hour journey to Ban Phe Pier. From there it is a 30-minute crossing by boat to the island.

Normally the last boat leaves the pier before sundown, but since there was a group of young backpackers all wanting to cross, the boatman considered it worth his while to make one more trip.

As we were the last to arrive, four or five other boats were already lined up horizontally between us and the jetty. To disembark, we had a choice – either jump off and land waist deep in water before reaching the shore, or, as was the case, clamber over the other boats with various gaps of one to three feet of sea yawning between us. Busy counting his money, the boatman was no help, but the other passengers were a cheery lot; although making no concessions to the old duck desperately stretching short, puny legs across the murky water, they did at least hold on to each other's and my bags which had to be lobbed across, so that we had free hands to pull ourselves over to the jetty. I removed my sandals to get a firmer grip and promptly and irretrievably lost one in the water.

The wooden jetty was old, with a rickety perpendicular and very narrow ladder to climb before reaching the landing. Limping along, the next step was to find somewhere to sleep for the night at that late hour. We were lucky to find transport in the form of an open truck which bumped and rattled along the only main track on the island – ten people with room for six, all hanging on for dear life!

The communal accommodation was not ideal, but at least I had a bed to myself, which was more than anyone else did – or maybe none of them wanted to, for all I knew.

We had arrived in Na Dan at the northeast end of Ko Samet, where there were a few open-fronted shops and food stalls, as well as the island's only school, health centre and temple. Samet's best beaches are along the east coast and that was where we found a bungalow resort. I had joined forces with two Irish girls and although we discovered later that these bungalows were accessible by walking a rough track between the trees, my new companions had been told to walk along the beach at low tide. So we did.

We had found Ao Hin Kok, a small uncluttered resort where there were only two bungalow outfits, and both overlooked the beach from a grassy slope on the far side of the track. Our accommodation was simple bamboo huts containing a mattress, mosquito net and a blanket, with limited toilet facilities. Samet has no fresh water, but water is trucked in from the mainland and although there may be a shower facility in the hut, its use is often very limited since electricity in the more basic places is rationed for evening consumption only.

Our group of huts shared a beach restaurant, a bar and an English-run cafe specialising in home-made bread and cakes. Around the next outcrop of rocks, the evenings were enlivened by the outdoor bar and an occasional disco, obviously very popular with the backpackers.

I found convivial company and cold drinks where I was, and was content to watch the amazing sunsets and listen to the geckos. The interior of the island is dense jungle, home to hornbills, gibbons, spectacular butterflies and, of course, the ubiquitous gecko. Even if you don't venture inland, and I didn't, you will see and hear geckos in every beachfront restaurant and more than likely they will turn up in your hut as well. I checked my room very thoroughly every night before I put my head down, and placed a towel firmly in the gap between the bottom of the door and the floor.

Samet harbours a huge population of the largest and most vociferous gecko, the tokay, named after the disconcertingly loud sound it makes. They can grow to up to 35 centimetres long, but they are completely harmless to humans – in fact, they are welcomed by most local householders as they eat insects and mice, and Thais consider it auspicious if a baby is born within earshot of a crowing tokay.

With its sparkling seas, white sand, secluded and peaceful bays, there was always somewhere else to investigate. I could walk barefoot along the unpolluted beach at low tide, sometimes scrambling over the low rocky points which were often all that linked one resort to another on that part of the coast. Each place was different – different sounds and smells, and different wildlife and fauna. I went there whenever I could; but now I was obliged to go to Penang.

8

PENANG

My original employment contract was for three months. It was, however, becoming increasingly evident that I would not be going home at the end of March as I had planned. No, Duangchai had other ideas. 'Go home?' she said 'you can't do that, I need you here.'

What she really needed was for me to hold the fort while she was in the UK on her first official TRIP! For six weeks from the middle of April until the end of May she and her newly primed flock would be away from the school. I had already done my bit to put in place travel arrangements and organise accommodation for her and the children. I had also alerted the various agencies of the impending visit and sincerely hoped that they too would do their bit at their end.

To stay on in Bangkok for this extra time meant I would have to leave Thailand to go to Malaysia to renew my visa for a further three months. Most foreign nationals working in the city had to do the same, so the 'Penang run' was the thing to do, 48 hours there and back.

Not for me. 'If I am going to Penang then it will take me a week,' I informed Duangchai. 'I am not going all that way and then have to rush back.' Reluctantly, she agreed.

The train station was packed, with entire families picnicking on the unswept platforms, obviously prepared for a long wait. Rail travel is comparatively cheap but the trains are crammed, a seat only more or less guaranteed if booked days in advance. My trip to Penang was enhanced by having a sleeper booked for me; all I had to do was find it!

I took the perfunctory survival food with me – water, bananas, sweet bread, withered ham and cheese (bought at the station), and my liquor flask. I had been assured I would be able to buy dinner and breakfast on the train. Hmm.

Once away from the outskirts of Bangkok, the vegetation is lush. We passed little communities of people living anywhere where they have a remote chance of work – in the salt pans, paddy fields, logging, anything, but mostly it is farm land. In patches of ancient common land the people live in clusters of little thatch and timber stilt houses, raised high enough to keep the occupants dry, if that is at all possible during the monsoon season. Children and chickens run about under groups of palm trees and riotous, multicoloured bougainvillea, providing shade for them and the lonely goat or cow usually kept for milking.

Even these humble abodes will have their spirit house, inhabited by the power of the spirits, known in Thai as San Phra Phum. These little houses, built like miniature temples, are about the size of a doll's house. Their ornamentation is supposed to reflect the status of the humans' building; therefore, if a home has been enlarged or refurbished, the spirit house would be improved accordingly. They are often brightly lit at night, and during the day Thai families can be seen bringing rice, tea, orchids or other gifts to it, seeking the blessing of the good spirits.

Phra Phum is everyone's true everyday comforter, since he actually lives with people – not under their roof or in the shadow of a house, but very close by, usually on the northern side, so that he is never overshadowed. As guardian spirit of the household, his dwelling is an artistically fashioned wooden or papier-mâché shrine, set on a post at eye level with a narrow platform round it to hold the virtually daily offerings he receives.

On special occasions – at times of illness, birth, debt or the hope of winning first prize in the lottery – he finds his share of serviceable or entertaining tributes enriched by delicately fashioned paper or wooden horses and elephants, slaves and dancing girls. Phra Phum himself, leaning against the back wall of his little house, fly swatter in one hand and a big book in the other, can observe and watch over all that goes on through his open front portal; he enters family events in his register and punishes lack of respect with nightmares and sometimes even burglaries or fire.

It was a bit of a lark travelling alone through Thailand into Malaysia just to get a new visa; I felt like Mata Hari, observing my travelling companions as unobtrusively as I could. They were a right motley lot, I can tell you!

Across the gangway sat a man of indeterminate Asian origin dressed in

European clothes. Big, ugly and very fat, he seemed never to stop eating. Rice, chicken wings, rice again and more chicken wings, occasionally washed down in noisy gulps by what smelled like fish soup, all supplied by the woman facing him from plastic boxes and cups. She was thin, middle-aged, wearing a dreary sarong and faded blouse, and her clothes hung on her. Her eyes hardly left him, her face devoid of expression, while she silently produced his food from a large rattan bag placed between her feet.

Opposite me, to my consternation, sat a monk in saffron robes, with sandals and a shaven head, and wearing what I thought were pretty smart designer shades. I was disconcerted by his close proximity because from hard experience I knew it was forbidden for a woman to touch the clothes or belongings of a revered holy man, let alone sit next to him.

Almost every Thai male believer enters a monastery at some time in his life. Until 1945 this was for a minimum of three months, but now the – normally young – Thai man needs to spend only a few weeks there to enhance his knowledge of the teachings of Buddha. Even as novices the boys have to adhere to the three most important rules applied to monks: they must give up all earthly possessions and beg for their living; they must inflict no sorrow or suffering on any fellow creature; and they must deny themselves any sexual pleasures. The novice is allowed to bring to the monastery only the eight utensils of an ascetic – the three sections of the monk's staff; a needle; a razor to shave his head; a strainer for water; an alms dish; and a string of 108 beads which he allows to run through his fingers during meditation.

In spite of the obligation to beg for their basic needs for the day – although it is not seen as begging as such because the Thai faithful are happy to contribute their share – the monks will decline food or money proffered by a woman and will not touch anything that has been handled by a woman.

The two-tier bunks on the train were clean and curtained off with thickly woven fabric in a murky shade of pink; mysterious little lights were strategically placed but not strong enough to read by. The steward came along to set up this arrangement at 7 p.m. Seven? It was going to be a long night.

The chappie across the gangway began to perform his bedtime ritual. The sandals and socks (socks!) came off. He removed his vest, had a really good scratch – everywhere – removed his heavy medallioned belt . . . and horrors! As he clumsily climbed into his bunk, his baggy trousers became draped seductively below his vest, lower paunch and whatever else he had between that and his knees. The woman carefully collected his clothes from the floor and placed them at the bottom of her bed. She then got in herself and closed the curtains. Not a word had passed between them.

The monk on the other hand, used a grotty-looking rag to wipe his shaven pate, picked his large yellow teeth to his satisfaction, and with a final wipe round, began to swing his arms in a circular motion until his robe tightened around his body like a vast cocoon. He climbed the little stepladder to his bunk (I carefully lowered my eyes!), put his saffron cotton bag in a net attached to the wall, and placed his begging bowl artfully on top of it, along with his mobile phone.

I sat for a while with my feet dangling over the edge of my bunk, wondering whether there was any likelihood of a dining facility on the train. I doubted it. I was wide awake and too excited to sleep but reluctant to leave my belongings to investigate. The snoring, incidentally, had already begun.

A steward came by and asked if I would like a drink. 'Yes, I certainly would,' I told him, not optimistic about an alcoholic beverage. 'Follow me and bring your bags.' OK. Fine. I followed him, an endless trot to the very end of the long train. There, gracing the final carriage was a platform, open to the elements and surrounded by a semicircular iron railing with several young stewards sitting on the floor, with rice packs and bottles of whisky.

Thai whisky comes in two main qualities: bad and not too bad. The bad variety tastes of methylated spirits, and the other – Sang Thrip – is drinkable. After inspecting the label and contributing 100 baht to the festivities, I accepted the first of several bevvies. An English couple joined us and the stewards seemed fascinated by these 'farangs' (foreigners) at close quarters. Their command of English was sufficient for them to engage in conversation and we had a very pleasant night of it indeed. In the early hours I decided I was tired enough to sleep, and my new friends and I staggered our way back to our respective beds.

It was a little past dawn when we reached the border at Butterworth, where our papers were carefully scrutinised. To my consternation it appeared I had been reading the wrong date on my visa and it had run out the previous week! No problem, just cough up 1,000 baht and you are free to go. I gratefully touched my forelock, paid up and pushed off smartly, alert to the harrowing tales of anyone who has ever had the misfortune to be holed up in a Thai jail.

Another train and a ferry boat took us to Georgetown, the main city of Penang Island. Taxis, trishaws, rickshaws, pony and trap, all were available within the immediate vicinity of the terminal and their drivers were happy to pick up unwary passengers and deposit them wherever they wanted to go, at an exorbitant price.

It had not been difficult to persuade Duangchai that my journey to Penang could loosely be regarded as a business trip and therefore my expenses would be on the house, so to speak: 'Yes dear, of course, but please don't take that awful bag of yours, I will get you a proper suitcase.' She did, a huge bright red one (to match the T-shirts), and never a soul to miss a trick, bang in the middle of the top of it she had stuck the ghastly school logo. Very nice, I must say.

Logo or not, I decided I could avoid the downtown hostel accommodation, take a taxi and install myself into a decent hotel for a change. I had done my homework. 'Batu Ferringhi,' I instructed the cab driver. 'The Bayview Beach Hotel.' I had chosen well. The northern coast of Penang boasts some of the finest beaches in Malaysia. All along the coastal roads, from Tanjung Bungah to Teluk Bahang, can be seen exquisite scenes of rolling white sands and swaying palm trees.

The hotel was modern and tasteful, and catered for almost every whim. Quality bathroom commodities, big fluffy towels and plenty of hot water; a king-size bed all to myself; and a view from my balcony to die for. Nothing could describe the beautiful and fascinating sunsets; the wide, wide skies were illuminated by the sinking sun in ever-changing hues of gold, purple and bronze. I made sure I was there on the balcony every evening, armed with a large G & T from the mini-bar, so as not to miss the sun go down.

The first day after registering my passport at the Consulate, I decided to just chill out on the beach, with the luxury of a wide sunbed under the trees. I spent time studying the tourist brochures and realised I couldn't do everything in a few days. It was clear that I would have to get a taxi from the hotel to the centre of town, and from there I could hire a trishaw, the more ethnic way to get about. Anyway, I was in no hurry.

Penang derives its name from the betel-nut palm, which is found in great abundance on the island. Originally Penang was part of Kedah before Captain

Francis Light successfully negotiated with the Sultan of Kedah to cede it to the British East India Company in 1786. The British were attracted to the natural harbour which could provide anchorage for their trading ships, and the township of Georgetown was named after King George III. Penang remained part of the British Straits Settlements until Malaya gained its independence on 31 August 1957.

Today, the island bustles with commercial life, and a host of multiracial communities have settled harmoniously, accompanied by their colourful cultures, religions and traditions.

I went to most of the places I wanted to see on the island, starting with the botanical gardens, situated in a large valley surrounded by evergreen trees. At the end of the valley lies an impressive cascade of water with little streams and rivers flowing through the park. Hundreds of monkeys can be seen scampering all over the place, having fun with each other or begging for peanuts and bananas from visitors. The serenity of the park also provides a natural sanctuary for birds, butterflies and plant life, and a haven for people like me to wander about alone and undisturbed.

On the third day I decided that what I needed was a round trip and the best way to achieve this was to go into the middle of town and get a trishaw. These are one of the oldest forms of transport in Penang. They are tricycles pedalled by thin, scrawny men or boys, and because they are able to move around in the rather chaotic traffic on roads barred to bigger vehicles, it was possible to discover the really more fascinating sights off the beaten track.

I picked up my trishaw man after I had found a somewhat scruffy bar ambiguously name 'English Teahouse', where they did indeed sell half-decent cups of tea and beer. I had been sitting at a small circular table for only a few minutes when I became surrounded by a group of young Malays, first wanting to know how old I was.

They did not, of course, realise that it was disrespectful to ask a woman her age, but they always want to know. 'That is my secret,' I said, 'but I will share it with you.' I added fifteen years on for good measure. They gaped. 'Where do you come from?' I told them that most of the time I lived in London. 'Do you know the Queen? How did you get here?' 'I walked.' Yeah, 'course I did.

I became conscious of one toothless wonder really staring at my mouth.

'Those teef,' he said, pointing with a twiggy brown finger, 'are they yours?' Dear God, I sincerely hope so!

After I finally managed to finish my cup of tea, I was rescued by a very nice English gentleman from Manchester who planned to cycle – at the age of 66 – through Malaysia and up to the Thai border. As I said to him, the best of British luck mate, in this heat.

He wanted to share my trishaw, but I told him no, on your bike, I wanted to do this on my own. My driver, painfully thin and bandy-legged, was delighted to have the 'honour' of showing me the sights. He did me proud. For four hours he pedalled, grunted, and chatted in broken English, waiting every time I wanted to stop and look at the various ornate temples, fruit markets and anything else that captured my imagination. At the waterfront I bought him a drink and smoked one of his evil-looking, liquorice-tasting cigarettes and we had a lovely time.

He had three teeth, and obviously didn't miss the rest of them, judging by the way he chomped through a juicy pineapple he had bought at the market. He had cut it up into little bits with a penknife to share with me as we went along. I dared not look at his hands! He took me all the way back to the hotel at the end of our tour, jumping off his saddle to vigorously shake my hand with both of his. Ignoring the disapproving expression of the doorman, I paid him and gave him a big, sloppy English kiss.

9

BACK TO BANGKOK

My journey from Malaysia back to Thailand and to my work in Bangkok was uneventful. I had enjoyed Penang, its multicultural people living in peace and harmony, and the vibrant cosmopolitan ethos of the island. I had made time to have a good rest, to think clearly and to make up my mind, no matter what, I would go home to London by the end of June.

I needed to get back to the ineffable comfort of my own home, to be embraced by my family and my animals, and to be able to speak freely in the company of good friends who understood me and the ambiguity of English humour – that what is said is not necessarily what is meant!

While the cat's away the mice can play, so to speak, and, not to be outdone by my Penang trip, Peter had taken himself and his girlfriend to Laos, leaving no clear idea as to when he could be expected to return. One of his side-kicks had also left altogether, apparently aggrieved that he had too much to do without Peter. Pauline was bristling with outrage at the pair of them.

'I do not intend to play football,' she told me indignantly, 'and I will not supervise fifteen-year-old boys while they trash the bathrooms.' 'I don't blame you,' I said, 'I don't play football either, but they won't trash the bathrooms while I'm here.' And they didn't. I stood, arms folded, outside the open doors of the bathrooms while they showered and changed their clothes after games. They could not get out of there quick enough, taking their clobber with them.

It was now the middle of May, Duangchai was still in the UK, and we were short-staffed. It was costing me more to keep my apartment cool than it would to keep my house warm at home. It was also taking longer and longer to walk the mile or so to school every morning, where I passed several smiling street vendors; we had progressed from 'Good morning' to 'How are you?' and 'Has your dog had its puppies yet?' The children would say 'Goo morni' as I passed back again in the evening.

The heat was sweltering and getting hotter: I would arrive at the school sweating and clammy, with my clothes sticking to me. The monsoon rains were only just beginning, with short afternoon showers, hardly enough to settle the dust on the streets. It would be very different once the monsoon season really got under way, when unpaved roads would be reduced to mud troughs and whole districts of Bangkok flooded.

The work was demanding, and the students lethargic in the heat. Sometimes I felt I could by now teach English to a brick wall, because that was what I was up against much of the time. The Thais have so much trouble pronouncing their 'r', 'w', and 'l'. Even those who had already had some previous English tuition would say, 'Maireee iss 'ere soo les spe al a wunss' – no consonant sounds at the end of words, making life very difficult at times for them and for me.

Pauline had taken on a new 5-year-old boy who wouldn't open his mouth. Exasperated, she suggested I try with him; although I agreed to, I didn't hold out much hope. The child, nicknamed Champ, was overweight, short black hair standing up from his head like a broom, and he just stared at me, po-faced, from black, black, deep-set eyes.

In the Thai family, right from infancy, the young Thai experiences a great sense of togetherness. A mere whimper is enough for the child to be scooped up, soothed and rocked back and forth. As soon as a baby can crawl and toddle, it is carried everywhere, usually naked, perched on an older sister's hip or hugged by a nanny in the crook of her arm, a position in which the child can sleep, play, and even eat whenever it wants.

The children already possess perfect manners when they first start school, and they go on to show respect through school and college (if they get there) not only to teachers but also towards their parents and all grown-ups. Asian children are hardly ever scolded or smacked, nor is rejection a form of punishment. Gentle methods of conditioning are preferred – by appealing, to a child's sense of shame by saying, 'If you do that the others will laugh at you!'

Whereas Western parents try to encourage their children to be independent from an early age, Asian parents protect theirs from worries and conflict and keep them in the bosom of the family for as long as possible. The result, to a certain extent, is a collectivisation which manifests itself in later life as indecisiveness or shying away from conflict.

Strangely though, the Thai adult will not retreat from quite violent methods of retribution if the cause is right. Compared with Europe and America, crime is not rife in the country, but stealth, be it money, property or a wife, will inevitably invoke a tortuous death for the perpetrator. Retribution is usually supported by the family and ignored by the authorities; it is accepted, though not publicly, and rarely will a case be brought to court. An offensive comment, particularly by foreigners, regarding the Royal Family, who are greatly revered and respected by their subjects, will generate an almost frightening show of anger from the people of an extremely loyal and proud nation. Thailand is known as the 'Land of Smiles'. It must be advised to watch your back if they are not smiling.

Champ had not a word of English and I had not a word of Thai. We went, just the two of us, for a walk in the gardens. The pond now looked lovely, lotus flowers skimming the surface of the water and the ducks bickering happily to each other. I chatted away to the child as though he would understand every word. 'Quack, quack,' I said, imitating the ducks. 'Quack, quack,' he replied, sounding his consonants clearly. We were off.

That morning I read the story of the Ugly Duckling to him from a book with beautiful illustrations. He could not get enough of it, and every day for five days, I read the same story while he pointed at the pictures. By then he could read all of it by himself, his enunciation almost perfect. An exceptionally bright little lad, he was a joy. He would draw, paint, write his letters and play – to some extent – with the other children, but he never smiled.

Two or three weeks after my return from Penang and Duangchai's return from the UK, Connor, my fellow crooner at the Oriental Hotel, turned up at the school. I was amazed to see him in her 'office', admiring her plants and obviously completely at ease. That man could charm the birds out of the trees, I thought. He had evidently come to tell Duangchai that through his Connections, he had two colleagues anxious to enrol their children in the Little Professors as soon as possible. Duangchai agreed without question. 'Would you like to discuss this with Ben Mairee?' Indeed, over lunch.

Dressed casually in a bone-coloured safari suit and open-neck shirt, he appeared younger and thinner than when I had met him several weeks before. 'Let's go,' he said with his warm, easy smile, and we fairly skipped away down the drive to his car.

'Can we go somewhere where I can use a knife and fork?' I was becoming almost skeletal, constantly struggling with friggin' chopsticks. 'We are having steak and chips today, but tomorrow I am taking you to friends, downtown,' he informed me, 'and there you will use chopsticks, your fingers, or starve!' I can't wait, I thought gloomily.

Gloom was despatched in the company of this man. He was fun, interesting, had impeccable manners, and was also gay, in every sense of the word. We ate heartily and drank moderately with our meal, talking all the time. He had lost his long-term boyfriend to AIDS a year or two before, and deeply understood the grief and loneliness of the bereaved. I felt I had known him for ever. He raised my spirits and my self-esteem and the long, extended lunch seemed to pass in no time. 'Tomorrow,' he said. 'And wear trousers.'

He arrived at the school late the following afternoon, and we were off again, this time through back streets hardly wide enough to accommodate the car, passing concrete shop openings and seedy bars and tired-looking people, on our way to an area that certainly was downtown.

We entered a three-storey building of tenement flats, stepping around small children sitting on the stairs, to be greeted on the second floor by a young Thai family and their elderly parents. I used the *wai* greeting, hands straight, pointing directly under the chin, as they did, and Connor grinned, obviously very impressed.

Ordinary Thai families generally live in one main room, two at the most, wherein there is usually a sleeping pad or two, a corner set aside for a primitive shower and toilet facility (I prayed that I wouldn't need to go), and a balcony which serves as a kitchen. Cooking utensils amount to a rice cooker, a wok, a couple of sharp knives and a few bowls to eat from.

Packdee and his wife Celadin were charming. While Packdee fussed over water and containers for us, Celadin was busy preparing food with her mother-in-law. I was fascinated – garlic, lemon grass, wonderful-smelling herbs were being bashed with a bottle on a wooden board, balanced on the railing of the balcony overlooking the busy street.

The food was imaginative in its variety, wholesome, and very tasty, although difficult to eat with the chopsticks while sitting on a bare ceramic floor. My bum was frozen and I had to be very careful not to point my feet in anyone's direction as this would be considered very rude in Thai company.

We were subsequently joined by a variety of neighbours and their children who also sat on the floor, picking at the food, while steadily gazing at me and Connor as though we were people from another planet. There were so many people sitting around that in the end the entire company, food, drink, everything, was shifted out onto the landing, where once again I had to rearrange my feet and try to eat with their blasted chopsticks.

Eventually we went out with Packdee and Celadin, the elderly parents declining the invitation, and ended up in some dubious back-street Karaoke bar in Patpong. Karaoke is not meant to be fun in Thailand – it is taken seriously, and when one volunteers (and most of the patrons do) to sing along with the music provided from a list, no one laughs at some of the ghastly renderings from the participants.

Connor really pushed his luck that evening: his one-liners would have me in hysterics, and I seemed to spend the entire evening with my hand over my mouth to avoid embarrassment. We finally escaped in the early hours, I seemed to swing from the posh to the pitiful with this man; either way, though, he was great company.

We became firm friends. Every now and again when our time off coincided and he was in the capital, he would take me to places I would otherwise never have seen and it was always a big treat.

Although I rarely see him these days, he remains a cherished friend. He will send me a ridiculous card, caricaturing the pair of us or someone we knew or a place we had seen, and always he will only write 'Saw this and thought of you'. Even from far distant places he can still warm my heart and make me laugh.

10

I had spent much of my free time in Bangkok travelling east and south of the city and now, before leaving Thailand, I wanted to go north and west of the capital to the unwieldy urban mass of Greater Bangkok, which peters out into the vast well-watered central plains, a region that for centuries had grown the bulk of the nation's food, and has also been a tantalising temptation for neighbouring powers. The most densely populated region of Thailand, with large towns sprinkled among patchworks of paddy and sugarcane fields, the plains are fundamental to Thailand's emergence as one of Southeast Asia's healthiest economies.

It's rivers are key to this area's fecundity, especially the Nan and the Ping, whose waters flow from the Chiang Mai hills to irrigate the northern plains before merging to form the Chao Phraya River, which meanders slowly south through Bangkok and out into the Gulf of Thailand. Northwest of Bangkok, beyond the extraordinary religious site of Nakhon Pathom, lies Kanchanaburi, where the notorious bridge over the river Kwai draws visitors from all over the world. I wanted to go there too, to pay my own respects to the thousands of British young men, and others, who died there as Japanese prisoners of war.

I planned my trip to Kanchanaburi with the idea of stopping off overnight at Nakhon Pathom during the time of one of the town's major annual festivals, which is a gathering space for itinerant musicians, artisans and craftsmen, food vendors and fortune tellers. Nakhon Pathom is probably Thailand's oldest town and is thought to be the point at which Buddhism first entered the region of Siam, now known as Thailand, over two thousand years ago. Even today, the province of Nakhon Pathom retains a high Buddhist profile – aside from housing the country's most important Chedi, it also contains Phuttamonthon, Thailand's most celebrated Buddhist sanctuary and the home of its supreme patriarch.

I travelled on the early-morning bus from Bangkok's North Terminal, optimistically hoping I would get a seat; the buses are always crowded, even though they leave several times a day. Thankfully, apart from the monks, the Thai men are usually respectful towards women, especially older women (and I tried to look as old as I could), and will give up their seat for what is for most passengers only a short ride to their particular destination; but I was going all the way – and so was the luckless man who gave up his seat for me! I felt happier about it when I saw he finally found another place to sit.

Stopping and starting, people getting off and people getting on, I began to wish I had used the train, but I arrived at Nakhon Pathom before lunchtime, and even before I got off the bus I could see the enormous Phra Pathom Chedi, which dominates the skyline from every direction. Apart from the pyramids in Egypt, it was the most massive monument I had ever seen. Standing 120 metres high, it is as tall as St Paul's Cathedral in London.

Twice rebuilt since its construction, Phra Pathom Chedi's earliest fragments remain entombed within the later layers. Its true origin has become indistinguishable from folklore. Although Buddha never actually came to Thailand, legend has it that he rested here after wandering the country, and the original Indian-style (inverted bowl shape) Chedi may have been erected to commemorate this.

Local chronicles, however, tell how the original Chedi was built as an act of atonement by the patricidal Phraya Pan. Abandoned at birth because of a prediction that he would one day murder his father, the Mon King, Pan was found by a village woman and raised to be a champion of the downtrodden. Vowing to rid the Mon of its oppressive ruler, Pan killed the King and then, learning that he had fulfilled the tragic prophecy, blamed his adopted mother and proceeded to murder her as well.

To expiate his sin, the monks advised him to build a Chedi 'as high as the wild pigeon flies', and thus was born the original 39-metre-high stupa. Statues of both father and son stand inside the Viharns (sermon halls) of the present imposing Chedi, unforgettably eye-catching in sunlight and nowadays floodlit at night. I was glad I had stopped over.

I spent the evening wandering through the town, where scruffy travellers sat at the roadside plucking away on guitars. The usual vendors sold food and fruit under colourful awnings and gave demonstrations of cooking and fruit carving, all contributing to a lively night market atmosphere. But I was tired and wanted to go to bed.

Accommodation in the area was obviously no great shakes and I booked a ground-floor room in a moderately priced hotel near the bus station to allow for an early getaway in the morning. The air-conditioner was noisy, the shower slow as usual, and a cock-fighting pit just across the road was an ugly sight, which thankfully the punters had more or less finished with for the night. The generator, cheerfully humming as loud as it could, was housed in a room just below mine in the basement. In the middle of the night I wondered if my visit to the Chedi had been worth it.

Set in a landscape of limestone hills five kilometres northwest of Nakhon Pathom, the provincial capital of Kanchanaburi unfurls along the left bank of the river Kwai. Raft houses and riverside guest houses make attractive places to stay. I was tempted to put up on a raft house, which is little more than a simple rattan and cane hut, partitioned into two or three sparsely furnished rooms and balanced on a raft of planks and logs, moored close to the riverbank. In the event though, I had taken the precaution of booking myself into the Jungle Village Hotel before I left Bangkok. I had really scored here, it was lovely – a perfect room, excellent shower and bathroom facilities, and a balcony overlooking landscaped gardens leading to uninterrupted views of the river, set against the blue silhouettes of the craggy hills.

I had planned to spend five or six days in the area of Kanchanaburi, and the hotel provided interesting itineraries for excursions around the countryside. From experience I knew that these more organised outings were by far the easiest way to get around when time is at a premium.

However, my first foray into the unknown was alone, with only a boatman to keep me company. I had meandered down to the river on the first morning to have breakfast in the small floating restaurant, and chatted to a young waiter whose cousin (they all have cousins!) would take visitors upriver, away from the main drag, towards the Burmese border and to see a Burmese refugee village, which, from the river, could only be reached by taking a ride on an elephant. 'OK I'll go for that then.'

The boat was a shortened version of the longtail, with an outboard motor. It looked sturdy enough to me, and my waiter's 'cousin' was charming as he helped me to board. I was startled at his excellent command of English, and his looks – black wavy hair, grey eyes set in otherwise typical Thai features – were quite exceptional. Pity you are not a bit older, I thought.

'Was I alone? Where did I come from?' Usual inquisition, but this time with a genuinely polite interest. As we chugged up the river we had plenty of time to chat and for me to learn something about him and his background. Apparently Harri's father was English, married to a Burmese girl, and he was the product of that union. He spoke very respectively of his parents, appreciated his privileged education and was happy to be a boatman while he continued to study criminal law part time.

I suppose we spent a good hour or more quietly making our way on smooth waters, the river bending at intervals and passing little islands where small groups of monkeys frolicked in the trees, following us for a while and then finding better things to do. The solitude and isolation of the river was calming after the mad bustle and chaos of Bangkok.

Parts of the embankment were solid rock where, during the war, prisoners had been obliged to build a series of new embankments and trestle bridges, gouging at depressingly frequent intervals deep cuttings through the rock to allow the ubiquitous railway to progress further on to Konyu, 18 kilometres beyond Nam Tok Sai Yok Noi, where seven of these cuttings were made over a three-and-a-half-kilometre stretch.

The longest and most brutal of these was Hellfire Pass, which got its name from the hellish lights and shadows of the fires the POWs used when working at night – and it took three months of round-the-clock labour by prisoners of war working with the most primitive tools. Hellfire Pass has now been turned into a memorial walk, in honour of the men, who worked and died building that stretch of the railway.

The tracks of the railway were actually sited back from the embankment and could not be seen from the river. Now working along the river were elephants, nosing logs to various points of collection. All along the Sai Yai valley there were assemblies of fairly isolated communities of raft houses, occupied by river workers and their families. Nowadays, some of these are set aside for larky young backpackers who relish the primitive for a while.

Harri hove to alongside a small landing stage supporting an open-sided hut selling cold drinks from an enormous fridge. Workers were taking a break there, sitting on crudely cut bench seats. The landing was situated close to where the elephants were used to being fed. Asian elephants are smaller than African ones, and there they stood, knee deep in water, patiently waiting for their dinner. Harri gave me a huge basket of bananas to feed these beautiful, soft-eyed creatures, and whole hands of twenty or more small bananas were quickly lifted by the trunk and chomped up in no time.

We progressed further upstream until the river became wider and shallower and Harri turned off the motor and used a long pole to urge our little craft forward. From my seat in the prow of the boat, the sun shining low on the river, I could feel the impenetrable, infinitely dense jungle silence – there were no sounds, no birds flew here, nothing to disturb the intense, palpable quiet. It seemed to me there was an uncanny spirituality to this place; it was as if the drips from the trees overhanging the riverbanks were the tears of the thousands of souls who had died there. In that strange, unforgettable atmosphere, we finally came to where there was a Burmese refugee village.

Over hundreds of years, the Mon people – both Burmese and Thai – have endured an extended history of persecution and displacement. For various political and religious reasons, many Mons were welcomed into Thailand from Burma and whole areas of undeveloped jungle were given over to them. Because we were approaching the village from the river, the only way to reach it was on the back of an elephant.

Did I want to go? 'Course I did. Was he coming with me? No, he wasn't. Instead, Harri entrusted my care to a long-suffering, ageing elephant and his owner, who helped me to climb a vertical wooden ladder on what once had been a Japanese watchtower. From here I was able to reach across to sit on a thin rush mat immediately behind a young Thai boy. He was the driver, and sat almost on the animal's head, right behind the big flapping ears, to prod and guide him forward and upwards over a rough track to the village. Riding an elephant is not quite the same as riding a horse; the heel of a boot will urge a horse into a canter, but in the case of the elephant it takes a small tool, similar to a wallpaper scraper, repeatedly prodded into the top of its head to guide it and to keep it moving. The elephant didn't seem to mind, made no effort to hurry and was obviously used to this treatment judging by the tufty hair, like weeds sticking up from the top of its head.

We plodded and swayed upwards, threading our way through tough vines hanging from the jungle trees, all the time negotiating hazardous tree roots and rock underfoot. My arms were firmly folded around the thin frame of the boy-driver, and my knees and feet served more or less to keep my balance on this lumbering creature, stoically making his way along an almost undefined path to the village.

The village itself was clean and obviously well maintained. The stilt houses and several thatched roundels were spaced out over a clearing in the trees covering an area of possibly three or four acres. We walked on red sandy soil while chickens strutted and pecked at our feet; goats were tethered to wooden posts and a few cats and dogs were sleeping in the shade on a hot, humid afternoon. No mess, no debris, no loud music, an idyllic atmosphere of peace and calm prevailed in this haven for the misplaced.

An elderly man came forward dressed in a sarong and collarless shirt made of coarse cotton twill. We exchanged the *wai* greeting and again I was amazed to be spoken to in English – in this place, in this outlandish place! 'Welcome,' he said in a slow, well-modulated voice. 'Thank you for coming to see us, I will show you our village if you would like that.' Like it?! He told me that this well-established community was safe here, away from the endless skirmishes going on between the rebellious Karen people and their political or religious opponents on the other side of the Burmese border only a few miles away across the river, and said that with some support from the Thai authorities, these people were more or less self-sufficient.

They earned money from a variety of communal cottage industries; the young girls sewed sequins in lovely unique designs onto what were otherwise ordinary plain cotton T-shirts; their mothers knitted or crocheted hats and bags in an extraordinary rainbow of coloured cotton, silk and wool. Beads were strung together by the children, expertly knotted and tied, proudly and attractively presented on miniature trees fashioned out of bamboo. The men produced teak carvings representing ancient figures, and masks; chess sets, beautifully finished, smooth and tactile, while the older boys made wooden boxes in all shapes and sizes, inlaid in some cases with chips of mother-of-pearl.

A well-designed thatched showroom had been built to display these goods to the tourists who visited the village. Occasionally these people came, a few at a time by arrangement, in transit vans from the main highway, not usually arriving by elephant as I did, but obviously these visits did not generate enough trade to justify the work of the commune. However, it appeared they had outlets in the town where the sale price seldom reflected the quality of the goods.

I was offered refreshment, and I gratefully accepted the little glass tumbler of camomile tea. I gazed around as I sat on an old tree trunk and was utterly fascinated by these people. Plump and naked toddlers sat beside their mothers on straw mats, contentedly playing with each other, or still being fed from the breast. Everyone I looked at smiled at me, beautiful girls with thick, lustrous black hair braided or tied into a pigtail hanging long, in some cases to the waist, all with clean, healthy white teeth and slim, golden bodies.

My guide it turned out, was also the village schoolteacher. He was old and quite frail with clouded eyes and I wondered how he managed in a classroom. He invited me to see the school. It was yet another thatched roof supported by rough tree trunks and open on all sides, creating a room no more than twenty feet long by twenty feet wide, housing wooden desks and bench seats to accommodate maybe twelve to fifteen children.

I was introduced to a middle-aged woman taking the class at the time, and I was happy to sit for a while, observing from the back of the room. The children were working with chalk and slate, but of course I was creating a distraction from their lesson and their teacher got them to print the Latin alphabet on rice paper with a Biro that was being passed from one to the other as a present for me! They sang 'Happy Birthday' and I felt really humbled, and thought about the chronic waste in British schools, pencils which our kids can't be bothered to sharpen as they reach for a new one, paper hardly used before being screwed up and thrown away, text books and equipment constantly being replaced – the utter waste, all in an environment of smart classrooms and extensive playing fields, and all taken so much for granted. I resolved that when I returned to the UK I would see if there was anything I could do to help these teachers and the children, but they are a proud people, and they seemed to be managing very well in their own way. To this day, I still have that rice paper.

Kanchanaburi is a long ribbon of a town measuring about five kilometres from north to south. The war sites are sandwiched between the river and the busy main drag, Saeng Chuto Road, which, along with the area around the bus station, forms the commercial centre of Kanchanaburi.

I had been advised that traipsing around the town to see the main sights could be exhausting in the prevailing sweaty climate and that I would be better to get a bike. So I did. With a bottle of water and my guidebook placed in a basket conveniently tied to the handlebars, I set off, aiming to go the museum first and then on to the cemetery and the bridge.

The JEATH War Museum gives the clearest introduction to local wartime history, putting the notorious sights of the Death Railway in context, and painting a vivid picture of the gruesome conditions suffered by the POWs who worked on the line. JEATH is an acronym for the five main nationalities involved in the construction of the railway: Japanese, English, Australian, Thai, and Holland. Notably lacking, though, is any real attempt to document the plight of the conscripted Asian force.

The museum provides a shockingly instructive account of a period not publicly documented elsewhere, and is housed in a reconstructed Allied POW hut of rough wood and thatched palm. There I saw exhibits of newspaper articles, paintings and photographs recording conditions in the camps. When things got really bad, photography was forbidden and any sketches had to be done in secret, on stolen scraps of toilet paper, many by English POW Jack Chalker, whose works were later reproduced as paintings. The simple drawings and paintings of torture methods are the most harrowing of all the evidence. A tableau had been constructed, depicting plaster-cast life-size men dressed only in loincloths, gaunt, bruised and bloodied figures working with picks and shovels at the rock face. It was a pitiful, brutal sight, lit by low, flickering, realistic flame to capture the dreadful conditions of the time.

Reading from my guidebook, I learned that shortly after entering World War II in December 1941, Japan – fearing an Allied blockage of the Bay of Bengal – began looking for an alternative supply route to connect its newly acquired territories that now stretched from Singapore to the Burma–India border. In spite of the almost impenetrable terrain, the Japanese chose the River Kwai basin as the route for a new Thailand–Burma railway, the aim being to join the existing terminals of Non Pladuk in Thailand and Thanbyuzayat in Burma, a total distance of 415 kilometres.

About 60,000 Allied POWs were shipped up from captured Southeast Asian territories to work on the link, their numbers later augmented by as many as 200,000 conscripted Thai labourers. Work began at both ends in June 1942. Three million cubic metres of rock were shifted and nine miles of bridges built, using little else but cast-iron picks and shovels, dynamite and pulleys. By the time the line was completed fifteen months later, it had more than earned its nickname of the Death Railway; a conservative estimate of 16,000 POWs and 100,000 Asian labourers died while working on it.

I don't know whether I am being politically incorrect here or not, but I am going to tell you that the appalling conditions and Japanese brutality were the consequences of the Samurai code: Japanese soldiers abhorred the disgrace of imprisonment – to them, ritual suicide was the only honourable option open to a prisoner – and they considered therefore that Allied POWs had forfeited any rights as human beings.

Food rations were meagre for men forced into backbreaking eighteen-hour shifts, often followed by night-long marches to the next camp. Many suffered from beriberi, many more died of dysentery-induced starvation, but the biggest killers were cholera and malaria; it is said that one man died for every sleeper laid on the track. Ironically, when some of the camps were finally liberated, plentiful stocks of unused medication and rice were found on many of the camp sites.

It is said that 38 allied POWs died for each kilometre of track laid on the Thai–Burma railway, and many of them are buried in Kanchanaburi's two war cemeteries. Of all the region's war sites, the cemeteries are the only places to have remained completely untouched by the tourist trade.

The first cemetery I visited was the largest, with 6,982 graves laid out in straight lines amid immaculately kept lawns and flowering shrubs. Many of the identical stone memorial slabs state simply: 'A Man Who Died for his Country'; others, inscribed with names, dates and regiments, indicate that the overwhelming majority of the dead were under 25 years old.

I had to cross the river to the Chungkai War Cemetery, and took the two-minute ferry ride with my bike from the pier, then followed the road on the other side. A two-kilometre ride took me to a peaceful burial place built on the banks of the Kwai Noi at the site of a former POW camp. Some 1,750 men are interred there; hundreds more unnamed allied soldiers had been hastily disposed of on the various sites along the river. I left the bike in the hedge and walked very slowly around the graves, aching with all my heart for those young men buried there and their families left behind to suffer the grief. I thought of my own sons, both now in their thirties, fine, healthy young men able to get on with their lives, and I fervently thanked God for it.

By late afternoon I was very hot, sweaty and saddle sore. The mileage I had covered on this clapped-out contraption was minimal, but when the pedals were only metal bars and the saddle worn to a thin leather strip it did not make for comfortable cycling. I wearily pushed the damn thing much of the way back to the pier and decided I had had more than enough of tourism for one day. The bridge could wait.

The next day I simply wanted to relax in my immediate surroundings. Room service brought a late breakfast of tea and croissants, and after a leisurely bath and a good rub down I felt refreshed and somewhat more cheerful after the traumatic and unforgettable visits to the POW sites. I spent the morning wandering around the intricately landscaped garden, vibrant jungle plants of outsize proportions all meticulously tended and manicured, and whiled away most of the afternoon reading. A little shop attached to the reception area later drew me to investigate its goodies, and it took me no time at all to be relieved of a few hundred baht on good-quality handicrafts and souvenirs – some from the Burmese village – to take home.

Not wanting to get bitten to death in this jungle environment, I had dinner at the restaurant inside the hotel, where it was promised there would be a culture show at some point during the evening. As a very small eater, I could only pick at the massive, enticing array of food from the buffet – delicious soup, snakefish, fiery tom yan, beansprout-stuffed khanom buang (crispy pancakes), traditional curries, rice and noodle dishes, and, in an effort to please everybody, some European food – undercooked, barely warm, pallid-looking offerings which most thinking people concerned about their health wouldn't touch with a bargepole.

The evening show, a hotchpotch of Thai dancing by a troupe of local girls, classical music played by local students, and with a martial-arts demonstration thrown in, was colourful, enthusiastic and entertaining, and wildly appreciated by the twenty or so diners seated around the tables – Germans, Dutch, Australians and, uncomfortably, a small party of Japanese.

The new day dawned already hot and steamy. I abandoned the bike idea and took a taxi to the area around the bridge, the symbol of Japanese atrocities. I found the plain steel arches of the bridge over the river Kwai a disappointment; as a war memorial it lacks both the emotive punch of the museum and the perceptible drama of sites I had visited upriver, further along the line. The approaches to the bridge were seething with trinket sellers and touts. But I had to see it.

The fording of the Kwai Yai River at the point just north of Kanchanaburi known as Tha Makham was one of the first major obstacles in the construction of the railway. Sections of a steel bridge were brought up from Java and reassembled by POWs using only pulleys and derricks. A temporary wooden bridge was built alongside it, taking its first train in February 1943. Three months later the steel bridge was finished.

Both bridges were severely damaged by Allied bombers in 1944 and 1945, and now only the stumps of the wooden bridge remain, but the steel bridge was repaired after the war and is still in use today. People can walk across it or take the train. I took the train a few stops up the line and got off, disenchanted by the commercialism which has taken over, insensitively exploiting the POW experience.

Kanchanaburi is a profound and emotive place and I am glad I went, but it was time to leave, time to make my way back to Bangkok and prepare for my journey home.

11

VIETNAM

But when the days of golden dreams had perished,
And even despair was powerless to destroy,
Then did I learn how existence could be cherished,
Strengthened and fed without the aid of joy.

Emily Brontë, *Remembrance* (1846)

I decided to take the train back to Bangkok. Once out of the station and into the confused, ugly strata of the place, with the city fug obscuring the sun, the chainsaw drone of traffic and the sweltering heat, I already felt a million miles away from the tranquillity of the Kwai River. Then I saw Sangpong, or rather he spotted me walking towards the taxis, grouped willy-nilly around the terminal. How was I ever to thank this delightful young man for his many kindnesses, this man who had taken the time to meet me and to drive me in air-conditioned comfort through jam-packed streets, past dispirited slum communities permanently camped under bridges (when and where would they ever house these people?), all the way back to my apartment.

My landlord, known to me as Mr Kimono was there, his huge toothy smile stretched across his face, to greet me 'A big surpri' for you Ben Mairee,' he said, pointing at my mailbox in reception. I had already assumed he had a good old read of any correspondence of mine that wasn't sealed in an envelope. 'A Fax from your daughter, a big surpri'.'

It was a big surpri'. A lovely surprise from Fiona, my youngest daughter, to tell me that the family had delegated her to escort me home, after a holiday together somewhere – anywhere, but definitely not Bangkok – and what did I think of that?

What did I think of it? What a darling, what a family to think of such a thing! I loved them and had missed them, for what had been the longest period ever to have been separated from my sons and daughters, and I was by now utterly fed up to my back teeth with this aloneness.

I had also continued to miss my man, especially in the mornings and evenings, or in my bed at night. He had always been there to listen as I unfolded the daily journal of my life, telling it to make him laugh, to sympathise, or to just understand because he knew me better than anyone ever will. I had missed the secrets of his physical presence – his smile, his quirky habits – and his authority. Will I always have this endless gut-wrenching ache? Will I always be floundering on my own, searching for distractions, forever seeking new horizons, new ways to make him proud of me? 'You will be all right darling,' he had said. 'Don't be lonely.' Yeah, well, dearest heart, it's not all that easy at times.

Vietnam. That's where we will go. Neither of us had been there before. Although still only in her early twenties, Fiona was already an intrepid traveller, as was her older sister, Jacqui. Blessed with radiant high spirits, Jacqui had, at nineteen, travelled to India and back, journeying across Europe and Afghanistan to New Delhi, on the Magic Bus, worrying the daylights out of her father and me at the time. Now, I supposed, I was worrying them.

It only took a day or two to book our flights – Bangkok to Saigon (nowadays known as Ho Chi Minh), Saigon to Da Nang, and then on to Hanoi in the north, a trip spread over three weeks.

I met Fiona at the airport after a very fluid party given for me by the staff at the school. 'Promise,' they said 'we will get you there on time to meet your daughter, come what may.' They did. They dumped me off to sit on a very hard plastic seat at 4.30 a.m. to wait for the 6.30 a.m. flight from Heathrow.

We hardly recognised each other. There she was, tall and slim, long blonde hair swinging loose – she looked lovelier than ever, but she wept at the sight of me. 'Ma,' she said, 'you look terrible.' Even taking the all-night session with my friends and colleagues into account, I suppose I did. Slightly built at the best of times, the heat and consequential lack of appetite had reduced my weight, which, when I checked it, was now down to not much more than 6 stones. All the same, I felt as fit as a flea, I assured her. 'You'd better be,' she said as she hugged me so tight I could hardly breathe.

The single exit door from the small, uncrowded arrivals hall at Tan Son Nhat Airport was hemmed in from the outside by a gaggle of drivers clamouring to take us wherever we wanted to go. One optimistic young man took himself off with our luggage towards his van.

Seriously underestimating Fiona's sharp eyes and her wrath, by the time she had finished slagging him off, he certainly wished he hadn't been so presumptuous. A fellow traveller – a middle-aged American – came to our rescue. 'I can save you all this hassle,' he said, 'you are welcome to share my car – I work here and I can take you into the city.' What a gem!

He recommended a place to stay, reasonably priced, reasonably clean and safe, right there in the heart of Ho Chi Minh. We couldn't thank him enough at the time.

We soon had a key and a room number. We entered the room after a long haul up endless stairs to the fourth and topmost floor of the hotel (the higher you go, the cheaper it gets), and we were horrified. The furnishings were like those in a hostel for down-and-outs: two plastic chairs, a badly scratched Formica-topped table, and a bare electric bulb. There was hanging space in one corner, curtained off by a ragged floral sheet of fabric, and offering two metal hangers. The bed sagged sadly and damply and looked as though the entire world had slept on it at some time. Behind a thin partition lurked a daunting, grim-looking shower and toilet facility. The only source of natural light and air was from a doorway at the end of the bed, opening onto a communal balcony, shared by four other presumably similar rooms. The balcony, or the terrace as the hotel fondly described it, was surrounded by a balustrade of crumbling stucco; limp and neglected plants, struggling to survive in dried-out plastic pots, were scattered around, to cover the sight of cracked walls, and everything was covered in a thick grey dust thrown up from the busy main street below.

We were hysterical. We sat on the bed and absolutely fell about. 'We can't stay here,' I said, wiping my eyes, but we were in a strange place and it was getting late. Not daring to leave our stuff, Fiona said, 'You stay here, leave it to me,' and off she went. In minutes she was back. 'First floor, same price, not perfect, but infinitely better than this.' And it was – clean, reasonably well appointed, and certainly a more inviting place to sleep in. 'Looks like the bridal suite by comparison,' I said. My daughter looked me up and down, grinning. 'A bit late for all that, don't you think?' Oh yeah?

Food was our next priority. With our small packs holding our money, passports and what few valuables we had strapped and tied firmly to the front of us, we ventured down the curved, marble staircase to the foyer. Compared with some of the state-run hotels, this was a comparatively small, privately owned place, exuding an air of long-ago grandeur, boasting what were once intricately woven oriental carpets but now faded and threadbare, and creaking floorboards. Artistically crafted ceiling moulds and covings were defaced by water-stained and cracked plaster. The whole place seemed possessed of genteel decay.

The word RECEPTION was displayed on the ground floor, luridly lit by a harsh green fluorescent light, and here at least there seemed a more lively atmosphere. A few arriving and departing tourists were optimistically trying to locate their luggage, a gaggle of backpackers with their belongings safely strapped to their backs and several young business entrepreneurs cluttered the area as Fiona and I pushed our way tentatively towards the street in search of somewhere to eat.

Narrow sidewalks served as pavements and a working place for hawkers and young girls dressed to kill in grotesquely brief miniskirts and low-cut camisoles; they had so much mascara and lipstick plastered on their small pointed faces that they looked almost clownish. Some were selling cigarettes and bottled water; others were simply parading. It was hot, humid and noisy and everyone seemed to be fighting for space. To cross the road we had to negotiate rasping motor scooters, the occasional car, and many big, black, ancient bicycles, all with madly ringing bells, wobbling all over the road, with two and sometimes three people clinging on dangerously and racing to get past whatever vehicles obstructed their passage forward.

A short walk took us to a bar, situated on a big corner of the thoroughfare, teeming with people sitting outside at plastic tables covered in beer glasses and paper plates. Bikes and scooters all piled up together leaned against lamp posts. 'Hello,' said our American friend. 'You made it then.'

It is amazing how pitifully pleased one can be to see even a remotely familiar face in a strange and foreign land. Here was the man who had helped us at the airport and now seemed to be happy enough to offer a friendly hand again. 'What can I get you girls to drink? Have you eaten?' What a saviour! Fiona settled for a beer, and I told him I could murder a G & T.

It appeared that gin was not at the time readily available in Vietnam, but vodka was. 'But I still need tonic,' I whined. 'Get yourselves some food,' he said, 'and I will be back. My name is Daniel, by the way.' We introduced ourselves and off he went.

The cheapest and most fun places to eat are the street kitchens, which range from makeshift food stalls set up on the pavement to open-fronted eating houses and bars, as this place was. Most only specialise in one type of food, generally indicated on a board, and some simply offer rice dishes or noodle soups. There are the 'people's meals', comprising an array of prepared dishes, stuffed tomatoes, fried fish, tofu, pickles and eggs, all with rice. Fiona and I chose, with some difficulty, anything we could point to and sat down to a plateful of mixed vegetables and soup between us, which looked healthy enough and tasted very good.

By now Daniel had returned, complete with two polythene carrier bags. One held two bottles of vodka and the other a dozen or so cans of Schweppes tonic water. The bar staff cheerfully equipped us with glasses and we were away.

Replete and refreshed, I sat back watching this scene of noisy, confident young men and women, both European and Vietnamese, having a good time, and kept a close eye on my daughter. She is an attractive, very animated girl, and her long blonde hair may not be so unusual on our home patch, but in Asia it is, and draws attention everywhere she goes. I wondered about Daniel, whether he had any ulterior motives, even though he had indeed been very kind to both of us.

Suddenly from the crowded street behind me a package was lobbed over my shoulder and fell into my lap. I shrieked – I thought it was a bomb! Wrapped in newspaper and tied tightly with string, it measured roughly six inches square and two inches deep. Fiona saw it. 'Sit on it,' she hissed. 'Sit on it?' I was aghast. She whispered something to Daniel, and then she announced to me that we were going. Daniel offered to see us back to our hotel. Every inch the gentleman, he shook hands and thanked us for our company, and told us he was going to the States in two days' time. 'I will give you the conducted tour tomorrow if you would like that. I will call for you at ten.'

Back in our room, Fiona calmly informed me that the packet was probably drugs, and that Daniel had kicked it away from the seat and under the table. 'Why would anyone drop drugs on me?' I wanted to know.

Crime against tourists is very rare in Vietnam, and is known to be one of the safest countries in which to travel. However, the major cities have an increasingly bad reputation for pickpockets and con artists. There is also a fair amount of drug peddling, or dumping, and the criminals will then turn you over to the police. A substantial bribe might persuade them to drop the matter; otherwise, you are looking at massive fines or jail sentences for lesser offences, or the death penalty for smuggling large quantities. I reckoned my package could have been rated as a pretty large quantity had I been found to be in possession of it.

We were both shaken by this thought and my mind turned to Daniel who had dealt so swiftly with the situation. I wondered whether the package had gone under the table. I didn't need to know, and soon we saw the funny side of the event, especially when we realised we still had the vodka and tonic water – no law against that – and decided that now was as good a time as any to make a start on it.

Daniel was not there at ten, nor at eleven, nor, as it turned out, did we ever see him again. Deciding not to waste any more time, we pushed off on our own to discover this really vibrant place. We enquired at the desk for reliable transport and were told that the rickshaw man waiting outside was trustworthy and would stay with us as long as we needed him. 'Do not pay him until he brings you back.' Fair enough.

We were pleasantly surprised to see quite a smart rickshaw, freshly painted and complete with folded black leather hood. Our driver helped us up the step and hoped we were comfortable on his fine, deep leather seats. He looked strong and muscular, his long black hair tied back in a ponytail, his face showing the typical agelessness of the Chinese, but I guessed him to be around twenty years old. He had a fair command of English and informed us that this was his very own vehicle and that he intended to study the English language and be top Rickshaw Man.

He took us forward onto one of the main boulevards, where the occasional sleek Diplomatic limousine cruised past, as well as the little Citroën 2CVs and the blue-and-cream taxis, survivors from the days of French colonisation. Lines of spreading tamarind trees with bright green feathery leaves and dark trunks had also survived, like images of the colonial days.

Vietnam, with 2,000 miles of beautiful coastline, has had a tortuous history, beating off all the great powers that in turn have assailed them: China, Japan, France, and more recently that fruitless conflict with the

USA. Now more or less free of Communist control, at least in the south, its citizens are emerging once again as indomitable and resourceful entrepreneurs, using their considerable talents as chefs, artists, musicians and seamstresses.

Even though most of the streets have been renamed since the Vietnamese beat off the French, Ho Chi Minh clings tenaciously to its legacies of the past. Echoes of colonial yesterdays haunt the streets, with never-ending boulevards flanked by neoclassical yellow and white buildings, bright orange roofs, French shutters and hanging balconies, where the elite of Saigon once cut a swathe through the main districts. Anywhere and everywhere, pavement hawkers squat behind tidy displays of crusty French loaves, the twin spires of Notre Dame Cathedral looming large above. In the temples it is still customary to burn incense sticks placed on mounds of sand, held in wide, deep pans of brass or copper, ornately decorated with religious effigies. Little squares of gold leaf are placed reverently at the feet of Buddha, along with food and flowers. It felt to me that the city was constantly on the move, and altogether it seemed to hark back to the golden days when Saigon was the omnipotent capital of Cochinchina and known as the 'Pearl of the Orient'.

We stopped at one of the numerous markets, crowded and hot, with narrow walkways dividing the stalls selling luscious fruit and vegetables dried fish and fabrics, and live animals – chickens, rabbits, birds, incredible Siamese cats and tiny, whimpering puppies, all crammed in boxes or small cages.

The women at the fabrics end of the market plied us with an amazing selection of beautiful cloth and silk and offered to make us clothes 'ready for tomorrow'. As fast as we managed to avoid one stall so we were invited insistently by another to allow them to measure us – a dress? Suit? *Ao dai*? Fiona hates to be crowded or harassed but realised this was the name of the game in these places. Taking the least line of resistance, we both agreed in the end to have wide trousers and sleeveless jackets with Chinese silk fastenings made for us, in both silk and linen. 'Will we pay now?' With the help of our driver, we paid half and agreed to collect tomorrow.

We did collect our clothes the following day and were delighted with the quality and finish of the garments – they were lovely, and to this day I still find an occasion now and then to wear mine.

We continued our rickshaw journey through the city, past the red-brick

Cathedral of Our Lady of Peace and the white baroque public buildings of the French, towards the Saigon river. There a modern esplanade had been tastefully constructed, around an expanding zone of bars, where once the American troops were catered for. It was an attractive area, and the three of us sat on high stools to enjoy a drink.

Here on this esplanade was where the serious begging was apparent. Ivory-skinned girls, with wild jasmine woven into their long jet-black hair, peddled garlands and American cigarettes, and offered 'sweet lovin,' to any likely-looking male, at a price; street children in sibling groups held out their mucky little hands, and knew how to look sorrowful. A barefooted girl child, perhaps five or six years old, with two younger children hanging on to her skirt and watched by their mother from some twenty feet away, carried a tiny baby, which looked only days old – and which Fiona and I first thought was a dolly – clutching it by the neck with its feet dangling. We were appalled, and we instinctively reached forward to the child to help her hold the baby more comfortably. Our driver restrained us. 'Leave her, her mother will scratch your eyes out if you touch her, and don't give her money either, it just encourages them to beg.' He told us later that begging kept the children from going to school, and there was plenty of work for the mother if she wanted it – there was no need for begging in Ho Chi Minh. We just had to take his word for it.

It seemed that nobody slumbered in that swinging, restless city. At night the young are out until the early hours perfecting their karaoke technique, and the old are up with the lark performing mass aerobics under the eucalyptus trees in Cong Vien Van Hoa Park before they begin their day. It all had a gentle, ceremonious air: their movements were slow and elegant, and this is very often the time and place where individually they offer prayers according to their beliefs.

The moral and religious life of most Vietnamese people is governed by a mixture of Confucian, Mahayana, Buddhist and Taoist teachings, interwoven with ancestral worship and ancient animistic practices. Vietnam also has small Hindu, Muslim and Theravada Buddhist communities, as well as the second-largest Catholic congregation in Southeast Asia. No matter what its religion, virtually every Vietnamese household will maintain an ancestral altar for rituals associated with ancestor worship, which is based on the principles of filial piety and obligation to the past, present and future generations. Residual animism, plus a whole host of spirits borrowed from other religions, further complicate Vietnam's mystical world, in which the universe is divided into three realms – the sky, earth and man – under the overall guardianship of Ong Troi, Lord of Heaven. It is easy to see how in the park they are able to connect with all these elements and at the same time have a jolly good stretch.

We had by now named our driver Rick Shaw; he liked that and optimistically called both of us 'My Lady'. He had become our guide as well as our regular driver and we employed him on a daily basis at a price he was quite overwhelmed with, but to us it was a good deal and worth every penny. He was fascinated by Fiona's ready smile and endless chatter and by how easily we made each other laugh. He told us that Vietnamese women did not talk so much to each other. Mothers, he said, although very gentle and watchful, were quite aloof with their children, only really taking notice when a remonstration was called for, and even that was done in a quiet, non-confrontational way. Do you hit your children for bad behaviour?' 'Yes,' said my darling daughter, 'all the time.'

We were anxious to go to the Cu Chi tunnels. This was where, during the American war, the villages around the district of Cu Chi supported a considerable Viet Cong presence. Faced with substantial American weaponry, the villagers dug themselves out of harm's way, and the legendary Cu Chi tunnels were the result.

Rick took us to the Van Thanh bus station for the early-morning 49-kilometre ride to the town nearest the tunnels, and from there we would, apparently, be advised to get a motorbike for the last 10 kilometre miles to the site of the tunnels, turning right off the main highway when we reached the Cu Chi post office.

The road to Cu Chi passes between high stands of green bamboo sometimes forming tunnels of their own, and wide distances of paddy fields, and small settlements with low wooden shops and thatched huts like little haystacks, some with rusty iron roofs. The rural countryside was criss-crossed with canals and dykes, soon to be flooded by the monsoon rains, but for now resembling shallow lakes. We could see the workers in their plain black pyjamas, bending and stooping to do their traditional tasks, while motionless water buffalo stood patiently by. Tall wooden ox carts were piloted by old men in conical straw hats, and here and there at the side of the road peasants were planting in the paddy fields for the next harvest of rice.

As we arrived in the town, the day was promising to be hotter and sweatier than ever and we decided a coffee would be a good idea before going on. In a side road we stopped at a noodle shop with an auspicious Kenco advertisement attached to the red canvas awning. The proprietor, dressed in wrap-around skirt and bikers' T-shirt, was happy to take our order, achieved by much pointing at the Kenco advert, and in no time the coffee was produced with a flourish; very hot, very black, it was served in aluminium cups from drip filters. Mr Kenco would have had a fit!

We watched the other noodle sellers, in their straw hats, often with Buddhist amulets hung in pouches around their neck, this apparently to keep their thoughts pure. 'I know a few chaps who could do with one of those,' commented Fiona. Other men, seemingly not having much else to do, were standing by the bamboo huts closely grouped along the road, gold teeth clenched on cheroots of hand-rolled tobacco. Near them, there were reed mats spread about, and on them their women squatted under the shade of the flame trees, dressed in the dark cotton sarongs of the countryside, some holding exquisite gold-skinned babies, their large brown eyes gazing steadily at us from under tiny straw hats of their own.

It was debatable, judging by the derelict state of them, whether any of the mopeds, scooters or motorbikes on hire were likely to go more than a few yards up the road, never mind the ten kilometres it would take to reach the tunnels, and even less likely that they would hold together long enough to survive the journey back.

Deciding to play safe, we took a taxi, in marginally better condition, with a driver who assured us with a big, wide, multi-gap smile that it would be *no problem*, he would see us there and back.

Anti-colonial Viet Minh dug the first tunnels in the late 1940s, and over a decade later Viet Cong activists controlling this staunchly anti-government area also went to ground. By 1965, 250 kilometres of tunnels were dug in and around Cu Chi. These tunnels could be as small as 80 centimetres wide and 80 centimetres high and were, in places, three levels deep. Provision had been made for latrines, wells, meeting rooms, a school – which also served as a kitchen and eating area – and a crudely assembled hospital. Operations were carried out in the hospital by torchlight, and using instruments fashioned out of shards of metal. The operating theatre sported a trestle table, with two narrow planks and straps fixed at right angles to support the arms away from the body when amputations were deemed necessary. There were times when local inhabitants and their children had to stay below ground for weeks on end; the people often had to lie on the earthy floor in order to get enough oxygen to breathe.

The two of us were escorted around the site by an ex-guerrilla soldier, Le Van Phuoc, who showed us the trapdoors where people could enter and exit the tunnels. The Vietnamese are normally a slender people; he was quite a well-built man, but all the same he demonstrated how it was possible to get in and out of these very narrow secret entrances, artfully disguised and hidden beneath natural foliage and tree roots.

He raised his arms high and folded them across his face and head and dropped into the trapdoor of the tunnel and then heaved himself out again. 'The tunnels were built very small so that the fat Americans couldn't get in,' he told us. Naturally claustrophobic, I declined the invitation to try, but Fiona was up for it. I held my breath as she struggled down followed by Le Van, and I waited anxiously for them to reappear. They did, from behind me, having used another enlarged, more accessible entrance directly open to the skies. Bent low, he took us both to see the underground chambers, primitive rat holes but providing effective hiding places against concentrated enemy attacks; these tunnels must have saved many, many lives.

Outside, we were shown the booby-trap system of wires and sophisticated home-made bangers, strung low across the rough terrain surrounding the village. These served to trip American patrols and when they did trip the wire, loud reports of gunfire would seemingly be coming from all around, and the Americans would then fire off their machine guns, but only succeed in shooting each other.

The US forces employed sniffer dogs to trace tunnel entrances, but the guerrillas used captured American uniforms and soap to make the dogs think the humans they smelled were their own. Many of these dogs were found impaled on the spiked booby traps near the entrances.

All the American attempts to flush out the tunnels were ineffective. Eventually they evacuated villagers into strategic hamlets and then used defoliant sprays and bulldozers to rob the Viet Cong of cover in 'scorched earth' operations. Thirty or so years on, the plants, trees and wildlife of the area are only just beginning to recover.

Our cabbie asked us if we would like to go to the Cao Dai Cathedral at Tay Ninh, before making our way back to the town, and since we had the time we readily agreed. The cathedral is the Holy See of the Cao Dai religion, a fusion of oriental and occidental religions, propounding the concept of a universal god. Much of the terminology and structure is based on Catholicism. By following its five commandments, Cao Daists look to hasten the evolution of the soul through reincarnation.

The cathedral's central portico is topped by a bowed first-floor balcony, and a Divine Eye is the most recurrent motif in the building. Men enter the cathedral through an entrance in the right wall, and women through one on the left, and all must take off their shoes at the big, impressive doors.

Rows of pink pillars are entwined by green dragons that march up the chamber, and at the head stands the papal chair, its arms carved into dragons. Dominating the chamber, and guarded by eight scary silver dragons, is a vast sphere of duck egg blue, speckled with stars and resting on a polished eight-sided dais. The Divine Eye peers through clouds painted on the front.

By chance, we had arrived at the cathedral in time for the 6 o'clock service, which, far from being a gloomy affair, treated us to the music of the customary traditional band, playing enthusiastically as robed worshippers chanted, prayed and sang. It was all very uplifting.

However, my spirits did not remain uplifted for very long. I am not particularly religious, relying usually on the 'Do unto others as you would expect them to do unto you' code of practice. Therefore, I was extremely peeved that in my attempts to respect and observe other people's faith, my sandals had, once again, been nicked from outside a place of worship where I had been obliged to remove the sodding things in the first place!

Fiona, predictably, was sitting on a wooden post, holding her sides and laughing her silly head off at me looking very cross indeed. 'It's not funny,' I complained. 'Look what I am left with to wear.' I was holding a pair of badly worn rope soles, so flat and shapeless they looked as though they would fit a baby elephant. 'Oh well,' said Fiona, 'try to see it as giving alms to the poor.' '*Again*,' I muttered grumpily as I proceeded to make a rotten job of tying what was left of the strings round my skinny ankles. Still grinning, she chummily held my arm as I flapped my way back to the cab.

12

THE CENTRAL PROVINCES

Vietnam's narrow waist comprises a string of provinces squeezed between the long, sandy coastline and the formidable barrier of the Truong Son mountains, which mark the border between Vietnam and Laos. Da Nang lies roughly halfway between Ho Chi Minh in the south and Hanoi in the north, and although not considered to be particularly interesting in itself, apart from the impressive Cham Museum, it is the fourth-largest city in Vietnam, it harbours a dominant port, and it also provides a major hub for transport. During the American war it served as a massive South Vietnamese airbase and played host to thousands of US troups and refugees searching for work.

Fiona and I said goodbye to our trusty 'Rick' and he seemed genuinely sorry to see us go. I gave him my necklace of beads he had been coveting all week and Fiona bought him a bandanna to put round his head, and we both took a chance and gave him a great big kiss. He seemed hugely chuffed about that as he waved us farewell, and we then made our way to the airport for the short flight to Da Nang.

Our intention was to base ourselves in the city so that we could explore other areas all around. In the event we changed our minds so that we could spend more time in Hoi An and Hue.

Da Nang had established a People's Committee, a very entrepreneurial council that had discovered that decent accommodation at fair prices would keep visitors and their money in the city for longer, and the hotel we were recommended did indeed reflect that interest. The Tan Minh, near the riverfront, was clean and comfortable, complete with air-conditioning, and reasonably priced. Also, as we saw later in the evening, Da Nang's similarly entrepreneurial prostitutes were also very much in evidence. At virtually every hotel we passed, single male travellers were being beguiled with offers of 'a massage where you want it' or 'sex how you like it' and so on. It's a wonder the Council managed to keep so many beds in such good condition, considering how much wear and tear they were obviously subjected to.

Much of the city stil harked back to its colonial days with wide, leafy boulevards and yellow and white stucco houses and the distinctive cement street signs dating from the French period, although gradually these were being replaced as the streets were renamed to bring them into line with the sensitivities of the government of the time. Occasionally though, one of the new white-on-blue metal plaques would fall off, revealing the old French name.

Walking around the city, it was difficult to imagine the scenes of utter chaos that prevailed in 1975 when Saigon government's forces were ordered to abandon the area after Hue and Quang Ngai had fallen to the Communists, cutting South Vietnam in two. Desperate civilians tried to flee the city as soldiers of the disintegrating South Vietnamese Army engaged in an orgy of looting, pillage and rape. On 29 March 1975, two truckloads of Communist guerrillas, more than half of them women, drove into what had been the most heavily defended city in South Vietnam and, without firing a shot, declared Da Nang 'liberated'.

Our walk that afternoon led us to the Cham Museum, exhibiting the finest collection of Cham sculpture in the world. Its display of graceful, sometimes severe terracotta and sandstone figures and carvings of altars and images is absolutely stunning. All of it gives a tantalising glimpse of an artistically inspired culture that ruled most of southern Vietnam for a thousand years.

We found a very knowledgeable guide, who told us that the recurring image in Cham art is that of Uroja, the 'Mother of the Country', who gave birth to the dynasties that ruled Champa. Uroja, whose name means 'woman's breast' (he said it so reverently – *vooman's breaths*) in the Cham language, was worshipped in the form of the nipples often seen in Cham sculpture. Also common is the Linga, phallic symbol of Shiva, which came to prominence after Champa's contact with Hinduism.

Fascinating stuff, and with our heads reeling with all this culture, we decided that since we had been on the go since very early that morning, it was time first for a drink, and then, before our feet completely dropped off, to find somewhere to eat.

Past the cathedral, known to the locals as the Rooster Church on account of the weathercock on top of the steeple, we made our way to Christie's

Restaurant & Cool Spot, quite a smart eating house run by a Japanese/Australian partnership, where in the upstairs restaurant we had a choice of an amazing array of delicious spicy curries from across Asia, and down below on the ground floor, a promising-looking bar.

It was good to spend time talking to other travellers, and there in that bar there were several of them, mostly Australians and Dutch, also ex-pats who for one reason or another were living in Da Nang, and all were happy to give us plenty of sound advice. 'Go to Hoi An, and make that your base for a few days, so much to see in and around there.' They recommended a good hotel, good this, good that – 'Go early so as not to wait while the bus fills up' – and so, in the morning bright and early, we caught the first bus for the hour-and-a-half trip to Hoi An.

Hoi An is a riverine town 30 kilometres south of Da Nang, known as Faifo to early western traders and it was one of Southeast Asia's major international ports during the 17th, 18th and 19th centuries. In its heyday, Hoi An, a contemporary of Macau and Malacca, was an important port of call for Dutch, Portuguese, Chinese and Japanese trading vessels, and the Vietnamese ships and sailors based in Hoi An sailed to Thailand and Indonesia and to other ports in Vietnam.

Since the 15th century, commercial traders, including American and Indonesian merchants, called at Hoi An to purchase high-grade silk, porcelain, tea, Chinese medicines, elephant tusks, beeswax and a multitude of other commodities. The Chinese and Japanese traders sailed south in the spring, driven by winds out of the north-east. They would stay in Hoi An until the summer, when southerly winds would blow them home again. During their time in the port, the merchants rented waterfront houses for use as warehouses and living quarters. The Japanese however, ceased going to Hoi An after 1537, when the Japanese government of the time forbade all contact with the outside world.

As we found our way to our hotel, past a number of Hoi An's wooden buildings which date from the first part of the 19th century – or even earlier – it was not difficult to imagine a time, a couple of centuries ago, when the wharf was crowded with sailing ships, the streets teemed with porters transporting goods to and from warehouses, and traders from a dozen countries haggled in a babble of languages.

Until recently the Hoi An Hotel was the only place authorised to accommodate foreigners, but things have changed and we had a choice of several attractive options. The Vinh Hung Hotel was a well-restored Chinese merchant house with superb wood panelling and large airy rooms centred around a quiet, peaceful courtyard with a small swimming pool set in a garden of oriental plants and trees, and was within easy walking distance to the main town and about four kilometres to Cua Dai beach.

It was lovely, with a pool and a sauna, a bar and a small restaurant. Once we got there, Fiona and I decided to leave exploring until the following day and to simply enjoy the facilities of this charming and restful place.

It was easy and a joy to rest here – our room was sublime, distinguished by a high ceiling and evidence of past grandeur and exotic taste. Casement doors led to the courtyard, and there were two four-poster beds, complete with drapery in cherry-red silk tapestry, supplemented with white mosquito nets tied back with hand-crafted silk rosettes; damask bedspreads were ornamented with appliqué work of bold peacocks, and the original mosaic tiled floor was randomly covered here and there with animal-skin rugs. The mirrored bathroom with modern fittings was scrupulously clean and generously supplied with huge white fluffy towels.

We slept well that night and woke early to a wide eastern sky, pale blue and gold in the morning sunrise, with the promise of a fine warm day. We had breakfast of papaya juice, black coffee and croissants with other visitors who advised us to hire bikes to get around. 'Not again,' I moaned. We were told there was a hire shed just yards away at the back of the hotel.

It was a wonder we found it. Tucked away behind trees lining a beaten track, the 'shed' could easily have been mistaken for a small chapel. It had red pantiles, an elongated roof, high-vaulted beamed ceiling and rough walls painted in a strange red hue, and the place stank of oil and fumes. But there they were, the bikes.

There were dozens of them, some big, old and heavy, a few lighter, more modern machines; others that looked as though they had been assembled from an assortment of bits and pieces – some leaning against the walls, some in racks, some hanging on hooks from the ceiling, but all, without exception, immaculately clean.

The overseer of the bicycle establishment was a wiry, elderly gentleman of Chinese extraction who spoke in a rapid, sing-song high-pitched voice and quickly made it clear that *we* did not choose our bicycle, he chose it for us. After much rooting around at the back of the building, he finally emerged with a machine which was selected, judging by the way he sized Fiona up, according to her height, weight and possible reliability as to whether she would bring it back.

It looked all right to me, but Fiona now decided to play him at his own game. 'I don't want that one,' she said. 'I would like that one if you don't mind,' and pointed to a bright red bike hanging prominently on a chain attached to the ceiling. 'That is very expensive,' he sighed with a pained expression. 'How much?' Fiona enquired. He told her some exorbitant amount. 'I only want the bike,' she retorted, 'not the whole shed full.' To keep the peace, I settled for his first choice, complete with a wicker basket fixed to the handlebars with a leather strap, and Fiona did a reasonable deal for that and the red machine of her choice. We had to wait while he carefully wiped them both down with his oily rag, and only then could we ride off, leaving a very anxious proprietor watching us all the way up the track.

We were making our way to the Japanese Covered Bridge, but on the way, the narrow streets we were cycling through were lined with tailors sitting in the fronts of their shops making clothes, most apparently, for visitors. Hoi An is renowned for the production of garments, made to a high standard from best-quality silk, cotton and linen, and completed in a matter of hours at minimal cost. The number of places selling extra suitcases to overburdened travellers was an indication of the volume of this business.

It was interesting as we passed by to see the rolls of cloth, piled high on top of one another, and to pause and watch the tailors at their work. There was no plying for our trade, no harassment, just a quiet, polite acknowledgement from these hard-working people that we were watching them. Needless to say, in no time we were being meticulously measured – back to front, top to toe, from every angle – for our extravagant but irresistible order of a couple of silk dresses each, linen trouser suits and cotton skirts. 'You will be most happy,' our tailor assured us. 'Come back tomorrow.' He did not want a deposit, he simply gave us a bill for an incredibly modest amount to pay on collection.

We continued our ride to the Japanese Covered Bridge, which was first constructed on the site in 1593 by the Japanese community of Hoi An, to link their neighbourhood with the Chinese quarters across the stream. The bridge was built with a roof so it could be used as a shelter from the rain and the sun, and is very solidly constructed, apparently because the original builders were afraid of earthquakes, so common in Japan. Built into the northern side of the bridge is a small temple. Over the door is written the name given to the bridge in 1719 – Lai Vien Kieu – meaning 'The Bridge For Passers-By-From-Afar', but that was probably too much of a mouthful for the locals, and the bridge is still known simply as the Japanese Bridge.

According to legend, there once lived an enormous monster called Cu whose head was in India, whose tail was in Japan and whose body was in Vietnam. Whenever the monster moved, terrible disasters of floods and earthquakes befell Vietnam. The bridge was built on the monster's weakest point and, not surprisingly, killed it. The people of Hoi An were so mortified that the monster was slain they built a temple at one end to pray for its soul.

Both entrances to the bridge are guarded by a pair of monkeys on one side and by a pair of dogs on the other, and the whole structure, even with all the restorations over the centuries, has retained beautiful, restrained ornamentation faithful to the original understated Japanese design.

We pushed our bikes across the bridge towards the temple where many of Hoi An's oldest shophouses remain, still open during the day, and where artisans work and display their wares: painters, potters and wood carvers can all be seen beavering away and producing goods of a very high quality indeed.

Fiona bought a painting by a well-known local artist, an abstract impression of a traditional peasant girl smoking a long clay pipe. I wasn't particularly impressed with it at the time, but to see it now, tastefully framed and adorning her sitting-room wall, it looks stunning.

It seemed to me that Hoi An had managed to retain the feel of centuries past, and the more we explored, the more fascinated we became. We found the Tan Ky House, built almost two centuries ago for a well-to-do Vietnamese merchant, and still lovingly preserved as a private home. The present owner, whose family has lived in the house for six generations, speaks fluent French and English, and it is his pride and joy to open his amazing house to visitors.

The influence of Japanese and Chinese styles is very evident in the house. A crabshell-shaped ceiling, below which are carvings of crossed sabres enwrapped by a ribbon of silk, represents force and flexibility. Chinese poems written in inlaid mother-of-pearl hang from a number of the columns that support the roof. The Chinese characters on these 150-year-old panels are formed entirely out of birds, gracefully portrayed in various positions of flight. The carved wooden balcony supports around the back of the house overlooks the river.

As the only visitors at that time of day, we felt a little intrusive walking around what was still very much a family house, occupied by men, women and several children, all watching us. But they were nodding and smiling, anxious to show us their precious books and ornaments and traditional toys, things they used every day and probably worth a fortune while they lived quite a meagre, although seemingly happy and contented, existence. We came away feeling somewhat humbled and privileged for having been there.

Nearby we found a Chinese teahouse in a little square surrounded by trees, providing the perfect watering hole for us and a convenient place to prop our bikes. We sat in the shade, relaxed and entranced by this very unique town in central Vietnam, which amazingly had remained almost completely undamaged during the American war.

Later that afternoon, my aching calf muscles reminded me that I had been, in recent years, totally unaccustomed to pedal pushing and I was by now convinced that my bike was definitely one of the heavier models, although Fiona, of course, was quite comfortable on her bright red more modern machine. Mr Ra Lee, back at the bike shed, was pathetically pleased to see us arrive safe and sound, and told us how honoured he would be to let us have exactly the same bikes again the following day. 'Do you possibly have another one like the red one my daughter is using?' I looked around optimistically. 'No,' he said.

I tottered to our room in the hotel where we decided a sauna and a swim might go a long way to relieving my aching limbs. The sauna, housed in a wooden structure to the side of the pool, was supervised by a large, well-upholstered lady who took her job very seriously. The small charcoal fire was constantly splashed with water contained in a long-handled metal cup, raising the heat in that little hut until Fiona and I looked and felt like boiled lobsters. We had to tell her enough was enough, at which point she practically shoved both of us into the pool to cool off.

After a short late-afternoon nap, we felt refreshed and ready for our evening meal at the hotel, where the restaurant was prettily lit with Chinese lanterns; glasses and cutlery were sparkling clean and polished; pink napkins folded in lotus shapes, and linen tablecloths completed the inviting ambience.

We were joined at the table by two other couples, both Australian, and there was no shortage that evening of pleasant, interesting and sometimes hilarious conversation. They were moving on to Cambodia the following day and I think, if I remember rightly through the haze of an over-generous flow of French wine, there were kisses all round at the end of the long evening, and that Fiona and I wished them all a maudlin and heartfelt 'Bon voyage!'

The following day we collected our bikes, duly cleaned and wiped down, and confidently waved off by Mr Ra Lee, we left to find Cua Dai Beach, about five kilometres east of Hoi An. We had started early to avoid riding in the heat of the midday sun. We cycled a long stretch of sandy road, passing shrimp-hatching pools, built apparently with Australian assistance, to give the villagers an opportunity to learn new skills and earn money to educate their children.

We had been told that compared with other desperately poor countries, Vietnam's population is very well educated on the whole: most children receive primary education and about forty per cent go on to secondary schools, though a significant number of children are apparently barred from enrolling in school because of the parents' political background.

The fine sands of Cua Dai Beach were reached down a narrow track, and served a small community living in typical one-room wooden houses grouped together and shaded by tall bamboo trees. Several lads hanging out together were obviously taken by surprise by the sight of us riding bikes, the basket on the front of my handlebars overflowing with our gear, and Fiona riding free with her hair streaming in the wind; we must have made a conspicuous apparition not often seen, I imagine, in that isolated neck of the woods.

They jumped up and down and opened a gate for us to pass through towards a shaded kiosk on an otherwise deserted beach. We learned later that this particular sandy bay was a favourite with local people, who go there when there is a full moon and spend the night talking and swimming together.

A woman was sitting in the kiosk, inscrutably watching us as we changed into cossies for a swim in the calm waters of an inviting sea. It was warm in the shallows and we had to swim out quite a way for the water to cool down enough for us to enjoy a more invigorating dip. We swam around for ages and finally splashed out to find our towels laid out and a cold fruit drink waiting for us at the kiosk!

Three other women were now in the sea, paddling knee-deep, skirts tied up to their waists, with long-handled wide triangular-shaped nets which they were swinging from side to side in slow motion. The woman inside the kiosk was now on the beach and had lit a fire under a big circular pan suspended from a tripod, and gradually the smell of garlic and lemon grass cooking gently in oil began to make our taste buds quiver. The fisherwomen emerged from the sea and carefully placed their catch into a metal tray, and then into the cooking pan. It took a while for us to realise they were preparing our lunch!

It would be difficult to convey how delicious that food was. Served in round bowls, a mixture of seafood had been cooked in the garlic and lemon grass and goodness knows what else, and was absolutely the best we had ever tasted. Even the chopsticks seemed easy to manage that day. To this day I cannot eat seafood without remembering that afternoon, sitting on a deserted beach – other than those four delightful women watching us devour every mouthful – and grinning widely when we agreed that yes, we could eat a little more.

They didn't bother us for money – we had to go to them to pay for our meal. We gave them at least what we would have paid in a good restaurant, as we felt we were paying for the best, and very, very shyly they eventually accepted what to them was a small fortune.

Just as we were thinking we should make a move, the lads from the little hamlet up the road came down to the beach and obviously wanted to play. We obliged by chasing them and each other around in the water, and they showed off by climbing onto each other's backs and being thoroughly silly to make us laugh. It was great fun for half an hour or so, but reluctantly we eventually had to go, to find our way back to collect our new clothes from our bespoke tailor in the town.

It seemed to take much longer to pedal back along that dusty track towards the town. The hot, airless, mid-afternoon sun beat down on a water buffalo wallowing at the edge of the rice fields, a mule plodding wearily, slowly dragging a cart laden with a mountainous pile of heavy sacks, and us, already lethargic after so much swimming and riding. We thought we knew where we were going and that we would have no difficulty in finding the place we had been to the day before, when we had ordered our clothes.

The town didn't even look the same. We were nowhere near the Japanese Bridge or the maze of narrow lanes where our tailor was. Names and landmarks meant nothing – we saw nowhere and nobody we could recognise. Pushing our bikes we blundered on, up and down streets that became scruffy alleyways, and in no time we were thoroughly lost.

'Where's the bill he gave us?' I enquired of my now very ratty daughter. '*You've* got it.' 'No I haven't – I bet it's in the hotel.' 'Where *is* the hotel?' 'What even is the *name* of our hotel?' Fiona remembered it, although she was unsure where it was. The problem we felt sure, would be solved if we got a trishaw. No trishaws. A horse and cart? '*THAT* will do!' we said in unison as we spotted just what we needed coming along the alleyway towards us.

It was a small cart, driven by a wizened farmer swiping encouraging flicks to the backside of a long-suffering mule; they were evidently on their way back from delivering fresh grown vegetables and herbs to the market. Those Viets were amazing – the farmer didn't bat an eyelid when we waved a few notes at him and shouted 'Vinh Hung' in his ear. Straight away we were invited to clamber on to his cart, complete with our bikes. He straightened his bony shoulders and whipped the mule into action, who obligingly trotted us, in style, through the streets back to our hotel, safe and sound.

Cheered enormously by this exceptional cooperation, we pushed our luck a little further. Returning our bikes with a generous payment for their use, and clutching the tailor's bill and the money to pay for our clothes, we approached Ra Lee. 'Would you – could you be so kind as to fetch our purchases from this address on your bike?' 'Course he could. With an air of great importance and determination, he dragged a huge motorbike out from under a tarpaulin, gave it a good wipe down with his ever-ready oily rag, directed a final squirt of oil somewhere in the region of the engine, and off he went, in a great cloud of dust and smoke. 'I hope they wrap our stuff properly,' pondered Fiona, staring after him. I wondered whether we would be lucky enough to get it back at all.

We had booked a massage for this last afternoon in the delightful Vinh Hung. 'Who is going in first?' 'I will,' offered Fiona, and off she went to the little hut adjoining the sauna, nicely prepared in her towelling robe and flip-flops. She seemed to be gone ages and finally appeared nearly an hour later looking very pink and po-faced. 'How was it?' I ventured. 'Don't ask, just go in there and get beaten up yourself.' Crumbs.

The same lady who had attended to us in the sauna was waiting. She was big, her ample boobs well harnessed into a colourful bra, revealing wide, muscular shoulders and strong arms. Her legs, firmly planted at the side of a padded trestle table, were stocky, with well-developed calf muscles. She looked like a battleship. Without her saying a word, it was indicated that I should strip off *everything* and get on the table, face down. Thank God for that, I was thinking fearfully. She cracked her fingers and flexed her wrists and then got started.

Dipping her hands into a large ceramic bowl of oil, she began at the top. Her fingers – or was it her knuckles? – kneaded deep into my collarbone, dug purposefully between my shoulder blades and ribs, separating every bone, every muscle, and I was conscious of places in my torso I hadn't known I had. I chewed my fists to avoid screaming. My buttocks were pummelled, the backs of my legs were pinched and thumbed all the way down to my ankles. Just as I was about to plead with her not to touch my feet, in one movement, with both arms flexed, I was flipped over like a wet fish and the same process was repeated to the front of my body – kneaded and pummelled, ever so slowly, until my stomach felt like it was touching my backbone. At no time did she speak, and at no time did she meet me eyeball to eyeball, and my tenderest parts, thankfully, were carefully avoided.

As I staggered back to our room, there was Fiona, freshly showered, gaily going through our new clothes. 'I feel marvellous,' she said happily. 'Good,' I muttered. 'You might have warned me – I feel like a rag doll!' But I felt marvellous too after a shower and a while to lie on that luxurious bed to put my bones back together. Soon we were away to enjoy aperitifs before dinner, loose limbed and tarted up in our new frocks.

Tomorrow we would be leaving to venture northwards, but for now we were sitting in the courtyard enjoying the cool of the evening air before going in to dinner. Wide eastern skies have a glory all their own as the sun goes down, with ever-changing streaks of pinks and purples, blues threaded with gold, a breathtaking sight of changing colour and contour, and we felt privileged, calm and contemplative, as we enjoyed the moment.

'How do you feel?' Fiona asked me quietly. 'I feel fine,' I replied. 'On reflection, that massage has done me a power of good.' She put her hand out to hold mine. 'No, I mean how do you *really* feel, Ma – about going home and everything?'

How did I really feel? I had tried not to think about it. I knew I would at some point have to face the prospect of resuming my normal life in circumstances that had been far from the norm when I'd left home six months ago. I had taken a long pause to lick my wounds and privately try to regain my balance by exposing myself to new challenges, heading for a fall and feeling out of my depth at times, but nevertheless having had no opportunity during that time to dwell on my inner thoughts.

I had found, in a strange and surprising way, that I had discovered a new drive, that instead of sinking I could stay afloat, fresh enthusiasms gave me good reason to concentrate on what I was doing right now, keeping me focused in the present. Could I maintain this sense of riding on the surface of being, once I returned home? Until now I had avoided the question, but now Fiona was asking. 'I don't know love,' I said. 'We shall have to see – we haven't finished here yet.'

13

We hitched a lift the next day to Hue. People we had met in the hotel were going there anyway and seemed glad for us to join them for the 70-kilometre journey. Hue was on the way to Hanoi, our last destination in Vietnam, and we could fly on to there.

Unlike Ho Chi Minh and most other Vietnamese cities, Hue somehow seems to have retained a unique cultural identity, in spite of its calamitous history. It is a small, peaceful city, full of lakes, canals and lush vegetation, and has some really amazing historical sites, including the 19th-century walled citadel, the remnants of its once-magnificent Imperial City, and seven palatial royal mausoleums. Historically, Hue has been the heartbeat of Vietnam, a centre of political intrigue, cultural innovation, religious worship and educational excellence.

In 1885, when the advisers of 13-year-old Emperor Ham Nghi objected to French activities in Tonkin, French forces encircled the city. Unwisely, the outnumbered Vietnamese forces launched an attack and the French responded mercilessly. According to a contemporary French account, the French forces took three days to burn the Imperial library and remove from the palace every single object of value, from gold and silver ornaments to mosquito nets and toothpicks. Ham Nghi fled to Laos, but he was eventually captured and exiled to Algeria.

Hue was the site of one of the bloodiest battles of the 1968 Tet Offensive and was the only city in South Vietnam to be held by the Communists for more than a few days. While the American command was concentrating its energies on relieving the siege of Khe Sanh, North Vietnamese and Viet Cong troops skirted the American stronghold and walked right into Hue. Immediately on taking the city, Communist political cadres implemented detailed plans to liquidate Hue's uncooperative elements. Thousands of people were rounded up in extensive house-to-house searches, conducted according to lists of names meticulously prepared months before.

During the three weeks or so that Hue remained under Communist control, approximately 3,000 civilians – including merchants, Buddhist monks, Catholic priests and intellectuals – were shot, clubbed to death or buried alive. The victims were buried in shallow mass graves that were discovered at various spots around the city over the following few years. In the ensuing counter-attack the city was all but levelled. Some years later, in 1975, the northerners were back to liberate Hue, and the huge task of rebuilding the city received a boost in 1993, when UNESCO listed Hue as a World Heritage Site.

The people we had travelled with from Hoi An, Robert and Violet, his charming wife, were no ordinary tourists. Robert was an American war veteran, and had kept up a 30-year relationship with a family from an outlying village near the city. He told us that unlike the war heroes from World War II who returned to the USA and were greeted with joyous banners and bunting, the Vietnam veterans went home without victory and were seriously stigmatised for being unwillingly drafted into a war engineered by politicians.

In spite of the horrors and the aftermath of that war, by no means were all American soldiers drug sodden, not all of them were involved in the massacres of villagers, nor did they all commit rape, pillage and other atrocities: most of these young American men just wanted it all to end and to get home. When they did, many of them were desperately unable to forget what they had seen and left behind in Vietnam.

Our new American friends told us that they had every reason to maintain their friendship with the people of this village, situated not far from Hue. During the war, Robert and two other soldiers had been separated from their platoon during an attack. They had wandered off the beaten track, onto a trail that led into thick red mud that sucked their boots, making it hard and agonisingly slow to walk. After many hours ploughing through swampy mosquito-infested countryside, hungry and exhausted, they came upon this village, and prayed that the Viet Cong were not in control or hiding there. They decided to risk being seen, and very soon they were. The villagers fed them, treated their badly blistered feet, and, in Robert's case, gave him their local cure for the onset of malaria. They allowed them to sleep until dawn and then escorted them to the main

Highway l, where they were eventually picked up by their own troops.

Robert, of course, had never forgotten their kindness. 'They risked their lives to do that for us,' he said quietly, 'even when at that time, civilian men, women and children were being mercilessly massacred in places not far from here.' The village people had everything to fear from all around by helping the Americans.

Robert urged us to join them on their visit to the village. 'They will be pleased to have English ladies visit them. We can let them know you are coming.' Our friends drove us to the edge of the village, about three kilometres out of the main city, in their hire car. We walked the rest of the way to what was little more than a hamlet with a narrow dirt road running through the centre. The houses of this small and simple place were built of bamboo with pitched roofs; black pigs and chickens rooted and scratched in the yards surrounded by picket fences. All around were groves of fruit trees: coconut palms, guavas, papayas, and the big green sails of banana trees.

As we approached, the deep pink and bronze sunset glowed low on the skyline and we were greeted by an elderly couple and innumerable relatives, some clutching tiny barefoot children. 'Thirty years is a long time,' said Robert. 'We are grandparents now and our families have grown.' To our delight, we were told we must stay to eat with them, and they set about preparing a traditional meal, cooked and served in the traditional way.

On rush mats, everyone was seated outside, encircling large black rice pots hanging over wood-burning fires. We were invited to fill our dishes with rice, small slivers of fish, pork soup and cabbage leaves, and were served with dainty pots of palm-sugar juice. The little girls, maybe six, seven or eight years old, were fascinated by the strangers in their midst. They came and sat down next to us and reached out shyly to touch our light-coloured skin and to stroke our hair, so different to theirs. They were curious to know what it was Fiona carried in her capacious handbag. Fiona fished out a small hairbrush and nail polish, and with smiling permission from their mothers, we spent a very happy girlie time brushing each other's hair and painting the nails of the children – and the nails of their mothers!

Robert, over the years, had achieved a serviceable command of Vietnamese and was conversing intently with a thin, gaunt man, whose leg was twisted and withered, and who stood beside Robert supported by a single crutch. He, like so many of his compatriots, had seen and suffered the indignity of his country torn apart by the ravages of war. His eyes, set wide apart, held an unshifting gaze as Robert spoke. Their thoughtful faces, like those of the others sitting around, were tinged bronze, reflecting the flames of the dying cooking fires. From somewhere in the bamboos a night bird sang, and little monkeys chattered before finally settling down to sleep. It was an evening I shall never forget.

We had reserved a room for two nights at the small, friendly Thang Long Hotel in Hue, with fairly basic facilities in homely rooms, a tour information centre and an airport pickup service thrown in. Again, there being no lift in the building, it was a case of the higher you climbed, the cheaper it became; we were taking no chances, and cheerfully paid the extra to be on the ground floor.

A tour operator organised a boat trip for us along the Perfume River (*perfume* is not exactly a description that leaps to mind when weighed against the debris that settles along most of the riverbanks). However, it is one of the city's highlights, and we puttered in front of the citadel, past rowboats heading for Dong Ba Market. We stopped off to visit Thien Mu Pagoda, the oldest in Hue and has long been a focus for the Buddhist protest against repression. In 1963 one of its monks burned himself to death in what was then the city of Saigon in protest at the excesses of the regime at that time. The monk's powder blue Austin car is still on display there, along with a copy of the famous photograph of his 'self-immolation' that shocked the world.

We discovered a more unusual way to enjoy the river, and attended a traditional folk-song performance on its waters. In the past, under the Nguyen emperors, Hue was the cultural as well as the political capital of Vietnam, and artists would entertain the gentry with poetry and music from sampans on the river. We finally finished our day with dinner, accompanied by more entertainment of music and singing, with Robert and Violet as our guests on a separately organised river cruise.

We left the strange and interesting city of Hue the following morning steeped in cultural impressions and the memory of that wonderful evening in the village, and were fondly embraced by our new friends. We felt very blessed indeed.

14

THE NORTH

The flight to Hanoi was mercifully short, as the aeroplane shook and rattled all the way – the original white-knuckle ride, you might say – and it was with grateful thanks to our Maker and sheer relief when we landed, bumpily, but at least in one piece.

Hanoi at that time was not yet ready to dance to the capitalists' tune. From his glass sarcophagus in the bowels of a concrete mausoleum, Ho Chi Minh keeps a beady eye on the northern kingdom – unless it's October, in which case he can usually be found in Russia having his embalming fluids topped up. Throughout the rest of the year, thousands apparently make the daily pilgrimage to peek at the figure of their former president with his cap of white hair. Uncle Ho might have shuffled off this mortal coil, but he hadn't lost the knack of pulling the crowds it seemed.

Hanoi – literally, the City in a Bend of the River – lounges along the banks of the Red River, where at dawn a fleet of frail sampans glide off in search of fish. Water buffalo lumber down the road, carts clatter behind; an old man in faded green fatigues sucks on a bamboo pipe; a romantic city, you might think, retaining buildings from the 11th-century court of its founding father, King Ly Thai To. Some of the narrow streets in the Old Quarter still trade in the same speciality goods they dealt in 500 years ago.

In 1887 the French turned Hanoi into the centre of government for the entire Union of Indochina, replacing ancient monuments with grand colonial residences – many of which survive today – lining grand tree-lined boulevards again reflecting the French influence. Lakes and parks dot the city, providing the locals with a perfect place for a spot of dawn exercise. There prevail fleeting moments of Paris: the smell wafts in the air of warm baguettes sold on street corners; the beret is commonly worn; and you will hear 'Bonjour' given as an early-morning greeting in some parts of the city.

At the heart of Hanoi is Hoan Kiem Lake, which lies between the cramped but endlessly diverting Old Quarter in the north and the French Quarter in the south. Across the rail tracks, some of Hanoi's most impressive monuments occupy the wide-open spaces of the former Imperial City, grouped around Ho Chi Minh's Mausoleum and extending south to the ancient walled gardens of the Temple of Literature.

Hoan Kiem Lake is small – we walked around it in just over thirty minutes. A squat, three-tiered pavilion known as the Tortoise Tower ornaments a tiny island in the middle of the lake – 'Lake of the Restored Sword' – and the name refers to a legend of the great 15th-century Vietnamese hero Le Loi, whose miraculous sword was swallowed by a huge golden turtle in the lake. Across the red-lacquered Hue Bridge is another island where stands a temple, founded in the 14th century and rebuilt in the 1800s in typical dynastic style. In a room to one side of the temple there is a glass box, housing a giant stuffed, ugly and tatty-looking turtle, said to have been found in the lake, and the belief is that this was the original golden turtle. 'No wonder it doesn't look very happy,' commented Fiona, 'if it still has that jolly old sword stuck in its gullet.'

Walking around the lake, tranquil though it seemed, was not a comfortable experience for us. At that time, Hanoi was understandably still smarting from the effects of the American war and from the serious damage and loss of life sustained in the city from the infamous Christmas bombing campaign of 1972. Although the tourist business was just beginning to flower in the early nineties, the northern political isolation and lack of resources was still very evident in the minds of the people. Therefore, anyone with a round, pink face, a farange, was assumed to be a hated American. As a result, Fiona and I had bread and evil-smelling vegetation thrown at us in the streets; we were rudely stared at wherever we went, a cold hostility shining in the eyes of these northerners. They seemed almost possessed of an undisguised and fearful malice. The atmosphere all around was frosty and very intimidating and not at all what we had encountered elsewhere in Vietnam. And we didn't like it one little bit.

Nevertheless, we decided that the odd bit of stale bread and wet cabbage was not going to deter us from seeing the sights, and I particularly wanted to go to the Temple of Literature. We risked our necks to cross a main road, with the now-familiar ancient, stately black bicycles doing a constant kamikaze act, and bashed-up cars driven by youngsters fantasising about their chances at the Grand Prix zooming past rows of artisans scattered over the pavements outside a few cluttered shops selling pots and pans; here, at least, we were ignored.

The Temple of Literature is a rare example of well-preserved traditional Vietnamese architecture and is made up of five separate courtyards. The main entrance is preceded by a gate, and on it there is an inscription requesting that all visitors dismount their horses before entering. It is a quiet, serene place and the 11th-century courtyards are modelled on that of Confucius's birthplace in China. In the third courtyard there is a beautiful walled pond covered in lotus flowers – the Well of Heavenly Clarity – flanked by the temple's most valuable relics, 82 stone stelae mounted on tortoises. Each stela records the results of state examinations held at the National Academy between 1442 and 1779. This academy was Vietnam's first university, but that part of the temple was destroyed by French bombs in 1947.

After our disconcerting experience in the morning, we were surprised to find the services of an excellent English-speaking guide. He took us to the fourth courtyard of the temple, bringing us to the Ceremonial Hall, a long, low building with a sweeping tiled roof crowned by lithe-bodied dragons bracketing a full moon. Here, we were told, the King and his mandarins would make sacrifices before the altar of Confucius. When pressed, our guide was reluctant to tell us what the King and his mandarins sacrificed. 'I bet they were pink-faced Englishwomen,' whispered Fiona in my ear.

After his very interesting and detailed tour, we chatted to the guide and told him of our unpleasant experience during the morning. He told us they would have been street gangs, louts, and that they behaved like that to anyone who didn't look like them, that the authorities were aware of it and were trying to stamp it out. Hanoi, in spite of its troubled past, was anxious now to promote tourism. He explained to us that the long history of war continues to weigh heavily on the consciousness of all who can remember, but now the Vietnamese people are beginning to learn to be gracious and welcoming to those who come in peace. 'Anyway,' he said, 'you do not look American. You smile, but the Americans look guilty.' He added, 'you would not have had the tour if you had been from the USA.' Oh well.

Later at our hotel we enquired about transport to take us for an evening ride to the puppet show, and emphasised that we didn't want to feel fearful. 'You will have no problems,' we were assured. 'We have good people who will be happy to show you our city. You will travel by cyclo.' With that, we were escorted to meet a gentleman who was the proud owner of a three-wheeled cycling machine, with a posh open carriage on the back.

The ancient art of water puppetry was virtually unknown outside northern Vietnam until the 1960s and is reckoned to be at least 1,000 years old. Rice farmers carved the puppets from water-resistant fig-tree timber in forms modelled on the villagers themselves, animals from their daily lives, and more fanciful mythical creatures such as the dragon, the phoenix and the unicorn. Eleven puppeteers stand in the water behind a bamboo screen and have traditionally suffered a host of waterborne diseases, and it is they who manipulate the heavy puppets attached to long underwater poles. Some of the puppets have articulated limbs and heads, in the darkened theatre auditorium they look as though they are walking on the water. The performances are of pastoral scenes, battles between fishermen and their prey, fire-breathing dragons and a flute-playing boy riding a buffalo with menacing upturned horns.

The music is as important as the action taking place on the 'stage', with wooden flutes, gongs, cylindrical drums, bamboo xylophones and the fascinating single-stringed *dan bau*. The whole performance was noisy and great fun, even though Fiona and I, sitting in special concession seats in the front row, got thoroughly soaked.

The drive back to the hotel that evening took us past the central lake where we had been in the morning. At dusk the atmosphere was entirely different. Elders were there selling cassavas and sugar cane, their women vaunting black teeth, the result of an age-old fear that teeth in their natural white state resemble the fangs of an animal. As we strolled along the pretty lantern-lit promenades, bevies of Miss Vietnams paraded in their finest *ao dai*, the traditional long, fitted dress worn over trousers that covers everything but, being fashioned in fine, translucent silk, hides almost nothing. When night fell, all was silent, save the squeak of rusty pedalos propelling young lovers across the moonlit water of the lake.

There is only so much you can take in, and Vietnam is a magical mine of amazing historical sites. In Europe we regard anything built around the time of the birth of Christ as pretty ancient, but all over Southeast Asia, and in Vietnam in particular, there are remains of past dynasties going back thousands of years, and many are particularly well preserved unless they have been bashed up irrevocably by the havoc of war. Braving the prospect of being yet again assaulted by wet cabbage, we decided to give history a miss for our next day in Hanoi and visit the Old Quarter, locally known as the Soul of Hanoi.

Founded in the 15th century, the old commercial district consists of a maze of narrow streets and alleyways, some bearing the name of their speciality. So there is a street for rice, one for hats, one for silk, one for fermented fish, and so on. Fermented fish is the staple ingredient of a pungent sauce that is to Vietnamese cooking what soy sauce is to the Japanese. Incidentally, the real culinary delight of the north is giant snails, stuffed with pork and ginger, or fried with tofu and bananas. Hanoi's many lakes provide rich pickings for teenagers, who spend whole days shoulder-high in water, feeling for snails with their feet. Any surplus not required by their families is sold on to the restaurant chefs, who pay them a pittance for their trouble.

Our map of the district indicated that we were to pass the hospital on our way to the northern end of the central lake. We could smell the fetid, pungent odour of disease and disinfectant even before we reached it. A low, single-storey building to the side of a buckling pavement, its windows were wide open to a street where fresh air fought with the fumes and dust of passing traffic. The decrepit wards, iron beds and patients, some hooked up to a variety of medical contraptions, some bound and bloodied, were in full view of passing pedestrians. It was a sickening sight, and there and then Fiona and I decided that we would make this our last day in Hanoi.

We continued to walk on past the Martyrs' Monument, and soon we were surrounded by dozens of shoe shops, selling every shape and size of footwear, and quite clearly demonstrating how serious the Hanoians are about their feet and how little they concern themselves about competition. Nearby were several shop fronts where artisans were carving intricate gravestones by hand, most bearing images of the deceased. We investigated rows of clothing outlets, and snazzy jewellers exhibiting their wares to tempt everyone who went past, and we, of course, couldn't resist buying a load of cheap junk we could well have done without.

We came to a pagoda with a red funeral palanquin, fiercely superintended by guards with long white beards, who apparently spent their days sipping tea. Legend has it that the Ky King used the pagoda to pray for assistance in building the city walls because they persistently collapsed, no matter how many times he rebuilt them. His prayers were finally answered when a white horse appeared out of the temple and guided him to the site where he could safely build his walls. Evidence of his success is still visible at Cua O Quan Chong, the quarter's well-preserved Old East Gate.

One of the most interesting streets translates as Counterfeit Street, where imitation 'ghost money' is sold for burning in Buddhist ceremonies. The mind boggles as to where it actually finishes up, considering how naive the average tourist is when handling foreign currency! We passed tin-makers, shops selling towels, mirrors, boxes, and leather, and groups of shops all selling the same commodity – Buddhist altars and statues. The best was a fantastic row of herb sellers filling the street with succulent aromas.

'Do you think,' asked Fiona, still trying to get over the sight of the hospital, 'there might be a street for cups of coffee?' Lo and behold, she had hardly uttered the words and there it was – a street chock-a-block with coffee shops and cafes! What a sight for sore eyes (and feet)! We were utterly spoilt for choice, so we picked a cafe not too busy, with seats out on the pavement under an awning – a good place, we thought, to sit, rest our weary legs and watch the world go by.

The street, opening out to a wide cobbled square, bustled with people going backwards and forwards; everyone seemed to be carrying something, or pushing a bike loaded with goods tied to the seat, handlebars and back mudguards (if they had any). The men appeared to be uniformly dressed in dreary dark grey pyjamas and black caps, and the women's apparel seemed only functional and unattractive. Tired, forlorn, disenchanted people; no pretty smiles here, no lads giving Fiona the eye, just downcast, downtrodden and miserable. Our coffee was slapped down in front of us, and the waiter stood waiting for his money as though he suspected we might do a runner. Fiona and I decided that they had a long way to go if they were to entice tourists to visit their city.

On the way back we passed a series of massage parlours. The Government apparently had severely restricted the number of places licensed to give massage because of the concern that naughty 'extra services' might be offered (as indeed they are in many places), but there seemed a fat chance that anything unseemly was likely to take place at these particular venues.

Customers were laid out on the pavement alfresco, and treated in public by buxom masseurs. Weary taxi drivers and tired-out rickshaw pedallers patiently queued for their turn, rolling home-grown tobacco into thin, matchstick cigarettes to pass the time. We were reluctant to stop and stare, but we did, and in this instance nobody seemed to mind. Exhausted by his day of pedalling, one rickshaw man had opted for a full restorative overhaul. In a bid to exorcise his aches and pains, fifteen heated cupping jars had been symmetrically arranged on his back. Twenty minutes later, accompanied by a pop-popping, the masseur removed them, exposing a cluster of perfect pink circles. 'Good grief!' said Fiona. 'I don't fancy *that*!'

From our short time in Hanoi, so different from the southern provinces, I could not think of any place in Vietnam that remotely compared to this northern city. It is complicated and contradictory in so many ways, and yet a natural simplicity reigns over the everyday life of its inhabitants. On the surface there is a strangely erotic combination of art, literature and excellence, and yet . . . bitterness, grey ugliness and defiance defile whatever admiration one has for its unique beauty.

After all the trauma of the recent war, Vietnam became once again a unified nation in 1976. However, the north had no industry, a cooperative system of agriculture, and much of its land had been bombed on a massive scale. Hanoi was apparently intent on ushering in a rigid socialist state. Privately owned land was confiscated, collectivisation of agriculture was introduced, and as the state took control of industry and trade, work opportunities dwindled and there was precious little help at that time from the outside world. Not surprising really, when anyone with remote connections with America was interned to be 're-educated' along with Buddhist monks, priests and intellectuals. Hundreds and thousands of southerners were sent to these camps and many remained there for over a decade. Discrimination against those on the 'wrong' side in the war was continuing to hold back real progress in areas as diverse as health care and job opportunities.

So it was no wonder that many of the people were so dispirited. In spite of the change of heart of the Americans, who lifted their veto on aid in 1993, so that subsequently western cash began to flow in, the benefits of all that had yet to perceptibly filter down to improve the lot of the average man on the street or to change his attitude towards the people of the West. I am sure tourists who visit Hanoi today, so many years later, will find the northerners with lighter hearts, risen up as they have before from the ashes of war, striving to make their homeland great again.

15

My eyes already touch the sunny hill,
Going far ahead of the road I have begun.
So we are grasped by what we cannot grasp;
It has its inner light, even from a distance—
And changes us, even if we do not reach it
Into something else, which hardly sensing it
We already are.
A gesture waves us on, answering our own wave—
But what we feel is the wind in our faces.

Rainer Maria Rilke, *A Walk 1875–1926*

I love to travel by bus, boat or train, but I really do not like flying. It's all right for people who have more or less taken off from the cradle, but I was well into my prime before I took my first terrified flight. However, to get anywhere far beyond my home shores, I realise I have to bite the bullet and fly.

All the same, I am irritable and fretful the instant I leave my point of departure: the taxi is late, I shall miss my flight, I check and recheck I have ticket, passport, money, cards, keys. I can't stand the airport busyness, the moving mass of people, the luggage, the trolleys catching my heels, and the hanging about to check in. 'Your flight will be twenty minutes late, madam.' 'What?' 'Do you want a coffee?' No, I don't. I want to get going. The long walk to the departure gate (Am I going the right way?) with unnecessary hand luggage. I ask myself, What do I want all this lot for?

We board the aircraft. The cabin crew are there to greet us. 'Are you going to Heathrow?' I asked. I wanted to be sure. I enquired after the Captain's health. 'Is he well? Has he remembered to fill up?' Fiona rolls her eyes by way of apology; the pretty cabin attendant smiles broadly and informs us we have been upgraded, and shows us to our seats. 'Oh! Thank you!' I gush inanely as she stuffs my bits and pieces in the overhead locker.

Fiona and I held hands as we took off into the sunset, a beautiful golden horizon, streaked with red fingers blazing a trail for us high into the sky, and I knew we were both remembering being together on another long journey almost two years before, returning from Australia. A similar evening flight into a very similar sunset, but then we had her precious Dad and my beloved husband with us, strapped into a stretcher above the seats and below the lockers, desperate to get him home before his illness reached its final and terrible conclusion.

Then we had passed over Ayers Rock, at 37,000 feet looking like a massive and magnificent mound of seemingly burning copper set in a vast desert; a spiritual place for Aboriginal Australians. Looking through that tiny porthole window, I could remember thinking how my vision of the world was enhanced by the sight, and prayed that the spirits would do something for us.

That journey took 26 hours, and even with the help of a doctor sent out from the UK to escort us, it was the ultimate nightmare. Fear of flying never entered my head then; all I could think about was getting this brave man out of the stretcher and into a more comfortable seat for at least part of that long journey home.

Sludged by time and tempered by experiences that I had deliberately imposed upon myself since then, I could now recall that terrible homecoming with dry eyes, and not for the first time realise that those memories were not only my own. Fiona had shared the haunting burden of that harrowing journey with me, and the thoughts of it kept us both very quiet until the drinks trolley appeared.

'Champagne, please, if you have it,' she said to the attendant, 'and do you have proper glasses?' 'Your Dad would be proud of you,' I told her as we clinked our drinks.

Night hours spent sitting in a darkened cabin unable to sleep provide ample time for contemplation. How would I be this time when I got home? This had been the longest stretch away from my family and friends – friends? Yes, I now knew who they were, dear people who had hung in there with me when the going got rough.

But there were others who had made me feel as though I were in a kind of quarantine. I felt socially marginalised by many of the people I knew as friends – couples, who once cheerfully popped in at any old time with any old excuse. Fancy a walk? A drink? Whattayadoin' on Saturday? I remembered thinking at the time that I must have suddenly developed contagious warts when they no longer bothered to come now I was on my own.

Asking around a bit among other luckless souls, women, and some men, in the same plight confirmed a similar experience after the death of their partner – that the majority of friendships they enjoyed when they were a married couple were no longer there for them. I felt excluded from the social calendar. What I, and they, wanted to know was: Why? Had our former friends always lacked a generosity of spirit? Did they always suffer from an emotional stinginess that automatically compartmentalises the widowed? Had we grown horns? Was I a threat? Maybe they thought I would want my grass cut, the car repaired, a new tap washer, a plug – a *cuddle*? Crumbs, whatever next!

I reflected on how we had known these people for many years, raised our children together, shared holidays, family weddings – always entertaining each other and everyone had been glad to join in. We grew older together, waists thickened, hair thinned and turned grey, but it didn't matter one little bit, we knew how to enjoy ourselves. Did they then believe I could no longer laugh? It's true my sense of humour did take a nosedive for a while, but even in the blackest moments there are occasions when you just *have* to laugh. Was there a time limit on how long I was allowed to grieve, like some sort of test to get through? Perhaps you should go back to work, perhaps you should move house, perhaps you need a holiday – whatever, *get normal!*

I thought about all these things in the hushed quiet of sleeping people all around me, uncomfortably sprawled in inadequate seats, the cabin attendants occasionally doing the rounds to see that everything was all right during those long night hours. 'Would you like a blanket?' whispered our pretty girl with the wide smile. 'Or a drink of something?' 'Just a drink of water would be nice, thank you,' I whispered back.

The night hours are often difficult, whether in my own bed, in a strange bed or in an aircraft flying above beautiful lands unseen in the dark. The lying awake or half dreaming are usually accompanied by waves of introspection, which during the day can be put firmly at the back of the mind.

I was feeling kinder now. It wasn't really their fault. To understand a grief is to understand the relationship, and it takes courage to confront someone else's pain. I was so fortunate in the love and support I had from my family and those lovely people who did not lose their bottle in the face of my tears. They, bless them, were not too paralysed by the embarrassment that death can induce or to risk saying the wrong thing; although they knew nothing could put it right, they tried anyway, and came back time and time again to ride the nightmare of disbelief and bewilderment with me, with free gifts of time and thought, energy and space. I hoped they would still be there for me now, after all this time away.

I gazed around me in that restricted place. Fiona was sleeping, having made herself as comfortable as possible under the circumstances with two pillows, a blanket up to her chin and her feet in my lap.

I wondered where all these other people had been, what wealth of new experience they had enjoyed, and suddenly I felt very privileged. I no longer felt charged with hypersensitivity, I felt changed, less anxious about trivia, more resilient, mentally stronger, and I knew I could find new reasons to pick up the threads of my life. I had achieved strength and independence, I had coped with the difficult bits and had become reasonably adept at being alone. I also knew that for as long as I could, I would continue to travel, somewhere – anywhere; this world was too beautiful to miss. My mind was drifting . . .

I awoke to Fiona insisting that I move so that she could go to the toilet. Dawn was breaking and it was a lovely sight from our lonely place in the sky. Suddenly the cabin was busy. People moving, stretching, chatting, queuing for the loo; the breakfast trolley ready to offer us tea, coffee and sustenance to see us through the next hour or so before landing. I was excited, so excited at the prospect of seeing my children and their children, and the dogs, and my garden – would they have cut the grass? Had the window cleaner been? Who cared? I was nearly home!

I wept at the sight of them all waiting at Arrivals. As Fiona proudly marched me through, my two little grandchildren ducked under the barrier and launched themselves at me, bringing me to my knees to hold them close. The rest, all my family, wide smiles, big hugs, moaning that we were late (as usual), and a big car to take us to my house.

The dogs were there, Nicky's elegant and faithful Dobermann and my little Polly, ginger and white, a cross between an Irish setter and a border collie. She sulked only for a minute or two to let me know I had been out of order for leaving her for so long, and then, unable to stop her waggy tail, she went out of her way to let me know she was still my best mate.

We ate together, we drank together and we all talked at once; we had a lovely time around the table we had all shared so many times before. The warm afternoon fled in a flurry of excitement, until twilight descended and the evening air chilled, and although they emphatically denied it, the children were getting tired, and reluctantly they were taken home to their beds.

Alone again, I walked out into the garden, now cool and quiet; I plucked twigs from the rosemary, the sage and the lavender bushes, and sniffed the aromatic perfume from their leaves. I could hear the tall trees whispering in the still night. The bright new moon cast shadows across the lawn and illuminated the branches of the trees, home over the years to urban wildlife – squirrels, nesting blackbirds and not so long ago, an owl, his silhouette unmistakable against the night sky, and we would listen for him to gently hoot for us. Heaven for me is not up there above the clouds where the aeroplanes fly, it is nearer to home, in my garden – watching over me. Once again under that hushed night sky I wished I could have him back, if only for an hour, to tell him about all that had happened since he had gone, and for him to say, 'You're doing all right, love, you're doing fine.' The owl had gone now from the eucalyptus tree but the spirits were still there; reassured, I went inside and closed the doors.

I wandered through my house, my home for so long, an encircling cocoon of love, built on trust and freedom and an acceptance of each other's faults and differences. How could I leave all this? But of course I could, it was no longer the place I knew, now it was just me in it, and it wasn't the same.

I spotted the massive pile of accumulated post and junk mail. 'I'll sort that lot out in the morning,' I told Polly. Idly, though, I pulled out a promisingly thick travel brochure and sat down to read.

Part 3

NORTHERN INDIA AND NEPAL 1996

16

Ever let the Fancy roam,
Pleasure never is at home;
At a touch sweet Pleasure melteth
Like to bubbles when rain pelteth;
Then let winged Fancy wander
Through the thought still spread beyond her:
Open wide the mind's caged door,
She'll dart forth, and cloudward soar.

John Keats, *Fancy 1795–1821*

India – *In-di-ah*, land of palaces and maharajas! The very sound of it conjures up a country steeped in history, with its abandoned cities, ruins, monuments and old battlefields – all of which have their tales to tell. It is one of the world's oldest civilisations, dating back some 5,000 years, and it was, in its heyday, one of the richest, known as the Golden Bird of the East. Its role as the birthplace of two of the world's greatest religions – Buddhism and Hinduism – alone is enough to ensure the country's historical importance. Many of the social structures that exist today can be traced back through many centuries, and great empires existed far earlier there than anything comparable in Europe.

India, it is often said, is not so much a country as a continent. From north to south and east to west the people are different, the customs are different and the languages are different. It is a land of exotic enchantment, of religious mystique and of great beauty. It is also a place of squalor and abject poverty; of noise, chaos and ugliness, relieved when you least expect it by colour and vitality, hospitality and friendliness and even, at times, a quiet tranquillity.

Yet India as an entity is a comparatively recent invention put together by the British. But they were not the first European power to arrive in India, nor were they the last to leave. Those honours go to the Portuguese; in 1498 Vasco da Gama arrived on the coast of modern-day Kerala, having sailed around the Cape of Good Hope, and gave Portugal a century of uninterrupted control of Indian trade with Europe. Then in 1520 they captured Goa, which they controlled right through to 1961, 14 years after the British had left. The Dutch also had trading posts in India, and so did the French, and they too still hung on to their enclave at Pondicherry for quite a while after the British Raj lost its grip. Nevertheless, from the early 19th century, India was effectively under British control. It was a place to make money, and for the most part the Brits had the sense to leave Indian culture, beliefs and religions alone; indeed, it was said that the British didn't give a damn what religion a person held, so long as he made a decent cup of tea!

Four years had passed since that dark, miserable, painful time of bereavement. Four years since I made those first tentative steps to travel alone, to work in foreign parts and to get to grips with 'moving on', whatever that means.

I'd moved on all right. I had moved tons of garden rubbish, bags and bags of the stuff, the result of plucking and pruning, cutting and chopping in an effort to restore my garden to something like its former glory. I had moved a million broken tiles, to be replaced by an entirely new roof on my house. Furniture, fixtures and fittings had been moved to complete a manic makeover to my home, which was rapidly becoming a neglected shell. Major battles had been fought with broken fences, blocked drains, stroppy builders – 'I can't mend that, you need a new one' – 'No, I *do not*, it will mend' – all the time a relentless and sometimes resentful effort to manage on my own.

I couldn't be bothered with the trivia of life any more. I think I had become more resilient, more resourceful, and hopefully more tolerant. To my friends and family there was no visible trace of the unhealed wound to my heart that still lurked and lingered, and played havoc with my thoughts in unguarded moments, but I knew I was less fraught, less frantic, and much less fragile. I wondered sometimes if my husband would even know me any more as the woman he was married to for so long. I had found too, that life could still be fun, and I had not had to do anything particularly amazing to reactivate my life. But now I needed a holiday – a proper one – and to realise a dream, not a shared dream but my own. I would go to India.

From experience in Thailand I knew how difficult, long-winded and frustrating it can be to travel anywhere in oriental places. Clapped-out and irregular buses are overcrowded and rattle enough to shake your fillings loose; trains take forever, if and when you can actually get on. Nothing in Thailand was ever straightforward: any old time will do in a place where any old answer will do in reply to a question, rather than admit ignorance. I suspected India would be much the same.

I felt this time that I could do without the beaurocratic resistance, the formalities and the paperwork to be processed, the queues to be negotiated and all of the bizarre delays to be experienced getting the necessary documentation to be able to move about at all in India given that I would not have all the time in the world to do it. I decided to let someone else work it all out for me. I contacted a travel company known and recommended for their expertise in arranging holidays abroad for the more mature client. I have put that politely; what they actually do is to cater for anyone over fifty with an open mind and a quest for adventure. They provide for those wanting unusual itineraries and extraordinary destinations and in some cases, and what particularly appealed to me, they arranged special holidays for singles. There was indeed one such party departing for northern India in four weeks' time, the very nice girl on the phone told me. Brilliant!

17

It was a treat to be greeted at the airport by a smart company representative who escorted me to check in my bags without further ado. She directed me to a group of seats roped off near a small cafe to one side of the concourse where several people were already gathered. We had an hour and fifteen minutes, she said – time to have a coffee – and she added that she would be back to escort us to the departure gate. No messing about there then.

One by one people joined the group until there were twenty-one of us assembled, nine men and eleven women, some already beginning to chat together, others staring stonily into space. One gentleman had appeared dressed in a heavy tweed suit, expensively cut, the jacket with a back flap that strained over a pot belly and well-developed buttocks. His woolly waistcoat was buttoned firmly over a pale blue shirt, and tied tight to his neck was a regimental tie. He wore highly polished shoes of quality brown leather, and the whole outfit was topped off with a bold-checked flat cap. He leaned elegantly on a black ebony cane, both hands clasped over a silver knob. Altogether rather stylish, he looked impressive, already hot, and very, very snooty. Blimey, I thought, maybe he's a left over from the days of the Raj! 'Well done, m'dear,' he boomed as our representative reappeared to escort us to the departure gate. 'Right on time.' He snapped his pocket watch shut. 'Good gel,' he added, confirming her efficiency as though the entire flight arrangements had fallen on her young shoulders.

As we boarded the evening flight to Delhi, I wondered how many of these people had any idea what they could be confronted with on this trip. It was planned as a tour, and promised to be very tiring – moving on after maybe only two or three nights in one place, with long overland journeys in between. The wide cultural divide in Asian countries can be quite shocking to the uninitiated. Beggars and cripples, many of them children forced to spend their lives sitting on little wooden boards on wheels with their legs, badly maimed, folded under their thin, wasted bodies, shunting in and around the main streets to gather alms from intimidated and appalled tourists. Pitiful slum areas, where the poor and unblessed live and work out their lives, where material values are secondary to the business of simply existing. Many of the visitors' conceptions would undoubtedly go to the wall, and I sincerely hoped that my travelling companions had done their homework.

September in New Delhi is a month of brand new facility, the trees and flowers are refreshed and washed from the monsoon rains. But the air still seemed sticky with damp heat as we arrived at the Taj Palace Hotel, situated in a quiet road just outside the city. Our luggage was already safely installed in our rooms, and there was time for a short rest, a shower and a walk in the gardens before dinner.

Beautifully laid out, the grounds flaunted wide shingled pathways edged with manicured lawns and beds of flamboyant crimson canna lilies. Towards the road, splashes of shade were provided by banyan trees lining the perimeter railings surrounding the hotel. From the road outside a file of women with baskets of laundry on their heads passed through the security gate, and I could hear the sound of the muezzins from a score of minarets spread beyond in the city of Old Delhi. I felt a childish excitement at the prospect of meeting the real India.

I hardly felt like eating after such a long journey, but I made my way anyway to the dining room. As in most Asian hotels doing their best to cater for European tourists, the cuisine allows for European food as well as traditional local fare. Unsurprisingly, the Asian interpretation of western dishes can be vague and disappointing if you are expecting roast beef and Yorkshire pudding. The vegetables are usually overcooked and soggy, the meat bland and barely warm. The quality of meat isn't all that good either: mutton (the meat is usually mutton) is stringy, and the chickens were probably half-starved before they hit the pot. So as far as I was concerned, I was very happy to eat traditional Indian food – hot lentil soup, curries and rice, a selection of vegetarian dishes and the delicious oven baked *naan* bread, or the flat cupcake *idii* made from rice flour and eaten hot. Judging by the elegantly laid out tables, complete with knives and forks, we were at least not expected to eat in the traditional Indian way, with our fingers.

The round tables were laid out for groups of six people. Sparkling glasses, cutlery and linen were all immaculately clean, while hovering nearby, young, smartly dressed waiters pulled out chairs for us and took orders for wine – red or white? Or both? Bottled water too, all on the house. None of us knew each other, but six women seated together take no time at all to exchange Christian names and snippets of information about their background, where they are from, whether widowed, divorced or just plain single. We had amongst us two very smart young-looking fifty-somethings, two ladies in their sixties, and one very spritely, very articulate eighty-year-old by the name of Cherie; I took to Cherie immediately, enhanced by the fact that she was very anxious to know if she could smoke and whether they served whisky at the bar 'I've got a bottle of duty-free in my bag,' I whispered.' Don't pass it round.'

It turned out that Cherie's room was next to mine. We were tired, and I for one was more than ready to hit the pit. 'Come in for a nightcap,' I invited Cherie, and was thanked by a beatific smile. Our rooms were pretty much the same, with quality furniture and a big double bed covered with silk overlays, and a wide window that opened out to the night sky. A gentle breeze had softened the oppressive heat of the afternoon and Cherie and I kicked off our shoes to enjoy a cigarette and a small whisky poured into the glasses provided in the bathroom. She had had three husbands, she told me. 'Should have stuck with the first one really, the other two were both bastards.' The only good thing that came out of any of it, apparently, was her daughter, but she died before she was forty. 'After that I gave up trying to be happy, least of all with a man, and it's only now when I'm past eighty that I don't expect anything and everything else is a bonus. Like tonight.' She smiled, saluting me with her glass. 'Here's to India,' I responded.

The capital of India, Delhi, is two cities in one; first is the Old Delhi of the Mughals, created by Shah Jahan and still a medieval place of forts, mosques and bazaars; and second is New Delhi, built by the British, an elegant metropolis of broad avenues, stately homes, Government buildings, fountains and landscaped gardens. The old and the new coexist, a common feature of modern Indian cities, with the poor inner city leading a life of its own, while the rich and the political elite retire to their sophisticated diplomatic enclaves to debate the encroaching poverty from behind closed doors. Nothing much changes there, then.

No fewer than fifteen cities of Delhi are said to have risen and fallen since the 11th century, and it has seen many invaders through the ages. Tamerlane plundered Delhi in the 14th century, and in 1739 the Persian Emperor, Nadir Shah, sacked the city leaders of the time and carted off the Koh-i-Noor Diamond and the famous Peacock Throne to Iran. By the early 19th century India was effectively under British rule, but Delhi remained virtually in the backwaters until 1911 when the King Emperor announced the creation of a new city – New Delhi – and made it the new capital instead of Calcutta.

The new modern city sprang up out of a bare wilderness, previously inhabited only by wild animals. It was designed by two British architects, Edwin Lutyens and Herbert Baker. They were given carte blanche (and plenty of money generated from Indian produce and peasant labour) to create a magnificent new city to reflect the might of the British Empire in India. Completed in 1931, on the very eve of independence, it is today considered either the blindest folly of the British Raj, or more generously, its finest gift to modern, free India. However you look at it, New Delhi remains a fine monument to British architecture.

Our early-morning start for our first tour began shortly after breakfast. We piled into a smart air-conditioned bus and were driven along stately tree-lined avenues leading to Connaught Place, a vast, circular centre from where all the roads and avenues radiate. Here we were joined by our guide, a tall Indian fellow with an impeccable English accent. We walked along Parliament Street with him to see the observatory, built in salmon-pink bricks and mortar. Outside was a massive sundial, and this apparently is where many Delhi city dwellers come to eat a picnic lunch on the pleasant lawns, near the sound of water from elegant fountains. We passed the Laxminarayan Temple, a colourful pink and gold modern Hindu temple composed of several different coloured stone materials instead of the traditional red sandstone. But it is Krishna's shrine that is the real attraction in this temple, a mirror chamber where everywhere you look, Krishna's reflection is staring back at you. Weird.

Everywhere on that walk we saw gems of beautiful architecture, set in acres of well-kept gardens – the impressive Parliament House, a vast, circular colonnade-rimmed building; the Viceroy's Lodge overlooking a massive complex of government offices and we walked on to Qutb Minar. This most famous landmark, situated about eight miles south of New Delhi, is an amazing tower of victory, started in 1199 to mark the Muslim defeat of the last Hindu king, and it began life as a minaret. Now it has five storeys – three in red sandstone and two of marble and sandstone, and tapers to a height of about 240 feet, it is exquisitely embellished and is recognised as a masterpiece of perfect proportions. To this day, in spite of earthquakes and the ravages of time, it is still in reasonably good condition.

Below the Qutb Minar, there are the remains of a mosque built on the site of an old Hindu temple. The mosque was once richly ornamented with floral designs and text from the Koran – now eroded by time, of course – but within the mosque is an Iron Pillar. It is judged to have been cast in the 4th century; nobody knows where it came from, why it is there, or why it hasn't gone rusty. The pillar is so strong that someone apparently once shot a cannon at it and it wasn't even dented!

Our tour guide, now known to us as Raji, had arranged for us to have lunch at a house that had once been the home of a British diplomat. It was now occupied by an Indian official and his family – obviously somehow connected to Raji – and we found ourselves courteously welcomed by the man and his wife. In no time, we were being shown round the house in small groups by their daughters. I have to admit, I get enormous pleasure out of nosing around other people's homes, but this was astounding. In the hall was a fountain, softly splashing sparkling water under a bougainvillea plant as big as a young tree. We entered a huge drawing room, with long windows opening onto vistas of garden and furnished in impeccable colonial taste. In the corner of the room was an alcove filled with narcissi and vases of sweet-smelling cabbage roses. Persian carpets were scattered everywhere and again as we entered the cool dining room there were more carpets, richly coloured, with borders of leopards bounding away from hounds and horsemen, worked into a rich tapestry of muted turquoise, beige and pinks.

Lunch began with slices of golden papaya fruit and coconut juice. Elderly servants brought in hot food served on silver platters – prawn curry and poppadams – tasting like nothing I had ever eaten in England – as well as chicken spiked on wooden sticks and dipped in a dish of satay sauce; it was delicious. Little brightly coloured sweets appeared, delicately arranged in small baskets, and all washed down with ice-cold water.

On the wide verandah outside, as I smoked an Indian cigarette (which I have to admit nearly choked me), it was a magical place. Garden birds chattered, and a flight of green-winged parakeets landed nearby. As I delighted in the scent of sweet peas, jasmine and nicotiana plants, the quiet away from the city, and sharing the time to smoke, I was able to have a chat with Raji. He was obviously well educated; his connection to this family was through the service of his grandfather to the original English administrator who lived in the house before 1947. Raji was married to one of the daughters of the present occupier and effectively it was his home as well.

It was time to go. How to thank these people for their kindness and hospitality was beyond me, but Raji assured us that they took pleasure in entertaining us; evidently it was a way of showing *their* appreciation that we had come all that way to see them and their lovely city!

As the afternoon heat waned, we drove back to the hotel and gathered in the communal lounge, where very welcome pots of tea were brought to us before we retired to our rooms to rest and change before dinner. I didn't think I could eat another thing, but I could and I did, enjoying the company round the table as I did the night before.

Other than the usual early-morning greetings and pleasantries about the weather and so on, I had not really taken much account of my travelling companions, apart from those I had shared a table with at dinner. Two or three of the men I could identify by Christian name simply because they, for one reason or another, marginally stood out in the crowd, but everyone seemed to be getting on well enough together. Of course there are always those who make a point of being first on the bus so that they can bag the front seat, and then flap about as they sort themselves out, thus holding up everyone else. It didn't matter to me – it was a well-appointed vehicle, with plenty of room for everyone and wide, clean windows and I was quite happy to go with the flow.

Setting out for our tour of Old Delhi, the bus pulled away slowly from the kerb. Rene, seated somewhere in the middle, suddenly screeched out for the driver to stop. '*STOP*!' she cried. 'Stop immediately, I must get off, I have forgotten my water and my *PILL*!' Rene had a room on the fifth floor, the hotel lifts were heavily occupied at that time of morning and it was a long, patient wait before she finally reappeared clutching another vast bag. We were not to know then that this was going to be a regular occurrence more or less on a daily basis.

Raji, looking fresh and immaculate, gave us a potted history of Old Delhi as we drove along the main highway towards the city. We passed the International Dolls Museum in Nehru House where, according to Raji, a collection of some 6,000 dolls from all over the world is housed. We then passed the historic Fifth city of Delhi, with its old walls, once 30 feet high, now crumbled in places, but still an impressive sight.

A ten-minute walk along Mahatma Gandhi Road took us to Raj Ghat, a simple black marble platform commemorating the place of Mahatma Gandhi's cremation. Set in green, tranquil gardens, each corner of the platform is graced by an Indian woman, dressed in yellow sari and yellow scarf over black braided hair. Every day the platform itself is scattered with fresh marigolds and lit with tiny candles. It is a place for pilgrims, especially on Fridays, when a special evening ceremony is held. Surrounding Raj Ghat, lawns are tended by a scrawny bullock, slowly pulling along an old-fashioned mowing machine, guided b a young, gaunt-looking boy chewing sunflower seeds. At the rate they were going, it looked like a full-time job to me.

We strolled on to the Delhi Gate, past a remarkable pavement bazaar, and on to the largest mosque in India, the Jama Masjid. It is a massive structure built in red sandstone and apparently it took twelve years to complete. The inside cloistered courtyard can accommodate anything up to 20,000 people on special occasions, but even so, 'women not accompanied by a responsible male relative' are firmly ejected.

We left the mosque by the northern gate, where Raji had organised rickshaws for those of us who wanted to go on through the crowded 'moonlit crossroads' of Chandni Chowk. This 68-foot-wide road was once the richest street in all India and the most famous bazaar of the east. Now hopelessly congested day and night and a great contrast to the open, spacious streets of New Delhi, it is a seething, frantic, crowded place – full of covered arcades, tiny roadside temples, lucky palaces, tailor shops, novelty shops, buskers and beggars. The air was thick with the tantalising smells of restaurants and cookshops, curry and spices, overlaid with the cloying, pungent smell of decaying vegetables and orange peel, debris and the dung of straying sacred cows. Women in bright clothes and headscarves selling bracelets and cheap souvenirs, their teeth stained red with areca nut, sat on doorway steps gossiping and directing their children to waylay the tourists.

Six of us, including Rene, with a white man-size handkerchief clasped conspicuously over her nose and mouth, pushed our way for about half an hour through the mass of people, dodging carts, donkeys and barrows, past narrow back lanes where I suppose you could get lost for ever, judging by the close watch Raji kept over us. Still in his suit but with his tie loosened and his jacket undone, he was never more than a pace or two behind us, urging us to keep going, not to stop, until he finally led us to an elegant Jain temple, which had a charming central marble courtyard with a water fountain, and trees providing shade where we could sit for a short while recovering from our jaunt in Chandni Chowk. I shared my cigarettes with Raji, who looked mighty relieved that he had lost none of us in the crowd. Cherie and I mustered the energy to visit the Charity Hospital for Sick Birds just across the way before we met up again with the others to cross the road to the massive Red Fort.

Once one of the most monumental and glorious of all India's royal palaces, the Red Fort dates back to the 17th century at the very peak of Moghal power, when the emperors rode out on elephant back into the streets of Old Delhi to demonstrate pomp and power at its most magnificent. The battlements alone are one and a half miles long and in places 60 feet high; the Hall of Public Audience, where once the Emperor would hear commoners' complaints from a 19-foot-high marble recess, is decorated with pearls, jewels and golden embroidery work. All this finery, together with the beautiful bird, flower and fruit mosaics of the Emperors' seat, was apparently looted in the aftermath of the 1857 mutiny. Well, anyway, it is not there now.

Nowadays, the Fort is typically Indian and we were led away past pavilions and courtyards and on to serene, green gardens, light years away it seemed, from the chaos and confusion of Old Delhi's streets and alleyways. From here we could look over the way to the Yamuna River where on the banks, an assortment of entertainers were gathered. Rope climbers, magicians, contortionists and fakirs were all doing their bit and ripping off the tourists like mad at the same time. 'Look at them,' piped up the ever-judgemental Rene, 'they are so scrawny, I bet none of them have eaten for a week.' I looked at her. A lanky five foot ten or eleven she was, bony with stooped shoulders, concave chest, stick-thin arms and legs – and tight-fisted. 'Yeah well, maybe that is why they have to put so much effort into relieving the tourists of their money,' I snapped back at her. This woman was beginning to drive me nuts.

We passed one of the three royal bath areas, where the Emperor and his favoured guests took hot saunas around perfumed fountains fed by the marble 'Stream of Paradise'. Very restful, I thought, mindful that my feet were nearly dropping off. I wish the Emperor was still here – perhaps he would consider me as a favoured guest?

Back at the hotel, we collapsed into comfortable wicker armchairs placed under generous yellow umbrellas on the terrace. We were well attended by boys dressed in brilliantly white overalls, with belted and buckled red jackets with gold buttons and epaulettes, and a headdress which looked to me like an upturned red velvet breadbasket. They were very smart and very efficient, serving drinks and nuts to us while we relaxed after a fascinating but very tiring day. Up early tomorrow for the train ride to Jodhpur.

18

The internal flight to Jodhpur was uneventful. We were now joined by a representative from our travel company. Profuse in his apologies that he had not met us in Delhi, he assured us that now he would be accompanying the party for the rest of the trip to iron out any little problems we may have, and to smooth our passage as we go along. He was a confident and pleasant-looking man in his early fifties and he had spent many years working – one way or another – in India. 'Has everything been all right so far?' he enquired. No, it had not. Three of the group, two men and Stella, had already gone down with 'Delhi Belly', stomach cramps and diarrhoea – not a good start to any journey more than a yard from the bathroom door, and whichever way you went, it was a long way to Jodhpur. Our Ken was brilliant. Straight away, he organised proper medication and arranged for them to stay on in Delhi, miss out Jodhpur and join us later in Jaipur. The relief on the faces of our sick companions was very evident as they promptly went back to their rooms while we made our way to the airport.

Situated at the edge of the Thar Desert, Jodhpur is the second-largest city in the region of Rajasthan known as the exotic 'Land of Princes'. It is a barren territory, dotted with battle-scarred forts and palaces where, because of the harsh climate and rough terrain, the people who populated this area in the past are known as proud warriors of courage and valour, a people who opted for glorious death rather than ignoble surrender in their battles. Their descendents still take pride in their traditional love of colour, culture and pageantry, their beautiful gardens and lakes, and their celebrated festivals and handicrafts. They are proud of their Hindi language, and although many Rajputs can and do speak English very well, even today on initial introduction they will not speak to you in English. For all that, they welcomed us in friendship and hospitality when we arrived at our next port of call, the Umaid Bhawan Palace Hotel. Even Ken was excited at the prospect of staying in this splendid place for a couple of nights.

Built as a palace, designed by the then President of the Royal Institute of British Architects, it is comparatively new, completed in 1943 and commissioned by the maharaja of the time as a bright idea way of keeping his population busy during a time of severe famine. This was to be the last of the great palaces built in India before Independence. Now part hotel, part private apartments of the present maharaja, part is a family museum, open to the public at appointed times. Most of the hotel rooms afford fantastic views across the valley to another great landmark, the mighty Mehrangarh Fort, set on a plateau some 400 feet above the town.

Rudyard Kipling decided that this sprawling edifice where we were to stay was so magnificent that it could not possibly have been built by man. He said that 'it must have been the work of angels, fairies and giants'. It certainly dwarfs the houses below, which cluster together to form the equally remarkable 'Blue City' of Jodhpur.

As we arrived at the hotel it was raining roses. From somewhere above, from a balcony, someone was emptying baskets of petals into the air, falling onto our shoulders like feathery duck down. 'It is a traditional royal greeting,' a member of staff told us. We were ushered in to a large, well-appointed reception lounge where fresh fruit juice was waiting for us, handed round by charming and very pretty girls in traditional dress. It seemed to me in my somewhat jaundiced view that they were particularly attentive to our men, who were by now grovelling and drooling like a bunch of idiotic pimply schoolboys. 'I must say,' giggled one of them, 'that was a fine welcome.' Yeah, well, behave yourself.

It was indeed a fine welcome. The palace had been converted into a luxury hotel of only 45 rooms, without losing either its character or its regal ambience. It has one of the world's largest collections of 1930s' art deco, with items tastefully placed in alcoves or on the walls to enhance the immaculate furnishings. We were meant, we were told, to *live* like the maharaja and his family for the few days we were here. In that case, I thought to myself, I shall certainly try. Some of the rooms were deluxe, with old-style period pieces, while others were elite royal chambers, luxuriously fitted out with all the trappings and fabrics of royalty, and every room was tastefully and expensively furnished. My bedcover was of vibrant emerald green damask, embroidered in multi-coloured silk threads depicting an elegant peacock with his wide plume of feathers, all worked by hand. The design and the fabric were repeated in the heavy drapes at the windows. It was as extravagant as it was beautiful. The sheer luxury of the bathroom was a joy, massive fluffy towels, facecloths, soft slippers and dressing gowns, and all the lotions for everything anyone could possibly use or need in a month, let alone in two or three days. It had flamboyant black and white tiling, gold taps and fixtures, big mirrors everywhere, a big bath and a walk-in shower. I tell you, these maharajas knew a thing or two about creature comforts. I loved it; never mind about towns and temples, I decided right now was the time to start living like a maharaja. I rang room service. 'One large gin and tonic, with ice and lime,' I said, and then, remembering my manners, added 'please'. I wasn't sure if maharajas said please, but there it was in a trice, an ice-cold large gin and tonic with ice and lime, served on a silver tray. I could get used to this, I thought.

The facilities of the palace included an underground swimming pool, somewhat dark and gloomy but provided apparently, to prevent the royal ladies being spied upon. There were two dining rooms and a lavish flare-lit buffet area on the sweeping lawns. This is where we were to eat dinner on our first evening. Under a black, starlit sky, an exciting presentation of exotic food was laid out on the long tables, where we were invited to help ourselves, affording us the opportunity to mix and mingle more easily with the other guests, some of whom were Indian.

From our own party, personalities were emerging and we were beginning to talk about ourselves to each other. It turned out we had two farmers amongst us, one of whom was the posh flat-capped man at the airport. We had a Reverend, and Jim, who was a retired customs and excise officer; there was also Peter, who, for reasons of his own, had taken early retirement from his work as a detective inspector in the Metropolitan Police. 'I am known,' he said with a big toothy grin, 'as the bent copper.' OK, if you say so. In some cases, among the women, we had already established a friendly rapport but it was interesting to know a little of their backgrounds.

Not all of us were widowed or divorced. There seemed to be a variety of reasons for people's current single status. Two of the men had left their wives behind because they didn't like flying or because they couldn't eat food they had not cooked themselves. Rita had left her much younger husband behind to manage their thriving bakery business in Scotland. 'Well,' she said, shrugging her shoulders, 'someone has to do it.' Shiela from Sidcup told us that she and her husband always took separate holidays twice a year because that was the only way they could stay together the rest of the time. As for the Reverend Percy, well, he had never married. 'Been tempted to a couple of times m'dear,' he confided, 'but never too late y'know,' and then he laughed heartily at the prospect.

Valerie, however, had been widowed twice. She was chubby, with rosy cheeks and short, dark, curly hair, and she was already kitted out in ethnic dress. 'Where did you get that?' I asked her, remembering the scrimmage in Chandni Chowk. 'Oh, I brought it with me, I *know* India,' she trilled. 'By the way,' she added, addressing all of us, 'please remember to call me *Valerie* – I hate Val, it's *so* common.' She continued . . . 'Yes, I was very sorry to lose the last one, we were only married a month and then he died and we never really knew why. Created havoc in his family I can tell you; his children are *most* unhappy that I have inherited all his money.' I daresay they *are*, I thought. The rest of the gang sitting around were hanging on to her every word. It seemed that Valerie was a choir mistress in her local church and to my mind she had already caught the Reverend Percy's eye.

It was quite late as one by one we drifted off for the night. I fiddled endlessly trying to get the door open to my room, and then to negotiate the whereabouts of the lights. My bed had been turned down to reveal pristine soft cotton sheets; pink scented petals and two tiny chocolates had been placed on the pillows, and all I could feel was an overwhelming sense of loneliness. This big bed just for me and the old sad ache welled up inside.

It seems to me that we think we can get accustomed to mental pain, without losing our sensibility to it. It becomes a habit, and most of the time it is possible to forget the state of perfect ease in our minds, but now and again, the firm ground I thought I stood on suddenly shuddered and heaved. Perhaps it was guilt this time, because I was really enjoying this incredible journey in India, particularly this night surrounded by an almost unreal opulence that I felt maybe I really didn't deserve. Whatever, I finally buried my sense of loss under those lovely sheets and fell into a dreamless sleep.

Our new guide, Sanjay, was a local man and knew Jodhpur city inside out. He led us through a jumble of narrow, winding streets that here and there disappeared into dark alleys. We picked our way past bicycles, cows and camels, and through the bustling bazaars of the old city. It was an exotic, exciting and contradictory place. The poverty and squalor was there – tribal women in ragged but still colourful clothes portered huge bundles of thorny wood; goats chomped away at decaying guavas; pedlars pushed carts of bananas and tropical fruits, and some carried tall baskets of shallots and twisted ginger on their heads. Other women, glittering in embroidered dresses and veils partly obscuring their faces, along with head-sized earrings, bangles and bracelets on both arms rattling all the way up to their elbows, browsed the multitude of curio shops with their men – antiques, jewellery and paintings, were a tourists' paradise if only the traders would leave you alone long enough to think and to choose. They hassled obtrusively, offering their goods at four times the price they were likely to get, fetching brothers, uncles, and cousins to join in the business of persuading the unwary to be relieved of their money. Some of us genuinely wanted to buy in Jodhpur as we had been told that the skills of the artisan potters, embroiderers, weavers, carpenters and painters from this region of Rajasthan were world famous. But because it was too confusing, almost too menacing, we walked away with nothing.

Now as we threshed our way through, we could see that the old city was a wild potpourri of street traders – a mix of candle makers, incense sellers, glass and lantern shops. All the while inscrutable old men, leaning on canes, casually observed their offspring still making and selling from the same dark doorways as they had done in the past. Young boys playing with live rats, tossing them backwards and forwards to be caught by the tail, were chased away by irate shopkeepers and craftsmen working nearby and I was thankful for that. Rene was having the vapours and I could hardly blame her: flying rodents were not my favourite form of entertainment either!

Sanjay purposefully led us through the convuluted streets to a large open area, known now as the Ghasmandi Bazaar, where the atmosphere was calmer – still colourful, but infinitely cleaner, the air smelling sweet with spices and perfumes. It was lunchtime by now, and Sanjay wanted us to eat and rest for a while before exploring the bazaar to do some serious shopping. He guided us to a cool, air-conditioned restaurant serving continental, Tandoor and Mughlai cuisine and a wide variety of vegetarian dishes. He assured us we could take our time to order – apparently the waiters were used to dithering foreigners – but in the end he did it for us: a bit of everything, and everything was delicious. Rene however, opted for a 'stuff omelette and potato chop', and didn't eat any of it.

After coffee, Sanjay cautioned us not to go out of the area and asked us to meet him back at the restaurant in two hours, giving us plenty of time to browse the various sections of the bazaar, the separate market and quaint shop fronts, and the places for jewellery, cloth, silks, novelty goods and clocks, all of good quality, reasonably priced and with no serious pressure to buy. The vendors were helpful and friendly, and we were delighted. Cherie and I spent loads of money and only for a fleeting moment did we worry about how we were ever going to get this lot back to London.

On our way back to the restaurant, we passed old haveli-type stone-eaved houses built above the shop fronts, and went past the modern Krishna temple. By now Cherie was walking very badly. She admitted to me that she was plagued by a gammy leg and she hoisted her skirt to reveal an elastic bandage covering what looked to me like a very swollen knee. Sanjay was brilliant. He summoned a rickshaw and came with us to an Indian pharmacy where we were offered a Chinese solution to Cherie's problem. Within a day or two it was working like a charm. I know nothing of the content of the liquid she was given to drink, nor of the gungy pink paste she was instructed to rub into her knee twice a day, but the redness and swelling rapidly subsided and she was more or less free of pain in no time. All the same, she was obliged to miss the visit to the Fort on our next and final day in Jodhpur.

Built on solid rock and towering 400 feet above the city of Jodhpur, the Mehrangarh Fort is a majestic and very impressive 15th-century fort and is Rajasthan's finest. To get there we had a half-hour climb up a very long, winding road, but it was worth it. We were greeted by a uniformed guide who spoke good English. He pointed out the first gate scarred by cannonball and the last, the Iron gate, where to one side there are fifteen handprints, the sati marks of widows of the maharajas; six of them were the widows of Maharaja Man Singh, all of whom threw themselves on his funeral pyre in 1843. Crumbs, that's love for you!

Still run by the Maharaja of Jodhpur, the interior of the fort is a lesson in ostentation and opulence, with all the trappings of Indian royalty – it houses a collection of elephant howdahs, used in glittering royal processions through the capital of Rajasthan, finely crafted paintings, antique folk musical instruments, furniture and costumes, and everywhere was beautifully decorated. There was an amazing royal bedroom with brightly coloured Christmas balls dangling from a pure gold ceiling, with wall-to-wall exotic carpets, mirrors and mosaics and a vast bed placed under what seemed like a huge tent made of silk and velvet, commissioned by Shah Jahan, and where he entertained his thirty-five wives. 'Not all at once, I hope,' I remarked to Bryan, who had now, in the absence of Cherie, tagged on to me.

Everywhere had been superbly maintained. Mosaics of jewels and semi-precious stones were inlaid into the marble walls, ceilings and floors, miraculously still in place as they were when the fort was built, and the whole edifice rises high and formidably above the tenements and the bright blue houses in the Brahmin quarter that we had seen a day or two earlier.

As we left to make our way down the hill, we were entertained by beggar musicians, mostly turbaned boys playing sitars and fiddles, all frantic in their efforts to please – and they were indeed very entertaining. These poorer-class Indian men and boys had an innate musical talent I could only dream of, and it was lovely to listen to. They wanted money of course, and they got it – handfuls of coins placed politely in their hands, not thrown at their feet, as so many tourists do, to their shame.

I bought postcards for myself and Cherie, and looked forward to a quiet afternoon of leisure and a swim at the hotel. Tomorrow would be another long day, journeying by road to Jaipur, but for the moment my mind was boggling with the sights and sounds of the morning, the sheer, almost obscene contrast between the incredibly rich and powerful at the top of the hill who overlooked the abject poverty of the masses of people scratching a bare living in the slum ghettos in the city below. Yet it was there, down there in the ghettos, that the craftsmen exercised their skills to build and decorate that magnificent Fort on the hill. It was they who laboured in unforgiving heat to shift tons and tons of red sandstone across the sprawling site, and to move that massive iron gate into place. It was they who painstakingly cut and carved the jewels and the wood, and fashioned silks and embroidery with amazing skill and finesse under poor lighting and with primitive tools. And yet they will tell you that the Fort was built by Maharaja Man Singh in 1806 to celebrate his victory over the armies of Jaipur and Bikaner. I don't think so – I doubt this bejewelled monarch ever lifted a manicured finger.

19

It was a nightmare getting away the following morning. Ken, the travel company rep, had warned us it was necessary to make a really early start to cover the 200-odd miles to Jaipur by bus. It would be a deluxe vehicle he assured us, and there would be much to see on the way. Rene, as usual, had to make the double trip back to her room to make sure she had left nothing behind; Peter's bar bill, which could have been settled the night before, was left till the morning; Cherie took a little time to get organised into the back seat so she could put her legs up; and Bryan, farmer number two, had lost his belt and had nothing to keep his trousers up. He appeared, half asleep, hair sticking up on end, lugging his bags with one hand and clutching his waistband with the other. John, a slim, kindly man, offered his belt. 'I don't really need it, use it till you can get another one,' he told Bryan. Bryan was mortified that, try as he might, holding his breath to hold in his stomach, he could not make John's belt reach around his middle. I thought it was funny. Bryan glared at me until Ken told him to sit down, and then his trousers would stay safely in place until we could stop off somewhere to buy him a new belt. I couldn't help it though. I leaned across to tell him, 'I think you can buy belts by the yard in India.' I was only trying to cheer him up.

I like bus rides. It is an opportunity to sit and muse and watch the world go by, and this bus was very comfortable, with plenty of room to spread ourselves out. Thankfully for some of the party still with tummy problems, there was also a toilet – cramped, but adequate in an emergency. Bryan had deliberately parked himself on a seat the other side of the aisle to me, where he could continue to glare.

All aboard and we were off, only thirty minutes late, but Ken reckoned that with the wind behind us we could make up the time. He really was a very nice man.

Our journey from Jodhpur proved to be long and tiring but not without interesting sights to see. We passed clusters of small dun-coloured houses, smoke spiralling from dung cooking fires; lines of bright washing hung haphazardly from house to house. Away to the right was a village, surrounded by irrigated fields and clumps of palm trees, making it barely visible from the road.

We had stopped for coffee at a roadside shack which I imagined had been set up purely for passing busloads of tourists. The owner of this enterprise bustled about, aided by a diminutive lad pouring water out of a bucket into a big tin kettle. We were finally presented with small plastic cups containing nothing short of liquorice-tasting coffee. Worried about the state of the water, I opted for one of the few remaining Fantas lurking on the counter. This place had a toilet – of sorts: behind the shack, there was a roughly assembled lean-to, wherein there was a primitive Portaloo firmly bolted to the wet concrete floor. I really could not imagine anyone, not *anyone*, who would be remotely interested in stealing that horrible, malodorous contraption!

An ox cart passed by. The ox was a huge, coffee-coloured, curve-horned beast harnessed to a tall wooden cart mounted on two high, narrow, steel-rimmed wheels. Across the wide but scrawny haunches of the animal balanced a wooden yoke with a rope attached, serving as a lead for the driver. He, an elderly, weary-looking man with frail, bony shoulders and rough and calloused hands, wore farmer-caste clothes – white pillbox cap, cotton kurta shirt and dhoti. Generally described as a loincloth, the dhoti is actually a very modest and practical garment. A long length of cotton fabric, worn round the waist and thighs, and pulled up between the legs to serve as work shorts during the day for labouring in the fields, or loosened to become pantaloons, leaving only the ankles free. The dhoti itself moves easily with the contours of the body, capturing the cooling breeze at noon or protecting from the evening chill. I pointed out the dhoti to Bryan. 'You are a farmer, perhaps you could wear one of those,' I helpfully suggested. 'Save you buying a new belt.' Judging by the appalled expression on his face, I don't think he thought that was one of my better ideas either.

We visited a Bird Sanctuary, a calm, relaxing haven for storks, ibises, parakeets, mynah birds and dozens of other wildlife species peculiar to the region. We walked through avenues of eucalyptus trees, decongesting the hot, stuffy air, while climbing hedges of jasmine screened the sun. We rubbed the bark of dried-out desert trees to smell myrrh and frankincense, the resinous perfume buried deep in their trunks.

Lunch was at a small local eating house. No European food served here; instead, green pea or bhindi okra curry, with tandoori roti bread. It was pungent, hot and spicy, a throat-burning, eye-streaming blast of chilli saved only by the split coconuts, providing a rich milk drunk through a straw. The white flesh of the nuts was then passed across to us on a shovel fashioned from the shell itself. Altogether, not something I would want to eat every day, as the Indians traditionally do, but worth the try.

Our last stop was at the crocodile farm where rescued baby crocs are given a chance to survive. At six weeks old they can be held in the hand, and special facilities are provided for their growth until they are three or four years old. By then they can be anything up to 12 feet long – vicious menacing creatures specially fed by trained keepers, a job not particularly envied by the watching tourists. At this place it was possible to buy crocodile-skin handbags, wallets and belts. The money generated from these sales went towards the upkeep of the reptiles. Bryan made his contribution by buying (after much persuasion) a rather trendy buckled belt that actually fitted him.

As we neared the outskirts of the city of Jaipur, small communities and busy local markets gave life to the otherwise scrubby landscape. They were selling each other fruit and vegetables, rice, lentils and wheat flour, mostly locally grown. All that combined with stringy mutton, goat meat and the occasional chicken forms the mainstay of the Indian diet.

Finally we could see the fortified crenellated walls of the old city. It was late afternoon and already the sun was low in the sky as we passed through a guarded gate to get our first taste of magical Jaipur.

Surrounded on three sides by the rugged Aravalli Hills, Jaipur is the picturesque capital of Rajasthan. It is popularly known as the Pink City because of the pink-orange-coloured sandstone from which the palaces and buildings in its old walled city are constructed. This distinctive colour of the sandstone was enhanced in 1853 when Prince Albert visited and the city was painted pink for the first time, and pink it has remained ever since. The soft glow of its buildings and monuments, especially at sunset, is a fascinating sight.

Our first sight of it was of its wide, colourful streets, motorbikes jostling for space with camels, and turbaned elders rubbing shoulders with young people in jeans. Many little beggar children, some carrying smaller tots on their backs, held out skinny arms and dirty palms at our bus as our driver ploughed his way through to our hotel. As usual, Rene was having a fit. 'Look at that!' she exhorted. 'Will you just look at those filthy children. Where are their mothers, *that's* what I would like to know.' So would the children, I imagined. Only in extreme circumstances would an Indian mother forsake her children to fend for themselves on the streets.

The Jai Mahal Palace was once exactly that – a palace. The original building dates from 1772, when it was built to provide an elite residence for royal physicians and ministers. Now expanded, altered and tastefully renovated, it has become an elegant and very comfortable hotel indeed. Set in several acres of landscaped gardens, its main restaurant overlooking regal lawns; there is a quaint bar and also two or three very attractive, well-stocked shops. In contrast to buying goods at bazaars (where you rarely have time to stop or even touch anything), here in these small, quite exclusive hotel outlets, goods were well displayed, and there was no pressure to buy and plenty of time to decide. Superior-quality ethnic clothes, crafts and designer examples of sometimes quite exquisite Indian jewellery were all there for inspection. Obviously more expensive, but you did at least know you got what you paid for.

I was really appreciating the porterage on this journey; from the start, we had at no time been obliged to carry our luggage anywhere. As we moved on from place to place, our belongings were taken from outside our rooms and would miraculously reappear outside the door of our next abode. Now at the end of our first week, we were to stop over in Jaipur for three nights to allow a free day at leisure to recuperate from what had been quite an exhausting time travelling.

I unpacked and took my time to sort out my crumpled belongings. My clothes were a mess and the whole lot needed washing, so I stuffed everything into the laundry bag provided. Then I found the list. At the top: it said: 'Please to be so Kind as to item your Articles in the Boxes provided'. Whoever compiled that list was obviously not well versed in the description of modern western attire. For ladies, 'bloomers' and 'petticoats'; stockings were divided into two columns – silk and cotton. 'Brasseries' [sic] and 'corsets' were provided for, and most of the listed items bore little relation to the clothing I had rammed into that laundry bag. The important thing was that the list also promised 'Your cloths [sic] will be returned Next Day, Clean and Beautiful'. It was; for the price of a few rupees, it was returned immaculate – knife-edge creases in T-shirts, cotton trousers, skirts and dresses, knickers and all, and all carefully arranged on hangers.

Dinner that night was served in the dining room, a smaller, more intimate room than the main restaurant. It had been set aside for our party, and the tables were placed in alcoves, divided by bamboo screens and lit by a series of floating candles set in crystal bowls. It was very pretty, but as I arrived late I sat where I could – with Ken, Bryan, Rene and Audrey, who turned out to be Rene's sister! I hadn't once noticed them sit together or even speak to each other before. They could not have been more physically different. Rene was tall and rangy, and Audrey was a short, shapeless, middle-aged woman, although younger apparently, than her sister. Everything about her drooped: her mouth and eyes had a hangdog expression and her hair hung in a lank bob; but tonight both sisters had made a valiant effort to dress prettily for dinner. It was almost a transformation! Ken, courteous as ever, stood to hold out a chair for me, and I settled in between him and Bryan. Anxious about our day, he chatted away, admired Bryan's new belt and directed his attention to Rene and Audrey. 'I have to say,' he said, 'you both look very nice this evening.' They positively radiated. 'Is everything all right with you?' he enquired brightly. 'No tummy bugs? Coping with the journeys, are you?' Ken wished he hadn't asked after Audrey had answered him. 'Yes,' she said wearily, 'we are managing, but wasn't that dreadful, all those people sitting in piles of rubbish? Dreadful.' What they had seen was an area haphazardly set apart for barbers to work. They saw men crouched on their haunches patiently awaiting their turn for a haircut or a shave, performed out there on the street. 'Primitive, I agree, but that is what they do in these parts – we have to accept that it is their way of life,' said Ken. 'Well,' Audrey sighed, 'I shall never get used to it.' 'What made you come?' I asked the sisters. 'You must have known India was going to be very different from Ickenham?' 'We needed a change of scenery,' explained Rene. They had got that all right.

All the same, I could relate to Rene and Audrey's need. For me, this journey was yet another great 'escape' too, liberating me for the time being from what was becoming a colourless existence at home. Is life meant to be a series of choices, I asked myself, or is it really a random affair? Should I be waiting for fate to take a hand, and if it did, would I be content to follow a definitive path already set in stone? I didn't know, but already I knew I would never regret choosing to make this journey. The exotic sights and sounds, the ravishing and dramatic landscapes, all of this was really beginning to open my eyes to the heart and soul of indigenous India, although it was already becoming difficult not to feel a sense of personal outrage that so many people spent their lives living in such squalid conditions, working themselves into the ground simply to earn a crust. It didn't seem right somehow. I said as much to Bryan . . .

'They're used to it,' he replied. 'No point in worrying, wouldn't do for everyone to be the same . . . can't all be rich! Start paying 'em too much and they will come to expect it and start getting above their station. That wouldn't do, would it?' I opened my mouth to say something but he went on, 'It's all about knowing your place!' I was speechless.

Only a couple of days before, this man had been rattling on about 'gentleman' farmers, taking a pop at Reginald, who apparently was one such gentleman. I had picked him up on it. 'What is the difference, then? A farmer is a farmer, isn't he?' He prodded my arm. 'Listen,' he said, 'I started my farm from scratch, I worked day and night to buy more land to expand – it took years. He, on the other hand,' he said, jabbing his thumb over his shoulder in the direction of Reginald – who was fortunately out of earshot – '*he* inherited his estate – came down through a wealthy family – *he* doesn't have to work the land – it's all let out to tenants and they do it. All his lot do is to spend their time hunting, fishing and shooting the birds,' he added belligerently.

I had listened, very attentively. 'Balls,' I said. 'What about Hunt Balls?'

Cherie, knee firmly bandaged and assisted by a walking stick, gamely joined Stella and me as we left to catch the early-morning tour around the city by bus from the railway station. Ken had not been very happy about our plan when we told him, but agreed it was less tiring for Cherie to do one or two shorter trips than go with the full-day arrangements. 'We shall be back for lunch,' we assured him. 'And we shall bring you back a princess,' I whispered in his ear. Ken was overtly gay, and lovely with it. '*You* are my princesses,' he replied gallantly, 'so take care.' He knew how to make us girls feel good.

Jaipur was built as a planned city by Jai Singh II. He was a prince, a warrior and a dedicated astronomer, who made Jaipur his capital in 1727 after moving down from his fortress in the hills at nearby Amber. Our guide took us to the heart of the Jaipur city where, from the high roof of an 18th-century merchant's house, we could see amazing panoramic views of the whole city. So early in the morning, before the heat of the day took hold, there was comfortable space to move around on the roof-top terraces. We looked down to the Tripolia Bazaar, the wide central avenue, already bustling and noisy with camel carts, rickshaws, the inevitable sacred cows, incessant car horns and bicycle bells. We could see the Jai Singh Observatory, the clock tower, the city palace and, up on a hill, the Tiger Fort, once Jai Singh's treasury. We were treated to a puppet show up there on those lofty terraces, with brightly decorated cloth dolls in gaudy traditional clothes telling their story of battles and valour on the end of long strings.

'Would you like *chai*?' Yes, we would . . . but be warned. The word 'chai' is associated with India, but is not actually the decent cup of tea one would expect, unless it is served in a private home. In the vicinity of the markets and bazaars of a busy city however, the Indians, in spite of all the tea they grow, make the most hideously undrinkable tea possible. It is the most over-sweetened, stewed, murky excuse for that normally fine beverage that you ever tasted! Here, outside what was laughingly called a 'tea shop', it was being served in a dented enamel mug and known as 'mixed tea'. Apparently this means that it has been made by putting cold water, milk, sugar and tea leaves all into one big pot, brought to the boil, and then allowed to rest – for possibly a very long time, depending on the time of day. The result of this brew can only be imagined. The trick, evidently, is to ask for 'tray tea,' in which the water (almost hot), milk and sugar are all served separately. It was still horrible.

We watched black-faced monkeys peering at us from off the walls of the old buildings as we made our way to the Hawa Mahal, known as the Palace of Winds. Built in 1799, it is Jaipur's central landmark, although it is actually little more than a beautiful façade. The five-storey building looks out onto the main thoroughfare of the old city. Its pink-sandstone octagonal windows are delicately honeycombed to enable the ladies of the royal household to watch in private the everyday life of the streets and the frequent processions routed through the city.

Beggars, pedlars and children swarmed around Cherie, Stella and me while we waited for the guide to turn up. Making arrangements in India appears to be comparatively easy, as long as whatever is arranged is not expected to happen. An appointment, such as we had made with our guide, is merely an agreement to meet – the timing could be anybody's guess. The agreement was that he was to meet us at this spot, where he would secure the services of a taxi to take us back to the door of our hotel, thus avoiding the scramble of the local bus, which would only take us to the railway station.

We waited and we waited, all the time harassed by seedy-looking pedlars trying to sell cheap, badly made souvenirs; by kids plucking at our clothes; and by aimless dogs sniffing at our feet. It was hot and sticky, and standing there in the heart of Jaipur's street life, we were getting very uncomfortable indeed. Suddenly, out of nowhere, the guide appeared. All smiles, no apology, he just snapped his fingers at a passing taxi and helped us, one, by one into the back of it. We were incredulous. Why couldn't we have done that? 'This is going to cost us an arm and a leg,' muttered Stella. But no, the twenty rupees we had agreed to pay our guide included, to our amazement, the cost of the taxi.

Now we were all smiles again as we arrived back in the hotel lounge. 'Where have you been?' Bryan demanded as he stood up from his sofa seat. 'Out,' I said. 'We have had a lovely time,' added Cherie, aglow. 'We have done this and we have done that, came back in a taxi, it has been a marvellous morning.' Bryan continued to have his say. 'Well, I don't think it's a good idea, and I told Ken so when I heard. It's not right for women to go trotting off on their own in these strange places – you don't know what it's like.' 'Yes we do,' I retorted. 'We have just done it.'

After a shower, a change of clothes and a light lunch it was very pleasant sitting outside on the terrace in the shade. I was keeping a journal of my travels and impressions of this fascinating country, so with that to do and a book to read, I was more than content to be alone for the afternoon. Not for long though. 'Fancy a cup of tea?' Bryan was nodding in the direction of a small white building in the grounds. Yes, I did – it had to be better than the terrible *chai* we had had in the morning. We wandered across the lawns to an open-sided, white-painted Victorian-style folly, set among green-blossomed champak and other sweet-smelling trees. Several small marble-top tables and wicker chairs were placed about to enable visitors to enjoy the view of splendid gardens while having afternoon tea. Boys dressed in white collarless jackets, wide pantaloon trousers and red turbans waited on us with trays of tea and tiny macaroons.

'I don't think you like me very much,' Bryan said, munching his biscuit. 'What?' I was totally taken aback. Did I like him? Did it *matter*? I hadn't given it a thought. 'I like your clothes,' he added. 'You always look nice.' I grinned at him. 'Thank you,' I said, 'and *I* like this excellent tea.' Then I told him what I thought that morning's *chai* looked and tasted like: 'reminded me of something to do with cats.'

When I later returned to my journal it was hard to record the sights and impressions of Jaipur that I felt would stay with me for ever. The atmosphere was electric, exotic, and the Rajasthani people themselves are a brilliant splash of colour. The men top their outfits with huge pastel-coloured turbans, and almost all of them sport fierce black beards and droopy moustaches. The women shine in their bright mirrored skirts and chunky jewellery worn from head to toe, walking so elegantly, sometimes with pots and baskets carried on their heads, never seemingly in a hurry. The confusion of camels, cows, dogs and monkeys, rickshaws, bikes and carts all churned up together on those broad avenues of Jaipur. What a day! All that, and Bryan wonders whether I like him? He needs to get out more!

They were going down like flies. One after the other, my poor companions were suffering the onset, or in the throes of the dreaded lurgy. One or two of them had stayed in their rooms, while others were scattered around the hotel, stationed near a convenient loo. Only a few had departed for the city trip. Ken had gone with them in search of a pharmacy to buy further supplies of Lomotil. Andrex Softest was out of the question. Not many trees end up as toilet paper in India – it is very hard to find, and if you do, it is horrendously expensive. In spite of vague evidence of the days of British imperialism that still lingers and lurks from time to time in India, there is nothing British about their loo rolls, which are little short of waxed cardboard. Therefore, most of us unashamedly – although not openly mentioned – equipped ourselves with yards of the superior-quality paper provided in the hotel toilets (more suited to our tender, western backsides) every time we went out, just in case. I imagined that the hotel staff were used to it, since supplies were constantly being replenished.

Bryan had tagged along with Stella and me for our visit to the Amber Fort. Cherie had cried off, needing a day to rest. Bryan suggested we three take the auto-rickshaw, more fun than a taxi, but to my mind it was too far to go in the hot, dusty heat of early afternoon. 'It's only up the road,' he said. 'No it is not,' I replied. 'It is seven or eight miles, but you take the rickshaw if you want to, we'll take a cab and we shall see you there.' So he did.

In no time we passed him on the road, lording it on his own at the back of a clapped-out contraption with no hood. It was little more than a horse and cart, compared with the smarter rickshaws to be seen in the vicinity of the city. We waved vigorously as we went by in our taxi and he seemed happy enough with his mode of travel. However, that was definitely not the case when he finally arrived at the Fort nearly an hour later. Sweating profusely, shaken by the rattle and noise of the road, he looked very unhappy indeed. We gave him a bottle of water, mopped his brow, found him a seat and listened attentively to his whingeing. '*And* I forgot my hat.' Oh dear.

Leaving Bryan on the seat, Stella and I found a few members of our party already making their way up the hill to the huge Fort at the top. Others were waiting for the elephant to take them up. Miles away from their natural habitat, these majestic creatures were now obliged to trundle up and down this narrow cobbled path, carrying several tourists at a time seated in a heavy wooden howdah strapped to the animal's back. Decorated in ornamental drapes, with mirrored and embroidered half-masks over their heads, chain necklaces around their necks and anklets of studded leather about their feet, they looked sad-eyed and resigned. I preferred to walk

Amber Fort is stunningly situated on a hillside where its terraces and ramparts overlook a lake. After ten minutes we had reached near the summit where we passed through a gate to enter a small, busy square. There was a huge banyan tree, infested with chattering monkeys; to one side there were spice stalls, and a man selling hats from a long pole, and the elephant rank. Up more steps, past a small market towards the Kali Temple with its silver doors, carved pillars and walls containing the image of Shila Devi, brought from Bengal. Across the way, another white marble temple and the Maharaja's private apartments were on yet another higher terrace. Through a further gateway, decorated with mosaics and sculptures, was the Hall of Victory, noted for its inlaid panels and mirrored ceilings. Then the Hall of Pleasure, with its ivory and sandalwood door, leading to a channel running right through the vast room which once carried cooling waters into an ornamental lake outside. It was a glittering array of Indian history, wealth and mind-blowing ostentation.

Coming away, we looked out for the man selling the hats. I bought a khaki cotton safari titfer for Bryan, and the minute we got back to where he was still seated, now accompanied by others, I clamped it on his head. Pleased as punch, he wanted to know if it suited him. 'I don't care if it doesn't, just wear it,' I insisted.

Our bus took us on to the Maota Lake. The air was warm and still by the water, and we sat for a while on projecting boulders of rock enjoying the view and a quiet chat. It was very peaceful. A holy man came towards us carrying a long staff. Tall, lean, with nut-brown shaven head, his arms and neck adorned with beads and amulets, he was dressed in a coarse fibre shirt worn over a long skirt, and the strings of his rope sandals were tied criss-cross around his ankles. He walked slowly, and clasped his hands together under his chin and blessed us as he passed by. No begging bowl, just a blessing. I at least felt spiritually uplifted by that simple gesture.

The sun, now lying low on the horizon, was sinking behind a row of tall trees, as straight as pencils, and in the distance the rocky hills formed a silhouette against the ever-changing colours of the sky. The Amber Fort above us glowed like a golden jewel from the reflected light of the lake. I was fascinated; I didn't want to leave – I wanted to bottle the sights, the atmosphere and the sheer magic of Jaipur so that I could see it and feel it again and again.

Tomorrow? Another day and another journey.

20

All this moving on every few days was becoming a bit of a lark. Little routines were slotting into place: on the bus, some people were wanting to sit next to each other – the Reverend Percy was certainly on a mission with our Valerie the choir mistress! Jim, Customs and Excise, and Peter, the Bent Copper, seemed to have a lot in common. John the submariner had made a pal of Rita, whose husband at home was hopefully still getting on with his baking. Cherie and I had a double seat each to ourselves most of the time. The sisters sat together, and Reginald, the *gentleman* farmer, sat as far away as he possibly could from Bryan, the not-so-gentleman farmer. Ken had his work cut out at these times of a new journey! 'Rene, have you got your pills? Good, then don't move. Your trousers OK, Bryan?' and so on.

Finally we were on our way in good time to catch the train to Agra. Pandemonium reigned at the railway station: the platform was heaving with people, packages and bundles of belongings wrapped in cloth and tightly knotted. Children hung on to their mothers' skirts while men pushed and shoved to get dangerously nearer to the platform's edge. There was a raucous, unintelligible litany of station announcements – which may or may not have been in English – it could have been any language, so garbled were the words when amplified through ancient, distorted speakers. The last announcement, whatever it was, sufficed to galvanise the crowd, who, complete with their bundles and children, hurled themselves onto the train – inside, outside, some on the roof, it didn't matter, so long as they were on it. Out of the chaos a train porter appeared. A harassed little man, dressed in his uniform of sky-blue cap and shorts, he bore down on our assembled group, gathering us together, luggage and all, and unceremoniously dumping us into a carriage, meant to be reserved entirely for us.

The train finally lurched forward to grind its way out of the terminus.

It rattled on, and fragments of food, dog-ends, plastic containers and empty water bottles rolled from side to side in the compartment, now occupied also by other travellers, unable or unwilling to read the label RESERVED pasted firmly on the window. You couldn't blame them – all the other compartments were crammed with many more passengers than the space intended. Rolled-up luggage served as extra seats for the elderly – if they were lucky – or as pillows for women and children sprawled across laps and legs, and the very tiny were accommodated on the luggage racks where there was space.

Periodically, the train slowed and jolted to negotiate a rail junction. Sometimes it made it the first time and sometimes it didn't. When it didn't, the driver would be obliged to wheeze his engine to a complete stop, back up the line a bit and try again with the help of much good advice shouted by the occupants of the roof or, equally dangerously, by those hanging on outside the windows.

We passed unknown villages, and farmers working in the green paddy fields dotted with water buffalo. They were harvesting, standing knee-deep in mud, leading the animals on a short rope to shift long shoots of rice stalks that were tied in bundles ready to be collected by the women who were paced out on tracks cut out like grids around the paddies. Several times we stopped at decrepit outlying rail stations. As people got off the train, as many got on. All the time food was being cooked and served by local villagers from the platform. Little boys ran up and down with baskets of sweets and drinks, and little girls were shyly trying to sell beads and bracelets they had made themselves. Each stop was completely chaotic.

Although the entire journey was an experience to say the least – this was, after all, what we came for – it was for all of us a hearty relief to finally arrive at our next port of call, the Taj View Hotel, on the outskirts of the city of Agra. Cleverly and tastefully renovated, it was, once again, a restored – although minor – palace, originally built in the early 17th century. We were yet to find the twin swimming pools and the mosaic terraces, or to sample the excellent food at this place – it was enough for the moment to find my room. It was classily furnished and luxuriously comfortable, but absolutely the best of all, from my wide windows there was a magnificent view of the Taj Mahal. I can hardly describe that moment of wonder, the magic of my first sight of truly the most beautiful monument to love that has ever been built anywhere in India: there it was, visible from my bedroom window! I would have slept in a hut just to have that view.

Little is known about Agra city's earlier history, but a small settlement was apparently established around five thousand years ago. What is known and what Agra is famous for is that it is the home of the Taj Mahal, and to see it was the prime reason for my travels to India.

Agra rose to prominence in the early 6th century when the Mughals seized it from the Hindu Lodhi dynasty and made it the capital of the Mughal Empire. The city became fabulously wealthy around 1566, when it was described by the Commentator Abul Fazal: 'a great city having esteemed healthy air. Pleasant houses and gardens inhabited by people of all nations; and exhibited with the production of every climate built on both banks of the Yamuna river. A castle of red sandstone, the like of which no traveller has ever seen, has been built by the Emperor.'

Under the Emperor's talented but drunkard son, Agra became a major industrial and commercial city, but it was Shah Jahan who left Agra her most enduring monument – the Taj Mahal. This most beautiful (and most costly) monument to love remains, and is today considered the finest wonder of the modern world.

Agra is now a city of over a million people, a busy centre of education and commerce. However, it is impossible to walk anywhere far. An aggressive horde of rickshaw wallahs pursue pedestrians with energy and persuasive ability who seem to stop at nothing to separate tourists from their money. Around the Red Fort, whining beggars and pedlars touting cheap tourist emporia make it an uneasy place to be. By contrast, the old, typically British cantonment with its wide, spacious streets, its peaceful parks, its gardens, and several lesser palaces and monuments, is surprisingly very relaxing.

At breakfast Ken decided that the last thing we needed on our first day in Agra was to be embroiled in the mad hubbub of the city, so instead we would drive the short distance to the Taj Mahal. The night before I had stood at my window mesmerised by the sight – not far distant, bathed in moonlight, a white sepulchral dome, soaring above the trees. Bryan, stuffing his way through cereal, eggs, croissant and endless cups of milky coffee asked, 'Where are we going today then?' 'To the Taj Mahal.' 'That's nice, what's there?' I couldn't be bothered to answer him.

This most famous Moghal monument was constructed by the Emperor Shah Jahan in memory of his wife Mumtaz Mahal, his 'Pearl of the Palace'. It has been described as the most extravagant monument ever built for love, for the Emperor was heartbroken when his Mumtaz to whom he had been married for seventeen years, died in 1631 after giving birth to their fourteenth child. She was utterly devoted to him, following him in all his battles. At eight months' pregnant, she had accompanied him when he set off to subdue the forces of Khan Jahan Lodhi at Burhanpur, and even as the battle was raging, her baby girl was born, but she herself was dying. It is said that as Shah Jahan knelt by his beloved queen, she whispered to him to build for her a monument that would symbolise the purity and beauty of their love. A short while later she died and Shah Jahan, the great Emperor of the World, broke down and wept inconsolably.

For a week Shah Jahan remained behind closed doors. He neither ate nor drank; nor did he allow anyone in. He emerged on the eighth day, an old man. His hair had turned white, his back was bent and his face worn with despair. No forty-day mourning period would suffice for his dead beloved. The entire Kingdom was ordered into mourning for two years and a silent gloom spread over north India. There was no public entertainment or amusement and no music; no jewellery, perfumes and other such fineries were used. No brightly coloured clothes were to be worn, and anyone who dared disrespect the memory of the Queen was executed. His overwhelming and abiding love for her continued to endure until his own death laid him beside her, under this marvel of beauty he finally built for her.

The love story of the Taj I could understand, as most probably many others had understood it. Nothing changes in the emotional state of things – people fall in love and stay in love until one of them is wretchedly taken away. For those left behind there is no good time to die; to lose the one who is the completing half, the compensating force, whenever it happens, is devastating. For some they wither and die too; for others, the light simply goes out and they plod through the rest of their lives with a stoic, miserable determination, becoming a burden to their families and their diminishing circle of friends. Many find a reasonably happy compromise and start again, with whoever, or whatever chance provides. A few build a mausoleum.

Through the gigantic red-sandstone entrance gate inscribed with Koranic texts is a scene of canals and fountains and sweeping manicured lawns. The approach to the mausoleum is via two long gravel paths separated by a central watercourse. The stone bench with the Taj behind it in the distance is where Princess Diana had her famous photograph taken, sitting forlornly alone – the bench where many others have since sat having their experience recorded on film. Flanked by two red-sandstone side buildings, including a mosque, the Taj stands on a raised marble platform with tall white minarets at each corner. There are four smaller domes surrounding the huge, bulbous central dome.

The whole edifice, built on the banks of the Yamuna River, is an amazing, graceful sight from any angle, but it is the close-up detail that is so astounding. Red and blue semi-precious stones and mother-of-pearl have been inlaid by superb craftsmanship with precision and care, forming exquisite patterns in the white carved marble. The actual tombs of Mumtaz Mahal and Shah Jahan are in a vault below, once surrounded by a gem-studded gold screen, but this was removed and replaced by a plainer one in 1642 because Shah Jahan didn't want to encourage grave robbers! Inside, under the soaring dome, there is a central chamber where there are two false tombs, replicas of the ones below in the vault. Light is admitted through finely cut screens embellished with floral designs – the flowers are said to have been recreated with as many as sixty pieces of different precious stones: crystal from China, lapis lazuli from Sri Lanka, cornelian from Baghdad, turquoise from Tibet, agate from Yemen, coral from the Red Sea, onyx from Persia and chrysolite from Europe, all crafted on gold or black, or on red and green marble. This delicate floral motif is used repeatedly, reflecting the Moghal love for gardens and flowers. A Cairene lamp (donated by Lord Curzon in 1909) hangs from the dome above the screens.

Elegant and exquisite, it took 20,000 workers twenty-one years to complete this unique monumental masterpiece. But there is a sad twist to the story of Shah Jahan. His son Aurangzeb deposed and imprisoned his father after the death of his mother. Shah Jahan spent the rest of his life in the Agra Fort, sadly looking out along the river to the final resting place of his wife.

As I strolled outside, along the terraces and through the formal gardens, the Taj Mahal at high noon was blindingly white against an azure sky. In its perfect symmetry and its heartbreaking beauty you don't have to be a romantic to fall in love with the Taj. The smooth, white marble has a sensual quality to it – you want to touch it, to caress it, hardly believing it is real.

Once, in the 16th and 17th centuries, Agra was the capital of India and many of its great monuments date from that era. With its crowded alleys and predatory rickshaw riders, Agra is much like any other northern city, but it is known to be one of the smelliest. What does it smell of? No one thing identifies it. It smells of hundreds of cooking stoves; the waste of thousands of animals – cows, camels, dogs and rats; the decay of the past – temples, mosques, shrines and ruins; bazaars with the pungent smells of incense, spices, heady perfumes and freshly cut flowers. There is the smell of the stirring and sleeping of millions of humans – a mix of Hindus, Buddhists, Muslims and Christians. Agra's people have all of India's variety of different form and face – green, golden brown and black eyes, fairer skin and dark. We negotiated the inner city, in turn intrigued and sometimes overwhelmed by the chaos, the redolence and irritation of the over-enthusiastic touts, to reach the Agra Fort.

The Red Fort of Agra was built between 1565 and 1573, and this massive red turreted edifice is comparatively well preserved, its sturdy walls stretching fifteen miles around its perimeter, and encircled by a wide moat. It was very hot as we walked through to the the Hall of Public Audience, where they held court for the common people. Sometimes when proceedings dragged on too long, decorated elephants would be brought out to parade up and down in front of the Emperor to indicate that matters should be brought to a speedy conclusion.

We then passed the flower-laden garden of the central courtyard and went up the steps to the Musamman Burj, where, in a small, octagonal turreted room poor old Shah Jahan is presumed to have spent the last eight years of his life gazing at his wife's shrine just along the river. There is a fountain and sunken courtyard opposite the Mirror Palace. Composed of only two rooms, artificial fountains and a cascade, its walls enriched with what is now damaged mirror work, this palace was once the harem bath house and dressing rooms. Nearby are the Jasmine Tower, adorned with jasmine blossoms and surrounded by marvellous marble filigree screens, and the Diwan-i-Khas, remarkable for its mosaics – with all the original colours intact – and its flower-wreathed columns, inlaid with precious stones.

It would have taken hours to see everything at the Fort, but with vivid impressions of the day entrenched in our minds, it was time to go before our tired feet completely dropped off.

Dinner that night at the Taj View Hotel was buffet style. Stretched out on long tables covered in pristine white linen was an amazing selection of traditional dishes, regional specialities drawn from all over northern India and beyond. Rogan josh – curried lamb; gushtaba – pounded and spiced meatballs cooked in yogurt sauce; a rich chicken dish cooked in butter sauce; flounder-like fish and Bombay duck, which is not duck at all but another fish, curried and flavoured with ginger and turmeric; vegetarian dishes – thali, usually more popular in the south, but north or south, will usually be accompanied by mountains of rice, relishes, poppadoms or a rolled leaf stuffed with fruit and nuts. All this, complete with huge piles of fruit banked up and tastefully decorated with leaves and flowers, and still the faint-hearted looked longingly at the western-style food provided at one end of the table, but most of us were by now happy to sample the Indian cuisine. The attending waiters were patient and polite, happily explaining to us what the food was, what it was called and what went well with what!

Set aside on a small raised platform, a small orchestra of ageing musicians played familiar ballads. We were all well again, all in good humour, and probably for all of us this was the best evening so far. Several of us girls (?) had decided to celebrate the Taj. Dressed up to the nines in our new ethnic clothes, we had all descended the stairs en masse to go to the dining room. The men seemed appreciative of our efforts, made complimentary noises and accompanied us to our tables. After the meal, what with the wine and all, several of them invited us to dance to the music. Bryan, with his hand placed firmly in the small of my back, and light on his feet, was a surprisingly good mover. But he had to spoil it. 'Where did you get your kit from? I didn't see you buy it.' 'You don't see everything,' I told him. 'Well, it's very nice, but you won't want to wear it again in England.' 'Yes I will.' 'Where?' 'At the next Hunt Ball,' I replied. Give him his due, he really laughed and for the first time I found him rather attractive.

Other diners joined in the dancing; the sisters were up on their feet, and John our submariner, smoothly groomed, offered his arm to Rita, while Jim, Customs and Excise, marched Stella around the room, more or less in time to the music. The Reverend Percy was having a rare old time, clutching

Valerie very close to his chest; I wondered if her flushed cheeks were the result of being thoroughly overwhelmed by his overtures or whether she was simply finding it difficult to breathe.

Dear Cherie, not about to start her knee off again, sat chatting happily with Reginald, our Gentleman Farmer, heads together, sharing endless 'nightcaps'. 'Don't worry, Mary dear,' she giggled later as I helped her back to her room, 'you have rescued me, he really was a grand old flirt and I think *he* wanted to put me to bed.' My mind boggled!

In my own bed before falling asleep, I wondered why it should be so difficult to imagine that the old had once been young, with all the strength and animal beauty of youth. Why is it so surprising that those well past their prime can still be passionate, still optimistic, and still want to be loving and to be loved? Time's winged chariot does not necessarily have knives in its wheels.

As night gave way to day, the silvery leaves of the eucalyptus trees outside my window framed the Taj – the dome and the minarets were now bathed in the softest pinky hue reflecting the early-morning light. I have seen that lovely place now, ethereal in moonlight, glittering at noon and now gentle pink at sunrise. This evening I shall see it again at sunset. For now I had to get going. It was to be another busy day and Ken wanted us to make an early start. The morning excursion was an hour's bus ride away to the deserted city of Fatehpur Sikri. Several people cried off, preferring to rest, and I wasn't surprised after all that cavorting the night before! I looked forward to walking without the herd for a change.

Between 1570 and 1586 during the reign of Emperor Akbar, the capital of the Moghal Empire was situated here. Then, as suddenly and dramatically as this new city was built, it was abandoned, due, it is said, to difficulties with the water supply. Fatehpur Sikri today is a perfectly preserved Moghal city at the height of the Empire's splendour. Indeed, so untouched by time is this finest of India's 'ghost' towns, that it takes very little imagination to visualise how it must have been as a refined and elegant city 400 years ago. Legend has it that the city was originally built as a tribute to the Sufi Saint Salim Chishti, who successfully predicted to Akbar the birth of three sons to his childless wives. His first son was born on the site of the celebrated saint's humble homestead in a small village called Sikri, and it was from there that this vast Imperial city arose.

Beyond the entrance gate, past the Public Audience Hall, we came to the Pachisi Courtyard, blocked like a gigantic game board where Akbar apparently played sexist games, similar to chess, using his harem ladies as pieces. Through a vast maze of elegant pink-sandstone courtyards, palaces, royal chambers, balconies, colonnades, baths and minarets, we came at last to a huge quadrangle to see the Jama Masjid Mosque, a magnificent structure built to hold 10,000 worshippers. Inside the mosque, where the air is sweet with the scent of atta roses, is the glittering white marble tomb of Saint Salim Chishti. It is surrounded by ornate lattice screens, and visiting pilgrims from all faiths seal their prayers by binding strings to the lattice work, returning to remove the threads when their wish has been granted. Just as Akbar came to the saint four centuries ago looking for a son, so do childless women visit his tomb to this very day.

Facing the Jama Masjid is India's grandest gate. 'Grand' is an understatement. Known as the Buland Darwaza – the Gate of Magnificance – it stands a monumental 176 feet high and is reached by an equally impressive flight of steps. An Arabic inscription inside the archway includes the useful thought: 'The world is a bridge, pass over it, but build no house upon it. He who hopes for an hour may hope for eternity.' There you go.

Before we left I saw the glowing embers of the sun go down behind the Taj Mahal, now wreathed in gold, seemingly taking on a hundred new shapes, each perfect, each beyond description, reflecting its image on the waters of the Yamuna River, at the close of yet another day. This noble, sacred edifice, in its bewitching oriental setting, eternal in the sands of time, stands as a witness to the passage of centuries past.

21

Khajuraho, with its population of around 5,000, is a small place situated in the hot, dry plains of Madhya Pradesh miles from anywhere, but somewhere between Agra and Varanasi. The climate can be extreme, and during the hot season very dusty and uncomfortable. Nothing very much to recommend it you would suppose, so why were we there? We had come to see the most famous temple structures in all India, a remarkable symphony in stone erected in praise of love and women, known affectionately in some quarters as the Temples of Erotica. I have to admit my interest was aroused!

Originally over eighty temples were built, of which only twenty-two are still more or less intact. Apparently they suddenly appeared between the 10th and 11th centuries, seemingly as a hundred-years' burst of religious and creative energy. How and why they were built in such a remote place so poorly populated is still a mystery, yet to erect that many temples of such monumental size in only one hundred years must have required a huge input of manpower. But there they are, in quiet, peaceful Khajuraho, set in a surprisingly green pastoral environment. The town itself is modest, with just a cluster of hotels and restaurants and a few shops around the bus terminal giving employment to some of the inhabitants, but mostly the people continue to tend their fields and animals, seemingly unimpressed by the fact that one of India's greatest treasures, and now deemed a World Heritage Site, is right there on their doorstep.

I, on the other hand, was totally unprepared for the sights we saw that day! A few of our crowd were armed with guidebooks, so perhaps they knew something about these temples at Khajuraho, but I certainly did not. It was very hot, the ground rough and uneven under my thin sandals, and I wondered at the wisdom of this expedition; but, not wanting to miss anything, I, as usual, went along with the flow.

To enter the site we went through an entrance porch leading to a main hall supported by pillars, and then into an inner sanctum with an enclosed corridor surrounding it. All the main temples stand on a high stone platform, each having distinctive spires, some soaring to over 30 metres; when seen collectively, they look like high mountain peaks. The structures are spread out, north, east, south and west of the site, and we were advised to start with the Western Group and see how we went for time (and energy!).

The temples, dedicated to various gods, are indeed superb: they are high, gracefully erected monuments to fine architecture, but it is the carvings and the artistic embellishments with which they are so liberally decorated that have made them so famous. The sculptors have shown many aspects of Indian life all those years ago, including gods and goddesses, warriors, musicians, nymphs and real and mythological animals. Two themes appear over and over again – the celebration of women, and sex. They depict an alluring quality of romanticism, with sensuously carved, explicitly erotic figures adorning so many of the temples, reputedly shocking many visiting Victorian archaeologists and blue-rinse tourists. Nobody seems to know their purpose; the theory I prefer is that the sculptors were trying to recreate the culture of their time in their artistry, including joy and fun.

Our guide took us to see the main temples in the western enclosure and finally to Kandariya Mahadev – artistically and architecturally the most perfect of all the remaining temples in Khajuraho. There are 872 larger-than-life statues in all, lavishly carved on and around the Kandariya Mahadev to include, apart from the gods and goddesses, impossibly well-endowed, pouting and posing celestial maidens, all with wide, happily smiling faces, and all, without a doubt, having a whale of a time together in twosomes, threesomes, sometimes more, demonstrating a whole Kama Sutra of erotic possibilities and positions with the nobles and maharajas of the time. Apart from it all being dauntingly athletic, it looked pretty good fun!

The guide, a jovial Indian fellow, obviously very accustomed to escorting middle-aged parties, had us rooted to the spot gazing up at this huge wall of rampant sexual activity, deliberately taking his time to point out various aspects of the carvings. The Reverend Percy, the sisters and several others trapped in the situation, although appearing to be dutifully listening attentively, were uncomfortably scuffing their feet and looking everywhere but at that wall. Those who were actually looking at those phenomenal sculptures had solemn expressions and furrowed brows and frequently checked their guidebooks in an effort to be seen to be taking an intellectual interest, albeit with its overly explicit sexual theme.

I am afraid I just saw the whole scene as absolutely hilarious. I had to move away to laugh till I cried. Bryan spotted me (he would). 'What's up with you?' 'Oh dear, I'm sorry,' I said, wiping my eyes, 'but just look at them, you'd think they had never heard of sex!'

Our tour complete, we retraced our steps past other groups of temples and shrines to our left and right. Whatever impressions each of us had imprinted on our minds of that morning, there was no getting away from the sheer intrigue, mystique, imagination and incredible craftsmanship and size of the temples at Khajuraho. I, I have to admit, had the best laugh I had enjoyed for a fortnight!

The afternoon was earmarked for a village visit not normally on the tourist trail. The invitation was for a small group, of no more than six people. In the event, most of my companions were still recovering from the morning tour, so only five of us went to the village to see Indian women cook an everyday traditional meal.

A young man – Rajid – who worked at the hotel, but whose home and family were part of the village community, escorted us from the main road along a single track of compressed earth and sand. It curved between fields of millet and maize on either side towards a cluster of round houses, arranged, it seemed, so that no one house directly faced another across the narrow street, which led into a small square. There, we saw another group of homesteads, built mainly of mud plastered on the outside and distempered in pale shades of green, yellow, terracotta and pink. The roofs were pitched, supported by crudely cut rafters and covered in thatched grass. The houses were spaced around communal garden areas of parched rough ground, with verandahs providing a place for earthenware pitchers, water pots and jugs, farming tools, wicker baskets, and a spare bed or two covered in multi-striped mats.

Children were playing together in the square around a central water pump. A child of about three years old was being vigorously soaped and scrubbed clean. His little face was a picture – eyes screwed tight, mouth wide open, protesting loudly as his mother operated the pump handle, firmly holding the child under the cast-iron spout.

Across the way was a low prefabricated hut with an asbestos roof which appeared to have been constructed from leftovers from another more ambitious project. This, Rajid informed us proudly, was the new school. The schoolmaster, a tiny man with closely cropped grey hair, introduced himself. Although his teaching had finished for the day, he had a group of seven or eight children still sitting at his feet on rush matting. There were shy little girls of about five or six years old, with big, luminous eyes heavily lined with black kohl, their hair braided and tied with bright cotton tassels, but the boys were more forthcoming and showed us their pictures. These were crudely drawn with thick stems of coloured chalk, but were recognisable as a child's image of a cow, a dog, matchstick effigies of their parents or of their house.

'Most of our village people are illiterate,' the schoolmaster told us. 'There has never been a school before in the village, but now we hope to teach our children at least to read and write, and perhaps to learn the English language. They will need it for the future.' He waggled his head. 'Yes indeed, they will need it,' he added thoughtfully. Some, probably most of the elders and women, had never been further than the fields around the village. Nowadays the younger men find work in hotels or on construction sites in the city, leaving their homes and families for weeks on end. Others, if they are very lucky, go to the Seminary to be educated.

It was difficult to assess how many people lived here. Each of the houses would accommodate an entire family in one room, or at most two. Extra beds outside, made of coconut wood and strung with rope, helped ease the lack of space inside.

There were not many people about at that time of day; the men and some women would be working in the fields. In the communal area, a few women were sitting together in a semicircle. One, older than the rest, thin and wrinkled, wispy grey hair showing from under her headscarf, was nursing a tiny baby in her arms. Barefoot girls were passing by, carrying water pots or washing to be hung out on lines threaded between the houses. Here and there villagers were gossiping on verandahs or sitting on stoops, a few crouched on their haunches playing games with stones in the sand. They stopped what they were doing to stare gravely at us as we passed through their hamlet. Even the children paused from chasing the squawking hens to watch us.

Everything about a European is different to an Indian. In the cities they are more used to it, but in a rural village in the middle of nowhere, the people will stare at our colour, our clothes, our demeanour, everything.

When I thought about it, it is not much different from an English village where a stranger in their midst is quickly noted as a source of new interest, except that, sadly, sometimes there is a tad more malevolence there than in these country Indians.

We had been invited to the village by Rajid's uncle, a modestly affluent man compared with his neighbours. Sporting a very impressive black beard, he stood tall and handsome in his clean blue turban, checked shirt and khaki shorts. He greeted us warmly and saw to it that his wife, a lovely lady in a sari and with a head veil covering the lower part of her face, observed village courtesies and offered us water and tea.

We had walked through a bamboo arch to another square where more houses stood. Some were made of mud and plaster, still thatched and painted, but our host's house was a larger, more substantial abode built of sand-coloured blocks, the roof covered in old pantiles, set apart by a private courtyard. The house had verandahs all around, the rails hung with mats and bedding. The windows were small, with rolls of cloth tied up in rope, untied when necessary for privacy or just to keep the flies out. At the back was a yard of sun-baked earth with a charcoal fire in the middle, and bellows placed nearby to puff the embers into life for cooking. Suspended over the fire, supported by a tripod of rough wooden sticks, was a shallow metal pan. Inside the house the main room was dark and cool, the floor covered in tatami matting; there was also a cupboard, a table and two painted stools. Placed on a packing case, a television. Narrow beds lined the walls, covered in striped cotton blankets, they were used as seats during the day, but were for sleeping at night. The neighbours, invited or not, could also sit there to watch the only television in the village. There was another room at the back, circular and lined with primitive string beds; this was the women's quarter. Judging from the uneven earth-packed floor, it had not been so long ago that the livestock had been evicted!

The whole house was topped by a low raftered ceiling; above that was a hayloft, a grain store reached by wooden steps from outside. At the outer edge of the courtyard, only a few yards away from the living quarters, was a buffalo pen. Beneath a big tree were poles for tethering the milking buffaloes and a goat with her kid that would one day, like its mother, also supply milk and cheese for the family. Nearby was a mound of dried manure, later to be fashioned into the dung cakes used for fuel.

Born and bred in London and used to the city life, with all the hubbub of traffic and rush, I almost envied the tranquil, calm atmosphere in and around these simple homesteads: everyone seemed to belong everywhere; Rajid's extended family, including his own parents and a sister, his grandparents, our host's sister and her children, his wife and two sons and another lady – she may have been a widow, I don't know, I didn't ask – but they all lived as a communal entity.

Men and women were returning from their day in the fields, bringing vegetables and fruit piled into wooden crates. It was time to make bread and prepare the evening meal. Quietly and unhurriedly, everyone had a job to do. The fire was rekindled and brought back to life. Over the fire a heavy cast-iron griddle was suspended from a tripod of iron rods. A mixture of lentil flour and water was stirred into a thick paste ready to be fried in oil once the griddle was hot enough. Root vegetables were cleaned and chopped and more lentils were added, all to be cooked in another large pot balanced on a kerosene stove. All of this was laborious and time consuming, the grinding and pounding, the mixing of spices, and all was part of their daily domestic routine, fastidiously supervised by the older women.

It occurred to me that Rajid's uncle – our host – was aware of the entrepreneurial advantage of inviting us to the village, not only for himself and his family, but for the wider community. He took us to his 'shop', a small hut off the central square that served not only as an outlet for a few bare necessities for the local people but also as a potential attraction for occasional visitors. The shelves lining the walls were crammed with spices, nuts, and oils of sandalwood, musk and jasmine. Dried red and green chillies and onions hung from the roof; sacks of rice, wheat flour and grain cluttered the floor. The hut had been extended to embrace another larger area. Here, in an atmosphere heady with the opiate fragrance of perfume, there were colourful mats, silk scarves, trinkets, wood and jewellery expertly crafted by the villagers – all enticingly laid out for inspection. Of *course* we spent some money!

Before we left we were invited to sample their food. Sitting on mats in the shade below a verandah, we watched as the lentil flour and water mixture was transformed into small golden pancakes. Cooked on the oiled and buttered griddle over the fire, the pancakes were folded and wrapped around a helping of curried vegetables – *masala dosa* – and offered to us served on banana leaves. Easy to eat with our fingers – we were watched with great interest by a small army of children – this food was very tasty, very tasty indeed.

We had taken small gifts of sweets, colouring pens and pencils, little notebooks, and English magazines, as well as hairslides for the girls and balloons for the boys. We shared all of it out as best we could between these absolutely delightful kids. A donation for the school was very graciously accepted by Shyam Singh as he and Rajid escorted us away from the village. Going back along the sandy track, we could smell mimosa carried on the gentle breeze that was moving the branches of banana trees, their huge elliptical leaves swaying and arching to partner the wind in a floating dance.

There was plenty to think about and to talk about after dinner that evening. It is always the ordinary people and their way of life in foreign parts that has the most profound effect on me, and I was struck by the way communities in these Indian villages seemed to have a natural sense of integration. Their concept of family extends generously to friends, neighbours, and even to us as visitors, the initial wariness soon melting into a genuine warmth. At times they appear overzealous in their willingness to assist or to please, and their generosity knows no bounds when entertaining in their homes. Kindnesses were hard to refuse, and we found it would be so easy to offend by strictly adhering to our western ethics of individualism and materialism. I was beginning to understand that their natural leaning towards the altruistic giving and receiving of help was an integral facet of Indian culture.

In a country where day in and day out most of the population has to slog for very little remuneration merely to survive, particularly in the rural areas where farmers and their families scrape an unforgiving land for their living, at times only to see it all washed away by an excessive monsoon season, this interdependence is vital. They are able to receive and even to ask without shame or expectation, and to give without compulsion or calculation of reward. It seemed to me after a while that these ties of family and community dependence strengthened, rather than restricted, their lives.

22

This was to be our last journey to another city in India before the majority of my holiday companions would be returning to Delhi by air to connect with their flight back to London. Only a handful of us were going on to Nepal to spend five or six days in Kathmandu and the surrounding foothills of the Himalayan mountains.

Of the people going home several, for various reasons, were only too pleased to be leaving. Three of them had been unwell for the entire trip; no amount of medication or diet adjustment had alleviated their incessant sickness and stomach cramps, and for them it had been a very difficult time indeed. Others were clearly exhausted – early mornings, long journeys and fitful sleep in strange surroundings had taken their toll and they could not wait to get back to the comfort and familiarity of their own homes, particularly their own beds. Then there were the few who had simply found that coming face to face with the real India was almost an assault on their senses. They had spent much of their time appalled at the poverty, ugliness and chaos, which does of course prevail in most inner cities of India, but they seemed unable to appreciate the alternating balance that is at the heart of Indian society – the deprivation of the very poor contrasted with the luxurious lifestyle of the very rich; the ugliness of filthy alleyways, the open drains, the maimed and crippled beggars and the appalling slums where they live weighed against the profound beauty of the landscape, the ancient buildings, and the marvellous expertise and creativity of Indian craftsmen – woodcutters, silk weavers, glass blowers – so much evidence of fine art that goes back down through the ages. All this, not to mention the generosity, courtesy and hospitality of ordinary people. As westerners, we may find the extremes resulting from unequal distribution of wealth unacceptable, but we were not there to put the world to rights.

India is not an easy place to be; it is not a country you can 'do' as a tourist – it is a total experience. Love it or hate it, it cannot help but leave an indelible impression, however that manifests itself. Whatever, there was no doubt that of those going home in a few days' time, several would be very relieved to finally get on that London-bound aircraft and fly away. But for now, we were all to take the short flight to Varanasi.

Set on the banks of the river Ganges, Varanasi is considered the holiest place in all India and is one of the oldest living cities in the world. One of the seven ancient sacred cities, Varanasi has been a centre of learning and civilisation for over two thousand years and is the spiritual heart of Uttar Pradesh state. It was at Sarnath, about ten kilometres away, that the Buddha first preached his message of enlightenment twenty-five centuries ago.

As well as being a pilgrimage centre, it is also considered especially auspicious to die in Varanasi, ensuring an instant routing to heaven. So it is then, that the old and the sick – people who feel they are ready to relinquish their tenuous hold on life on earth – will visit the holy Ganges here for their final purification dip. Many of the other visitors who come to Varanasi are pilgrims who make a once-in-a-lifetime trip, some having walked many miles to get there, to bathe and pray in the river for a cleansing of all their sins. Here more than anywhere else in all India, religion is an intrinsic part of life.

In many ways Varanasi is all of India in a nutshell. It is a maze of winding streets and alleys, domes and minarets, pinnacles and towers and derelict buildings, many crumbling and sliding into the holy Ganges. It is the street life, a continuous slide show of crazy traffic, clamouring pilgrims, mucky kids, sacred cows, roadside barbers and funeral processions, and on the riverside, smouldering cremation pyres.

It is three o'clock in the morning and I haven't slept; crickets chirping outside my window, someone coughing in a room somewhere along the corridor, the sporadic barking of dogs, all this served to keep me awake. I read my book, wrote a bit in my journal, and finally got up. The shower was not up to the standard we had come to expect but it was adequate, and so I dressed and was ready to go as the wake-up call came at 4.30 a.m. Tea, coffee and a help-yourself breakfast revitalised us, and we took the short bus ride to the river – or as near as we could get to it.

The essential Varanasi can be found on the riverbank at dawn, when

Hindu pilgrims flock to the ghats on the bank of the Ganges to perform their ablutions, do their gymnastic exercises and have a ritual bathe in the river, rituals derived and evolved from thousands of years of worship and tradition.

The walk down to the ghats was via a narrow sandy street, lined either side with carts and barrows on the side walk. The only lighting was provided by a few oil lamps, and here and there a kerosene stove. It was quiet and not a little eerie at that early hour before dawn; it seemed that few people were about – until we noticed that the bundles piled onto the carts were actually moving! Sleeping families – adults on the top and children underneath tucked in between big wooden wheels – were waking up to begin their day. The carts and barrows were their homes at night and their workplace during the day.

A few minutes later we were engulfed by a horde of people – men, women and children; I felt myself pushed against a woman carrying a tiny baby, helplessly carried along by the procession. I could see a banner, lettered and hung with marigolds. Something (or someone?) was being carried, around it people were chanting and beating on miniature cymbals. Ken was walking near me. 'Who are all these people?' I asked him. 'I don't know,' he said. 'It could be a funeral, or a bridegroom procession, but probably it is pilgrims making their way to wash in the river.'

We arrived at one of a long string of bathing ghats that line the west bank of the Ganges. Ghats are the worn stone steps which lead deep into the river from where pilgrims make their sin-cleansing dip; there are also two 'burning ghats,' where bodies are cremated. Three long punts, lit by terracotta lamps, accommodated our party, guided out onto the river by energetic young men with long poles. We were each given a little candle set in a paper shell shaped like a lotus flower, this apparently to be cast on the water for us to receive a blessing. We could feel the current eddying around our flimsy craft, and it was not too difficult to imagine how strong these currents would be further out on the immense expanse of the Ganges.

The sun was rising, a huge red disc as it cleared the horizon, heralding the beginning of a new day. There was a procession of boats, some driven by paddle wheels, while others were old craft with tatty sails, silently plunging in and out of the muddy, polluted river. Our boatman skillfully kept our boat as near to the bank as he could, but even he could not avoid the vile assortment of detritus that floated on and just below the surface of the water.

With the coming of dawn, the misty grey steps suddenly burst into lively, colourful action. The ghats were crowded, teeming with men in various stages of undress, some practising their contortionist yoga exercises, others sitting like statues in deep stages of meditation, the rest milling about with the women, on their way to wash their clothes or to do their daily ablutions, all making their way down to wade into the river. They splashed and dipped, dunked their entire bodies again and again in this act of purification and cleansing – the women too, more discreetly dressed in their saris, their skirts swirling up and about them, their black hair streaming behind their heads as they immersed themselves in the filthy water to complete their religious ritual.

We watched, silently holding on to the sides of our frail craft moving all the time against the pull of the river, riveted by the spectacle, the whole scene cast now with a rosy hue from the rising sun and set against a crazy backdrop of decaying buildings and temples, some tilting precariously or in some cases actually sliding down into the water. It was a fascinating sight. Stella broke the silence. 'They must have stomachs of cast iron – I wouldn't put so much as a fingernail in that water, no matter how holy it is.' Nor, I suspected, would any of us.

It is believed that the omnipotent god Shiva was washed of his sins while bathing in the holy Ganges at Varanasi and this is why the city is associated with him and spiritual cleansing. It is believed that to die there or to free the ashes of a loved one into the river is to ensure liberation from the cycle of mundane life and to guarantee the attainment of eternal life.

Cameras and any other recording gadgets were strictly prohibited as we approached the Jalsain and Manikarnika ghats, where the main burning ceremonies are carried out. More than anywhere else in India, life and death in Varanasi are on constant public view, but relatives of the dead are understandably sensitive about the ghats. At the time we were there, we could see three funeral pyres. The actual work of cremating the bodies, which involves much poking and stirring of embers to keep the fire going – similar, I suppose, to the attention a bog-standard bonfire in the back garden requires – is attended to by outcastes, known as *chandal*, armed with long sticks – tools of their trade, you might say. You have to be a Very Important Person – or a very rich one – to have the privilege of cremation in Varanasi, but either way, the final journey would most likely be by bamboo stretcher or on the roof of a battered old taxi, swathed and tied in white cloth. The ashes and what is left of the bones of the dead are finally lobbed into the river – along with everything else that no longer serves any purpose!

We finally left the boat and the river and worked our way back up the steps and into the town towards the railway station, to find a special place to have lunch. The Chinese Mandarin Restaurant offered a wide selection of food served in the traditional Chinese way. We sat at a two-tiered circular table, which could be turned to enable diners to help themselves to the variety of dishes constantly being added to with more samples of their tasty cuisine. That meal, coupled with the local wine, gave us fresh incentive to indulge in a little retail therapy.

Varanasi's silks and brocades have been famous for centuries. The Buddha, when he was a royal prince, is known to have valued them, and even today, the world's finest dressmakers use brocades from the area for making elaborate garments. The silk and brocade is handwoven by master weavers, and is exquisitely decorated in gold thread with all-over designs of tiny motifs. Most of it is very expensive, by Indian standards, but it was possible to buy good-quality silk stoles and saris, wall hangings and gorgeous bedspreads at reasonable prices. We found the city market, near the fabulous Golden Temple, amid a real mishmash of crumbling ruins, market stalls, mosques and shrines. Here it was possible to buy beautiful lacquered glass bangles, carved walking sticks and wooden toys, and silk-embroidered cushion covers in all the richest peacock colours imaginable. Importantly, they would also fit quite snugly into a suitcase.

Bryan, who had more or less been at my elbow since we left the boat, suddenly picked up a couple of scarves and engaged the attention of the stall holder. 'How much?' he demanded to know. The vendor gave him a price not too much above what could be considered reasonable. 'How much for two?' He was given a fair offer for two scarves. 'I only want two scarves, not the whole bloody cartload!' Bryan retorted. The young man conducting the deal marginally reduced the price again. 'I tell you what, I will take three scarves for that price, how about that?' The vendor shook his head. 'No sir, you can have two for that price,' he said politely. Bryan stood his ground and picked up another scarf. 'Three.' And so it went on, and on. Bryan was raising his voice and the young man looked embarrassed and exasperated. Richard, who had been hovering by, interceded and told Bryan that they were cheap for such good-quality silk. 'Oh, go away, they like to haggle,' he responded. 'Do you really want those scarves?' Richard asked him. 'No, not really, I'm just having a bit of fun.' Richard, normally a mild-mannered man, was clearly irritated. 'Well,' he said, 'while you are having your fun, this man is unable to attend to other people who really *do* want to buy, and he has to earn a living.' With that, he took the scarves from Bryan's arm and bought them himself. Bryan turned away, stomped off and disappeared into an alleyway. I hoped he would get seriously lost.

Bryan was conspicuous by his absence at dinner that evening. Richard and Reginald had joined our table – Stella, Cherie and me (Cherie had been to the river with us, but afterwards had gone straight back to the hotel, reluctantly giving up the idea of any shopping on account of her bad knee). I began to wonder what had happened to Bryan – it was unlike him to miss a meal (because, he would say, he had paid for it!). I thought perhaps Ken should know he hadn't turned up. 'Don't worry,' he said, 'he only has to tell a taxi driver the name of the hotel and they will bring him here.' I wondered whether Bryan would even *remember* the name of the place as I took my seat again at the table.

Richard fished around in his pocket and produced three silk sachets, tied with ribbon. He passed one to each of us. 'One each,' he said, 'one each for three lovely ladies,' he added gallantly. We found inside the little bags a beautiful silk scarf, the very ones we had seen in the market during the day, and the very *same* ones that Bryan had been haggling over. 'I paid that nice young man a bit more than he asked for, and he gave me an extra scarf and those little bags to put them in, so there you are, a present!' We were delighted, and told Cherie the story of Bryan's unsuccessful haggling. There and then we put our scarves round our necks, and there is nothing like the touch of real silk to make you feel glamorous. At that moment Bryan appeared, looking very cross and unhappy.

There was something about that man that either really annoyed me or really made me laugh. He was stockily built, barrel chested and looked every inch a picture-book country farmer. He had a large domed head, with a generous fringe of curly hair badly in need of a good cut; his bushy eyebrows were usually drawn together in a disapproving frown over deep brown eyes set in a broad, high-cheekboned face. He was good-looking in a rustic kind of way – quite magnetic, in fact, when he smiled, but he certainly wasn't smiling now.

Unkind though it may sound, this, I am afraid, was one of those times when he really made me laugh. He looked hapless and harassed, still in his street clothes, hair standing on end, and accused me of leaving him in the market! 'All those bloody back alleys – there are too many people in India – they ought to sort it out – I had a terrible time finding a taxi – then I couldn't remember the name of this place, so the driver took me around until I found somewhere I recognised.' 'That was very kind of him,' murmured Cherie, also desperately trying not to laugh. 'I had to pay him,' retorted Bryan. 'Oh *dear*,' said Stella. Richard placated him, offering to find him some dinner and get him a drink. 'Have some of this wine,' I offered, trying to keep a straight face. 'It's all right for you,' he growled. 'Anything out of a bottle puts the world right for you.' I was so, *so* tempted to ask him if he liked my scarf, but I thought better of it, and went out to watch the snake charmers in the garden.

23

This was to be the last day of the holiday for those leaving for home later in the evening and everyone wanted to make the best of it. There was time after breakfast to make the short trip north to the ancient city of Sarnath. It was here that the Buddha gave his first sermon, taught his first disciples, and introduced the world to his doctrine of peace. This initial message of the 'Middle Way' (the path of moderation leading to nirvana) became the cornerstone of the Buddhist religion.

Buddhism is not the major religion in India but it is still of great importance, not least in Sarnath, because here it was born and there are many reminders of its historic role. Buddhism is not really a religion in the accepted sense, since it is not centred on a god; instead, it is a system of philosophy and a code of morality, but I have to say that for many people like me, not particularly atheistic or agnostic, it is perhaps easier to follow a more individualistic pursuit in looking for a way of keeping the faith, or a 'middle way,' as the Buddha himself believed. However, what does impress me is that there has never been a war in the name of Buddhism.

Over the years, archaeologists have had their work cut out to establish much of the ancient history of Sarnath – the ruins there *are* pretty ruined – but it seems probable that the first monk communities came to the site around the 3rd century BC. Ashoka, the warlord who became a man of peace, patronised Sarnath as a centre of the Buddhist religion and erected several magnificent stupas and buildings. Describing it as it was all that time ago, the Chinese pilgrim Hiuen Tsiang, after visiting Sarnath in AD 637, wrote that it was:

> in eight divisions, all enclosed within one wall with tiers of balconies and rows of halls, extremely artistic, inhabited by 1500 monks. Within the great enclosing wall was a temple above 61 metres high, surmounted

> by an embossed gilt amra; in the brick portion above were more than 100 rows of niches, each containing a gilt image of the Buddha; inside the temple was a bellmetal image of the Buddha in the attitude of preaching, large as life.

Well, that's how it was, but as early as the 3rd century AD Buddhism had fallen into decline, and was eventually reabsorbed into the mainstream Hindu faith and philosophy. Today, sadly, the ruins of Sarnath afford only a glimpse of the magnificent monastery described by visiting Chinese pilgrims.

Sarnath is a pleasant and peaceful place; a few seats were placed around to enable people to just sit, maybe to achieve some spiritual comfort or to look at what is left of the ancient edifices of the past. A charming Chinese temple points the way to the outstanding Archaeological Museum, housing several fine recoveries from the Sarnath ruins. Of the two original huge stupas raised for ceremonial public worship, only the Dhamekh remains standing. Dating back to around AD 500, it is 338 metres high and is covered with interesting swastika and floral motifs. This apparently is the spot where the Buddha gave his first sermon. Near here is the Jain Temple, built in the 19th century, and then there is the elegant Mulagandhakuti Vihara, erected in 1931. This is a modern temple enshrining many relics. In this place is a silver casket, which it is said houses the original remains of the Buddha, that was recovered from a 1st-century BC temple during a 19th-century archaeological dig. That is why this has become a major Buddhist pilgrimage spot – the interior of the temple has a wall of frescoes depicting scenes in the Buddha's life and also houses the shrine of a graceful gold replica of the Buddha himself.

I was glad I had been to Sarnath, and that Cherie had been able to come too – it was a fitting end to our visit to India before I left for Nepal and she returned to London. It had been lovely sitting among the ruins, with the abundance of flowers and birds, and groups of people quietly strolling about and looking very relaxed. But it was time now to return to the hotel, have a light lunch and pack for our departure. A farewell dinner had been arranged, followed by a troupe of Indian dancers performing for us. It was going to be sad saying goodbye to our companions who were going home. Over the course of three weeks or so, much of the initial reticence and reserve had broken down and on the whole I felt I had been in good company with interesting and very nice people. I would be particularly sorry to see Cherie go; on the one hand, I was relieved that she now realised her leg needed specialist medical attention, but on the other, I knew I would miss her. She had been such fun during the daytime, and again in the evenings, when we would indulge in a nightcap while chatting and chewing over everything and everyone before we went to our rooms. Holiday friendships are usually just that, but I felt sure I would be in touch with and care about Cherie long after this particular holiday was over.

Most of my stuff was rolled and packed and I decided I had time for a short siesta before dinner. No sooner had my head hit the pillow then there was a loud knocking on my door. It was Bryan, looking utterly fraught. 'What's the matter?' I asked him, somewhat alarmed at the sight of him. 'Do you have a spare suitcase?' I had never heard anything so ridiculous in my life. 'Of course I do not have a spare suitcase, what's the matter with yours?' 'I can't shut it.' I followed him to his room, along the corridor and up the stairs. He had shut himself out. A visit to reception eventually sorted out that problem and as we entered his room it looked as though a bomb had hit it. His suitcase was on the bed, exploding with all manner of shoes, odd socks, underwear, shirts – nothing folded, just a massive heap of clothes. He stood by as I tipped the whole lot out. 'Have you had any washing done lately?' He muttered something about thinking he would have enough to see him through. 'Getting the washing done is expensive in these places,' he moaned. 'Yeah, well, it's very difficult amongst all this clobber to tell what is clean and what is dirty. I suggest you send the whole lot to the laundry when we get to Nepal – it will be worth the expense.' In the meantime I set myself the task of repacking for him. At the bottom of his case he had no fewer than six toilet rolls, all obviously nicked from various hotels. 'Are you expecting a major eruption of your innards?' I enquired sarcastically. There were jumpers, all looking as though they had been worn while he mucked out his animals on the farm, countless odd socks, shoes individually wrapped in several sheets of the *Oxford Times*, and a wooden box containing shoe polish and dusters. 'What did you bring this lot for? You havn't worn jumpers or shoes since you've been away!' He stood lamely by while I rolled and folded, sorted the clean from the dirty where it was possible, and finally packed one toilet roll. 'I can't leave all those behind,' he bleated. 'Yes you can – give them to the others and let them take them in their luggage.' We had got the lid down without too much trouble when he piped up again, 'I want to do some shopping when we get to Nepal.' 'Good,' I replied. 'Then you can pack it!'

Dinner was alfresco that night under an inky black sky lit by a thousand stars. It was a warm, sultry evening and romance was in the air. Looking across the table, I noticed that the Reverend Percy was gazing fondly into the eyes of Valerie. She, prettily winsome and coy, batting her eyelashes at him provocatively, made the pair of them look decidedly soppy. Every day she had somehow managed to find a shop to buy more beads, bangles and any ethic gear she could lay her hands on. Tonight she was wearing the lot. Gold hoops the size of cartwheels dangled from her ears, tinkling bracelets and beads jangled on both wrists, gold and silver chains and yards of baubles, like big gaudy gobstoppers, hung around her neck. Her dress was beautiful, embroidered silk in vivid crimson. In spite of it being a tad too much of everything, I had to hand it to her, she looked quite stunning. Richard leaned across to me. 'Are they coming on to Nepal with us?' 'Yes,' I said, grinning at him. 'I think this might be the beginning of something big!' 'Poor blighter,' muttered Richard.

At that moment a troupe of dancers, men and girls swaying to the sounds of loud, discordant music, arrived to entertain us. Immediately the previously still atmosphere of that balmy night came alive, and everyone sat up, mesmerised by the sight of those glamorous, exotic dancers, shimmying and swaying to the deafening sound of that awful music.

Indian music is very different from the melodious and harmonic sounds that we are accustomed to in the West. The classical Indian musical group consists of three players who provide a background drone, and what passes for melody and rhythm. The musicians, who are basically soloists, seemingly select and play their own personal repertoire, only coming together at times before diverging once again to provide an undefined beat only the dancers understand; not easy on western ears. Even Yehudi Menuhin had to devote much of his time and energy to understanding Indian music. He said that Indian music is much like Indian society, working individually but every now and then meeting at some common point. Menuhin contrasted it with western society, where a group of individuals (the orchestra) surrender their personal freedom to harmonise with the whole. All a bit too academic for me. I just enjoyed the colourful sight of the players, dressed in traditional Rajasthani clothes. One enthusiastically attacked what looked like twin bongo drums, another twanged away on the large stringed instrument known as a sitar, and the third musician seemed happy enough to provide the drone, two basic notes repeatedly played on the tamboura, vaguely reminiscent of a cello.

Indian dancing, where every movement of hands, feet, eyes and body tells a meaningful story, apparently relates to Shiva's role as the King of Dancers. Lord Shiva's first wife was Sati whose father, disliking Shiva, dared to insult him. So mortified and ashamed was Sati that she committed suicide in a sacrificial fire. Outraged, Shiva killed his father-in-law and danced the Tandava – the Dance of Destruction. Sati, reincarnated as the goddess Parvati, married Shiva again and danced the Lasya. The Tandava therefore became the male form of dance, and the Lasya the female form.

Dancing was once part of the religious temple rituals, and all of the dances had a tale to tell. Although temple dancing is no longer practised, classical dancing still has a religious background, and every element of expression is brought into play. The Lasya involves a huge repertoire of eye, facial and hand movements, with statuesque gestures of head and neck, arms, legs and feet elegantly posed and postured by female dancers, all designed to illustrate Indian legends and mythology. Then there are the different forms of Tandava, always performed by men. These forms tell dramatic tales of epic battles of gods and demons, expressive and dynamic choreography depicting courage and bravery and showing how good always reigns supreme in the end. These dances are noted for the elaborate make-up and painted masks worn by the male dancers, and the eyedrops which turn their eyes a bloodshot red.

Inevitably, the audience was invited to learn a few techniques of Indian dance. To my horror, Bryan was first up, quickly joined by Valerie, and then one or two others from our crowd. Bryan was waving at me to join them. My hands went up in a big, emphatic 'No!' It was hilarious to watch them though. Valerie twirled and cavorted, showing off her nice new dress a treat, beads clanking away as she girlishly hung on to one of the male dancers, who looked totally out of his depth with this rather large lady, so different from what he was used to. Bryan clumsily strutted his stuff, treading on everybody's feet and desperately trying to get one of those lovely girls all to himself. All the time the music got louder and faster, and the volunteers got redder, sweatier and more out of breath, until I was convinced that before the night was out the entire party would finish up at the local medical centre.

The excitement finally died down, everyone had enjoyed a super evening, and now it was time for those going home to leave for the airport. It was sad to see them go, and I promised Cherie I would get in touch on my return to London the following week; I knew I would, as she had become very special to me. After many hugs and handshakes they were off. For all of us, one way and another, it was the end of what had been an epic experience.

Those of us who were left watched until the bus turned the corner. Feeling very flat, we wandered back into the hotel together and gravitated to the bar. Now there were six – Richard, Bryan, the Reverend Percy, Stella, Valerie and me. Ken had gone back with the others and we were due to get a new tour manager when we arrived in Kathmandu the following day. If he was half as good and half as nice as Ken, we would be all right.

24

NEPAL

It is not difficult for me to remember as, when children, I and my classmates were obliged to stand on a cold blustery day in the playground of our village school, to celebrate Empire Day. Through the timbered tones of a large megaphone, our head teacher exhorted us to be proud of our country as the motherland of all those colonies (marked pink on the globe) that make up *our* Great British Empire. We waved our Union Jacks – supplied by the School Authority – enthusiastically, making as much noise as we could, while a bemused huddle of villagers watched us from the school railings. Later, after a dinner of mince, mash, treacle pudding and pale custard, we gathered in the hall to sing lusty patriotic songs from song sheets (also provided by the School Authority), accompanied by our music teacher, the elderly Miss Busby, fervently thumping out patriotic music on her pianoforte. In no time, as usual, I was unceremoniously sent to the back because I couldn't sing in tune; I didn't care, I had a rotten earache and a snuffly nose and all I wanted to do was to go home. All the same, I can remember staring at the large map on the wall and wondering what it must be like to go to these places, lands which might just as well be on the moon, as far as I was concerned at the time. Yet here I was, so many years later, stepping off a plane in mystical, exotic Kathmandu, as agog and excited as I would have been as a child.

Nepal, which, incidentally, has the distinction of never having been ruled by a European power, is a Kingdom, where the adventurous go to climb mountains, or to risk their necks rafting and kayaking in the fast white-water streams, or simply to trek, for days or weeks if you like, carrying a backpack and a small tent, through the scenic trails in the foothills of the Himalayas. It is a place where pilgrims go to visit the historical birthplace of the Buddha at Lumbini, to meditate in the monasteries surrounding one of the most important religious sites in the world. Others know that in Nepal it is possible to experience a vast range of diversity, from the wildlife reserves of the lowland jungles, to the Buddhist and Hindu temples, to the amazing architecture of the historical buildings. Instead of culture and artistry, however, some go to Nepal simply in pursuit of bodily calm and spiritual truth. There is no lack of practitioners of massage, of Ayurvedic and Tibetan medicine, and of astrology, and you would not have to go far to find new ideas in meditation and yoga.

Then there is the Yeti. This elusive, shaggy man-ape is the most mysterious of all Nepal's creatures, rumoured but never proven to inhabit the remote eastern Himalayas. It is known by some as the Abominable Snowman, and described as a 'hairy wild man living among the eternal snows', but actual sightings are inconclusive, in spite of tantalising scraps of evidence, including tufts of strange black fur, mysterious droppings and piercing screams that frightened the daylights out of members of one expedition. The Yeti is said to have an acute sense of smell, so it can disappear when foreigners approach, but the possibility of coming across this unlikely character would indeed be another excuse to visit this extraordinary country.

Nepal has always fascinated people in the West, the British in particular, with their affection and respect for the Gurkha soldiers who equal to their reputation as the world's finest infantrymen, they fought in both world wars, and many were highly decorated for extreme bravery. We also remember Hillary and Tenzing, – household names in Britain, as in many other countries – for being the first men to reach the summit of Mount Everest.

Measured in terms of miles, Nepal is a country which covers an area not much bigger than the size of England, but in terms of surface area it is in fact much bigger than it seems. Crowned by eight of the world's ten highest mountains, its variation of massive heights and lush tropics, forested hills, and high-altitude deserts fosters a wild and incredible variety of flora and fauna and packs more into its limited span than most countries many times its size.

Less than sixty years ago, a way of life persisted in Nepal which had scarcely changed since medieval times; western visitors were very few and far between. In 1951 the King abandoned his country's policy of splendid isolation, and with that, help arrived from western aid workers; increasing tourism, too, brought money into the country. In spite of all that, Nepal remains one of the poorest countries in the world. Most Nepalis are subsistence farmers. They farm tiny plots, using traditional systems and techniques tested over the centuries and expanded to the limit. They mostly manage to grow enough to feed their families and sell a small surplus which buys a few necessities, such as salt, tea and cloth. However, around half of all farming families, particularly those in the western mountain and hill districts, produce only enough food to keep them going for six or seven months of the year; the rest of the year they have a very lean time of it indeed. It is then that many of the male family members migrate to India in search of temporary labour.

Nepal's location between India and Tibet and the diversity of its ethnic groups and its different languages have resulted in a complex pattern of customs and beliefs that makes it hard to generalise about the nature of the people. The dominant culture is that of caste and status – caste determines not only a person's status but also their career and choice of marriage partner. There is a hierarchical system that extends even to the family, where everyone knows their place in the order of things. Nepali life depends on the demands of the family, the ethnic group and the caste. To break these traditions and customs is to risk being ostracised not only from the family but also from the community. In most ethnic groups, joint and extended families live in the same house; in some smaller villages, an extended family could make up the entire village.

Religious beliefs are surprisingly flexible in Nepal. There is almost no religious tension, and Nepalis are generally tolerant, good humoured, quick to smile and slow to anger. Their view of the world is dominated by prayer and ritual, and they believe the gods are not placed remotely, high up in the heavens, but are living, present beings, who can influence their day-to-day affairs in very direct ways. Nepalis perceive the divine everywhere, in the spirits and gods present in trees, in their rivers and mountain peaks, and in people. Their greeting '*Namaste*' literally means 'I greet the divine in you'.

It is not unusual to see Hindu women walking through the streets in the mornings carrying a copper plate filled with an assortment of goodies. They are taking part in an important daily ritual called *puja*. The plate might contain flower petals, rice, fruit or sweets and it is an offering to the gods, made at the local temple. Each of the items is sprinkled onto a temple deity and a bell is rung to let the gods know an offering is being made. It is then transformed into a sacred object and a portion of it returned to the giver as a blessing. Returning to her home, the woman will give a small share of the blessed offerings to each member of the household.

There are about 24 million people living in Nepal, the vast majority centred in Kathmandu; many are refugees from Tibet, but all in all there is a remarkable mosaic of diverse ethnic groups who have learned to live together, albeit with their different religions, languages and dialects. Kathmandu is the largest city in Nepal and the nation's historical centre, and its inhabitants are a blend of the country's diverse population. It is not surprising then, that Nepal's distinctive, age-old religious influences show up everywhere in the daily life of the inhabitants.

Skirting the old city of Kathmandu, we arrived at the Hotel de l'Annapurna in time for a late lunch. Not this time an old, restored palace as we had come to expect in India, but a comparatively new, uninspiring four-storey building situated on an expanse of five or six acres. Wide gravel paths led through the manicured gardens, allowing for a pleasant walk before arriving at the main road. We were situated near the embassies and key government offices and in close proximity to the city's financial district. The location was to prove ideal for walking into the city independently, but we were yet to discover the magic of the real Kathmandu.

For the moment, we were quite overwhelmed by the initial hospitality. Evidently the code of the management and staff was to exemplify the nation's philosophy of 'Guests are like Gods'. Well, I don't know about that, but although in no way obsequious, the welcome we received was extremely helpful and warm. The bellboys attended to our luggage while we were served with ice-cold fruit drinks in long glasses, shown around the lounge, bar and reception hall, and then directed to our rooms. No ostentation, just clean and comfortable, a pristine bathroom, and, in the distance, from my tiny balcony, a view of the mountains.

Bryan was over the moon. We were all on the same floor, and he was right next door to me. 'We can have a nightcap and go down to breakfast together,' he said gleefully. I was horrified, not quite sure of the implications of what he was saying. 'Valerie is the other side of you,' I told him. 'You can go down to breakfast with her, and if you are very, very good, I might let you buy me a nightcap in the bar.'

Stella and I got together over lunch and decided to make our first foray into the city. We walked along Durbar Marg, a wide street flanked by restaurants and expensive hotels leading towards a busy shopping area which, inturn, led into Kathmandu's old Durbar Square. My first impressions of this place were mind-blowing. This was the other side of the world, strange, vibrant, alive, and all my senses kicked in at once above the noise, bustle, sights, sounds and smell of the place, giving me an instantaneous sensory overload. It was so exciting, so exhilarating, and Stella and I really didn't know where to start – not surprising, since, without our maps, we hadn't a clue where we were. It was enough for the moment to take in the scene.

We found ourselves in a narrow lane leading to a bazaar in full swing, crowded with shoppers, and then to smaller shops brimming with brass pots, bolts of cloth, mountains of nails, sacks of lentils, herbs and spices. Here you could buy a sari, flowers, huge brown cannonballs of soap and Tiger balm. Taxi horns merged with the sound of solemn temple bells, and the scent of flowers and spices mingled with the stench of a filthy open sewer. We made our way back to the main square which, we later learned, was the place where the city's kings were once crowned. It is the traditional heart of the old town and Kathmandu's most spectacular legacy of traditional architecture. We worked our way up to the terraced platforms of the towering Maju Deval Temple, a wonderful place to soak up the atmosphere and to get a grip on ourselves before making our way back to the hotel.

Through busy, heavily polluted streets, we negotiated a crazy melee of cars, rickshaws, taxis, bikes with very dead chickens hanging by their necks from the handlebars, and carts piled high with straw or vegetables, with none of the drivers seeming to have any regard for the right or wrong side of the road. Everyone appeared to aim their vehicle in the direction they wanted to go and just went for it, only slowing down to avoid the cardinal crime of hitting a sacred cow, one of which we saw contentedly chewing the cud in the middle of the roaring traffic. As we finally approached our hotel we had to hold back to allow a herd of sheep to pass by – and this on one of the major roads in Kathmandu!

Dinner that first evening at the Annapurna was served in the attractively decorated garden room. Long glazed doors opened to the back gardens and to the swimming pool, filled to overflowing with undisturbed shimmering water lit by blue and green underwater lighting. We sat together at a round table, with plenty of space for the six of us – it seemed strange to be without the rest of our companions. The meal was vegetarian, varied and wholesome, but once past the lentil and coriander soup, I had had enough. I was too tired really to eat, but Bryan made sure I turned nothing away, and between him and Richard they saw off the rest of my meal. 'You don't eat enough,' commented Bryan. 'I've noticed it, you eat like a sparrow, no wonder you are so scrawny.' 'Thank you dear,' I murmured, 'you have such a winning way with words.'

At that moment our table was approached by a very attractive lady in a smart blue skirt and jacket. Tall and slim, with blonde expensively cut bobbed hair and immaculate make-up, she announced in clipped tones that she was Susan Kimberly, our tour manager. As one, our men stood to greet her and to offer their chair, but a seat was already being provided by a waiter. Bryan's eyes were on stalks, as were the Reverend Percy's, as she sat, elegantly revealing a pair of very nice knees. She was offered a drink . . . a coffee . . . 'No, no,' she declined, 'I have just come to introduce myself and make sure everything is in order for you. Are we all here?' We looked around at each other. 'Yes, I think so,' concluded Percy. 'You have your itineraries—' 'Bryan doesn't, he has lost his,' interrupted Stella. Ignoring Stella, she went on, '—you have your itineraries and tomorrow morning we shall visit Godavari Botanic Gardens, leaving here at 8.30 a.m. prompt. I am afraid I am a stickler for punctuality and the bus will not wait if you are not on time. I do hope you enjoyed your dinner, and now I must go, I have an engagement.' As she rose to go Bryan piped up with a conspiratorial smile, 'Got a date, have we, Susan?' She retorted sharply, 'What I do when I am not on duty is my business, Mr Lacey, I'll thank you to remember that,' and with a back like a ramrod she stalked out of the room. 'Who *does* she think she is?' Valerie wanted to know. 'Not like our Ken, is she?' grumbled Bryan. Richard just sat, looking very thoughtful.

The following morning I was up with the lark after a really good sleep. The day looked promisingly bright and sunny, birds twittering away outside, and I was off for an early breakfast, giving Bryan a knock as I passed his door. 'Come in,' he invited hopefully. 'On your bike, see you downstairs.' I was joined by Richard, and we enjoyed fresh croissants and endless coffee before Bryan arrived, looking half asleep, and then Percy and Valerie appeared looking as though they had not slept at all. As we gathered on the forecourt Susan was there, complete with clipboard, the blue skirt replaced by smart black trousers. We were on the bus in good time and at 8.30 a.m.

sharp Susan tapped the driver on the shoulder. 'OK, we can go.' 'Hey,' I called to her, 'Stella isn't here.' 'I am afraid we cannot wait,' insisted Susan. 'Then *I* shall get off the bus and wait for her.' And with that, I gathered up my stuff, shoved past her and got off. The bus left immediately, and within two or three minutes Stella appeared. 'I am so sorry,' she said, 'I got caught on the phone – Ian is having trouble with his ovens.' 'Well, there's not much you can do about it here, is there? Come on, we can get a cab.'

Godavari Botanic Gardens was about fifteen miles from our hotel, and the route itself was interesting, only because our cabbie took the trouble to tell us about it. Speaking good English, he was a charming young man and pointed out with pride the National Potato Improvement Centre, and then a Newar village, the site of a notorious temple where human sacrifices were apparently being carried out until the beginning of the twentieth century. It is still served, apparently, by priests of mystical leanings who dress in the old-fashioned long white pleated skirts, their uncut hair tied in buns. Fascinating stuff, and Stella and I looked out hoping to see one of these strange people. 'Perhaps they are not up yet,' she said, 'they won't have had a bus to catch.' We could see in the distance the Shanti Ban Buddha, a huge golden statue of the Buddha on a hillside behind the village, and then the Godavari Kunda – a sacred spring – and there on another hillside there were dozens of colourful prayer flags and a Tibetan monastery. Periodically, thousands of pilgrims visit this place to bathe and test their sin levels by trying to squeeze through a tiny gap in a rock.

The park itself was a peaceful green sanctuary, far removed from city dust and noise. The grounds were well maintained and had lovely exhibits of orchids, impossible-looking cacti of every shape and size, ferns and succulents, a lotus pond in full bloom and a Japanese garden. It was a paradise of rare and beautiful plants all in prime health, due to constant tender loving care and the advantage of this area receiving the highest rainfall in the Kathmandu valley during the monsoon season.

We caught up with the others enjoying a coffee near the herbarium, set in a quiet wooded area of the park. 'Where is Susan?' I asked. 'We left her at the entrance, and we are to return there at 12.30,' said Richard, 'but I am in no hurry, and I doubt we know the way back there anyway.' In the event, Susan was still waiting for us at 12.55, looking mighty testy and short-tempered. 'You are already late for lunch,' she said, heading towards the bus. Richard's next comment did not improve her disposition. 'We understand we have a free afternoon, so between us we have agreed that we would like to be dropped off in the city, where we shall have lunch in a local restaurant, if that's all right with you?' Susan gaped at him. 'You can't do that, the bus driver won't like it.' 'Tough,' said Richard, holding his ground, 'he is paid to do as he is told, and anyway, he will only have to stop once on his way back to the hotel.' With that, we all piled in behind Susan, who very reluctantly gave the driver his new instructions.

Lunch was fun. We sat on cushions round a low table and left it to Richard to choose the meal. We were served with a variety of à la carte individual dishes of traditional Nepali food. The meat, it turned out later, was either buffalo or goat or even wild boar, but whatever it was, served with a mixture of curried vegetables, pickles, yogurt (or curd?), crispy fried pancakes, rice, spicy potatoes, weird and wonderful steamed dumplings covered in hot sweet sauce, and piles of unleavened bread, it all went down a treat. Watching Valerie trying desperately to be dainty while eating with her fingers under instruction from a very obliging waiter was an absolute hoot! I reckoned Bryan was so good at it that he must eat with his fingers all the time at home. Give that man his due, he was really good natured about my digs at him. I said to him, 'You should be pleased you are getting so much of my attention.' 'Yeah, well,' he replied, 'I can think of better ways you can attend to me.' There was absolutely no answer to that.

Drinking the local booze was a matter that had to be approached warily, as I found out to my cost that afternoon. Encouraged by our men's approval of the locally produced Nepali beer, and in the absence of wine, I went the extra mile to try the harder stuff. *Arrak*, fermented from potatoes or grain, looked harmless enough, but in fact was a cross between firewater and paint stripper. A few sips of that and I could hardly breathe. 'Serves you right,' said Bryan. And so it did.

While we were gathered round the pool later in the afternoon, Richard disappeared for a few minutes and came back escorting Susan, who looked irritated and tense. Ordering more tea and placing a chair for her he said, 'There are one or two little matters we would like to run past you Susan, while we are still in the early stages of our last week on this trip.' 'I don't have much time' she said, as she sat bolt upright in her seat. I was amazed at Richard. He was normally quite reticent in his manner, always very pleasant, enjoying a joke and a chat, but he was not usually the first to voice an opinion or make a comment. Now he took the floor. 'First of all, it was very out of order that we left this morning leaving Mary and Stella behind,' he reproached her. 'Mary took the decision to get off the bus herself,' she retorted. 'Yes, she did, but it was your responsibility to ensure that Stella was not unwell. We are aware that we must let you know if we do not intend to turn up for a particular trip, but her room should have been checked before you left.' Susan opened her mouth to say something but Richard went on. 'And then, where was the tour guide? As you know, all our excursions are greatly enhanced by informed knowledge of the area.' 'We only went to the park,' Susan said hotly, 'and anyway, tour guides are not always available and when they are they are expensive.' Richard reminded her that the hotel receptionist kept a list of professional guides for every place we were likely to visit, and that the cost was borne by the client when paying for the holiday in the first place. 'You seem to know a lot about my job,' Susan flung at him. 'Yes, I do. I have worked for your company for many years, most recently in southern India. I'm now retired, and I'm on a hospitality trip as a guest. I do not intend that I shall be bullied into your standard of punctuality. I can assure you, none of us will let you down when time really matters.' Clearly miffed, Susan got up to go. 'Is there anything else?' she said. 'Yes.' Richard bowed courteously. 'We would be very pleased if you would join us for dinner.'

It had to be an early start the following day if we were to complete all the sightseeing planned for us. We congregated on the forecourt in good time and now we, together with a posh air-conditioned transit bus complete with driver, were waiting for Susan. Suddenly she appeared, accompanied by a drop-dead-gorgeous-looking middle-aged Nepali gentleman who turned out to be our brand-new tour guide. 'May I introduce Anwar – he has kindly agreed to escort us on our excursions.' (You may introduce him to *me* any time you like, I thought!) Susan was transformed. Still in the blue jacket but now worn over a pretty floral dress, she wore no stockings and only flat sandals. Gone were the brittle tones; she looked relaxed and comfortable as she settled into her seat. 'We are off,' she said, turning round to smile at us, 'to Swayambhunath, where the monkey temples are.'

At dinner the previous evening much had been achieved. We had placed her between Bryan and the Reverend Percy, and had made her laugh. We told her we understood her job must be difficult at times, and then she told us this was her first assignment in Nepal and she was finding the humid weather difficult to cope with. 'I have a horrible rash all across my stomach,' she confided. Bryan, never one to miss a trick, said, 'I have got just the right ointment for rashes in my room!' I butted in, 'Don't even go there!' I warned Susan, 'What he has in his room is shoe polish, and that won't do your rash any favours at all!' Caught in the crossfire of laughter, he was unable to add to his audacity, but just sat there enjoying the moment. Now the hatchet was truly buried.

It was only a short ride to our first destination where, leaving the city hustle for quieter neighbourhoods on the grungy banks of the Vishnumati River, we were to see one of the most recognisable symbols of Nepal. On top of a hill, offering fine views over Kathmandu and the valley, is a great stupa, the most sacred of Buddhist shrines, built and rebuilt over the centuries with no expense spared, and where fervent Newar Buddhists crowd together to pray at festival times. During the sacred summer month of *Gunla*, hundreds of pilgrims come here daily to worship – one act of worship here is said to carry 13 billion times more merit than elsewhere. Crumbs! Atop its soaring whitewashed dome, a gold-coloured block depicts the watchful, painted eyes of the Buddha gazing out across the valley in each direction, but first you have to get there, using the traditional pilgrim route – up 365 stone steps to the top.

The main gate to Swayambhunath, affectionately known as the Monkey Temple, is of brightly painted Tibetan-style plaster and there, enshrined in a small room, is a giant prayer wheel where Tibetans perform prostrations on the flat stone slabs beside the steps in front of three huge orange and yellow Buddhas carved out of stone blocks. Gamely, we approached the unforgiving staircase, but I had the strong impression that none of us aimed to get right to the top. I suppose we managed about half of the steep rise of the worn steps, but there were enough places to pause and rest under shady trees on the way up, as well as small Tibetan craft stalls to investigate, clusters of *chaityas* – small, delicately carved minor stupas – to admire, and the monkeys, dozens of them, yakking and screeching to each other, to amuse us as they endlessly ran up and down, playing the game of sliding down the railings. We had spotted a reviving cafe a little further up, and it was there that Susan and Anwar caught up with us. He was so interesting, and he sat under a small canopy drinking ice-cold Coke, telling us the fascinating history of Swayambhunath, which, legend has it, goes back over two thousand years. We hung on to his every word.

By the time we had made the slow descent, passing families going up with picnic baskets, and astrologers giving horoscopes, it was time to move on to our next port of call at Pashupatinath. Nepal's most sacred Hindu shrine, a sprawling collection of important Shiva temples raised over the centuries, stands on the banks of the holy Bagmati River on the eastern fringes of Kathmandu, drawing devotees and sadhus from all over India. The essence of Hinduism is found here, in a rich brew of pilgrims, yogis, priests and devotees, all worshipping Shiva in the form of Pashupati, 'Lord of the Beasts' and divine protector of Nepal.

Pashupatinath's supreme holiness is due partly to its location on the banks of the sacred, if slimy, Bagmati River. Not much more than a trickle in the dry winter months, the blackened waters flow past stone ghats where worshippers and mourners mingle with pilgrims doing their laundry and dishwashing. Devout Hindus plunge into the murky waters, immersing themselves, much as they do in the Ganges, to assure themselves of release from the cycle of rebirth. Given the extremely polluted state of these waters, I imagine it could also hasten progress out of their present life!

The river is also a sacred cremation site. Shrouded in cloth and placed on a bamboo litter, the bodies are delivered by barefoot pallbearers, accompanied by male relatives. The eldest son, if there is one, performs the rites to ensure the soul a smooth transition into the next world. The body is placed on a log pyre, and the white-clad mourners retreat to a nearby porch to watch its slow destruction. Later, the ashes are swept into the river, which eventually joins the Ganges.

Susan had excelled herself. She had organised a packed lunch from the hotel, including a cooler with fruit drinks and bottled water, and had arranged for the driver to take us to the riverbanks, where from the terraced hillside we could look down into the Pashupatinath Temple and the surrounding area. On our way we passed the Panch Deval – 'Five Temples'. Anwar told us that from being a shrine complex it had now been converted into a social welfare centre, a place to help the local elderly who were deemed destitute. Without a family, old people are left to exist without any support from any quarter, and from what I saw in and around the city, there are many of them looking very frail, very tired and certainly very hungry.

The air up there on the hillside was clean and cool, a restful place to have our picnic. We could see below the ripening fields of farmland, and small settlements dotting the countryside, the houses huddled together to maximise precious land. The temple of Pashupatinath, with its golden spires and stacked roofs of pagodas, was an amazing sight, and the shimmering track of the sacred river was infinitely more appealing from the hillside than it was at its banks. The remaining forests of oak and bamboo, and the flowering rhododendrons, now depleted from what they once were due to the increasing demands for fuel wood, were behind us and the mountains were visible in the hazy distance. With few people about it was a lovely spot, but we could not linger too long: we had one more historical place to visit before we were finished for the day.

Boudhanath, on the eastern side of Kathmandu, is home to one of the world's largest stupas, and the village, known as Boudha, is the religious centre for Nepal's population of Tibetan exiles. Simple, massive and powerful, the Great Stupa of Boudhanath rises above a huddle of buildings, its huge, bow-shaped, hooded and painted eyes gazing solemnly into the distance. The narrow side streets are full of maroon-robed Tibetan monks, shiny monastery roofs and shops full of Tibetan texts and yak butter. Among the most important Buddhist sites in Nepal, Boudha draws a cross section of society, including Himalayan pilgrims; tall Khampas from Tibet carrying big knives and with red tassels woven into their hair, Ladakhi women with seed-pearl earrings and winged hats, and others from remote Nepali regions wrapped in striped blankets. For all that, Boudha is a squalid mixture of muddy roads, heaps of rubbish and groups of shanty dwellings.

The Great Stupa itself, however, remains a magical sight, particularly at dusk when the long horns blown from monastery roofs resound with their deep booming tones, and the gathering crowds circle the stupa in a steady stream of murmured prayers and creaking prayer wheels. It creates an atmosphere of cultural timelessness and spiritual curiosity; even I felt an uncanny presence which I could not even begin to explain at the time.

Around the stupa are shops that used to house Newar gold- and silversmiths fashioning Tibetan jewellery and ritual pieces. Today, although some have resorted to the sale of junky souvenirs, there are still places where good antiques and old carpets can be bought – at a price, of course. On the way back to our transport taking us to the hotel, we went through the back streets where skilled metalworkers were hammering at silver altar bowls, carpenters were carving wooden tables, and women were expertly knotting woollen carpets. It was tempting to buy a trinket or two, but all of us were too tired to think about it, our heads full of history and strange cultures; there is only so much anyone can absorb in a day.

25

After our long day of sightseeing, we had a day of leisure before going on the trek, that was starting at Nagarkot, a small hilltop village at the edge of the Kathmandu Valley, from where it was planned that we would take a two-day hike into the foothills, staying overnight in a lodge. In the meantime it was lovely to spend time hanging around the pool having an occasional swim, reading or chatting, or simply getting ourselves together for the energetic couple of days ahead.

I was in good company; although we were not necessarily like-minded all the time, all of us were there for our own reasons. Increasingly I felt myself in an encircling cocoon of friendship where it was possible to stay as private as felt right for myself, even in the close company of others. This suited me, for as much as I enjoyed the good-natured banter and humour that had developed between us, I was not particularly interested in the intimate details of their lives, nor did I want to get involved in them. However, although we are taught in childhood not to remark on the remarkable, age and practical experience allows us to at least sometimes question what is different or unusual if we want to without fear of intrusion, because by now, hopefully, we have learned the art of diplomacy and respect. For that reason alone, it became possible for us to all get on very well together.

We were prepared for two days' hiking to Sundarijal from Nagarkot, ascending to around 2,000 metres, on a trail that follows the valley's rim, with an overnight stop in a village inn. We were up and ready to go before dawn – in time, we hoped, to see the sun rise over the Himalayas from Nagarkot village, located about 30 kilometres east of Kathmandu. Good comfortable walking shoes, practical clothing, a warm jacket or jumper for what could be a chilly night, and anything else we might need carried in a rucksack was the order of the day.

Bryan was ready, waiting in reception, unbelievably smartly dressed in a tweed jacket, collar and tie, with polished shoes and dragging a small suitcase on a long handle. I was aghast. '*Where* do you think you are *going*?' I said to him. 'Whaddaya mean, where am I going? I am coming with you.' There was no time to argue. 'Get in the bus and give me your keys, you can change your clothes on the way.' I left it to Stella to tell him how unsuitably clad he was and how absurd it was for him to think he could drag a suitcase about on rough, rocky trails. In his room I found amongst a pile of clothes on the floor his usual sensible walking shoes, thick socks, long shorts, anorak and the little backpack he normally carried. I was back in no time. Everybody was in stitches as poor Bryan was sent to the back seat to change his clothes. 'I *told* you I had lost my itinerary,' he bleated to Susan. We tried to empty his suitcase into the backpack, but even only allowing for the loo roll (which he adamantly refused to part with), his packed lunch and a water bottle, it was quite obvious the bag was not big enough. Anwar was brilliant. 'Don't worry,' he said, 'we can buy one more suitable in the village.'

We arrived at Nagarkot just before dawn, and as the night gave way to day, we watched as the sun slowly rose above the mountains, a pale, buttery light spreading from the east, glinting on the snowy peaks. Gradually the blurred shades of grey and blue and ochre in the sky were absorbed by the brilliance of the sun's rays, throwing a wide, magnificent, golden panorama of light reaching from one end to the other of the mountain range and beyond. The sight was utterly breathtaking.

We had breakfast before starting the uphill walk south of the village towards a lookout tower on a ridge. The trail was little more than a dirt track to begin with, but before long we were on rougher stony ground, the rise not particularly steep but difficult to walk on. Here and there were junctions for other trails, and without our special trekking guide, it would have become very confusing. The surrounding countryside, with its rich kaleidoscope of different-coloured wild flowers against a serene backdrop of verdant meadows, was quiet and peaceful, but our attention was on that path; we walked for a good hour or so before stopping to rest, just below the lookout tower. Sitting on little hillocks of coarse, tufty grass, we could see a vibrant vista of hills and valleys below us, a canvas of strong greens and yellows, the dark blue of pine trees in the distance, set against the red earth. Little huddles of secluded farmsteads were scattered across the countryside, and around them lay the terraces of cultivated land. It was a different world; in spite of its isolation, it seemed there was a rhythm of life that must have prevailed here for thousands of years.

We continued to walk uphill on a dirt track covered in shale and stones towards a pine forest until we reached the top of the ridge. High enough now to see for miles around, the wonderful views over the valley to the Himalayas, we followed the ridgeline, passing the odd hamlet or two until gradually we were descending to the village of Changunarayan. Nearby, in this unlikely place was a beautiful and historic temple, Changu Narayan. Standing on a hilltop, it dates from the very early 18th century, when it was rebuilt after a fire, but its origins go back to between the 4th and the 9th centuries, and many of the stone sculptures date from that time. It is an extraordinary building, with its double roof and intricate roof struts on which are depicted gods, reincarnations of man-birds with snakes around their necks. Stone lions guard the wonderfully gilded door flanked by detailed gilded windows. Ancient images cast in stone are dotted around in the courtyard, set in scenes depicting the underworld, the world of man and the heavens. One of these images is said to be 1,500 years old.

Enterprising locals had set up a small covered arcade near the temple to serve tea and cold water from an icebox connected to a Calor gas bottle, and we took the opportunity to rest here and eat our picnic lunch before tackling any more hiking. The air was thin and clean where we sat. A silky grey mist stretched here and there across the valley below, and as I lay back on the grass I could see high fluffy clouds drifting above across a clear blue sky. It was a few minutes of bliss I could not have shared with anyone – well, yes I could, but he wasn't here any more – treasured moments of a deep sense of peace and tranquillity.

We took a short and steep path upward before descending again to walk across fields to the Manohara River, which in the monsoon season, has to be waded across, but for us the temporary bridge was open. I hate temporary bridges. This one was particularly primitive – it was a contraption of wooden planks supported by netting, with ropes serving as handrails which were spaced almost too far apart for me to reach. Crossing it was horrible; the bridge swayed and tipped with the movement of people on it, and I was terrified. I prayed that we would not be obliged to do it again on the way back! We were heading towards Bhotichaur, where it was planned that we would stay overnight in a village inn.

Well away from the sprawl of Nagarkot, this small inn had the feel of a rural retreat. It only had fifteen rooms, some of which were quite basic bamboo cabins, while others were larger cottage-style rooms. All had simple shower and toilet facilities, adequate for an overnight stop. The proprietors were a friendly couple, anxious to please and to be sure we were comfortable. Were we happy with our cabins? Of course we were – dog-tired, with aching bones weary from unaccustomed exercise, that night we would have dossed down anywhere that was warm and dry. We were shown into the restaurant, with plain wooden chairs set at plain wooden tables, lit by candles, and leading to a small verandah with wooden benches to sit on. We were supplied with a kettle of tea, small glasses and wine, served from plain glass bottles. I eyed it dubiously, but not one to hold back in such matters, I had to try it. Tell you what – whether it was the mood or the need I don't know, but it was delicious! Asking about food, we were told that if we would be so kind as to tell them what we would like, we could have it, once they had cooked it! We looked helplessly at our guide, who after speaking to them in an unintelligible language, sent them off, seemingly happy to follow his instructions.

As we waited for our food to be cooked the sun began to set, illuminating the distant mountain scene and the valley below the ridge to a deep, vivid rose. It seemed at that moment the whole world was aglow. As I reluctantly turned away to go in for dinner, I tried to etch the scene on my mind so that I could recall it again and again, to tell it as it was. By now it was turning chilly and I was glad of my new warm Kashmir jumper, bought for a comparative pittance in the old city bazaar. I was almost too tired to eat the good, plain food served to us, but the whole family was standing by to watch us eating with specially provided plastic knives and forks, while we made genuine complimentary noises of appreciation.

It was to be another long day tomorrow. Bryan gave me a nice kiss as we bade each other goodnight. 'Thank you for sorting out my stuff this morning. Have I got a clean pair of socks?' Glancing down at his feet, and through gritted teeth, I said, 'Put it this way, sunshine, if you haven't, please make a point of keeping well clear of me all day tomorrow.' He went off to his bed laughing his silly head off.

Well rested, and up early with only a couple of minor blisters to attend to, I spent a heavenly hour catching up on my journal and absorbing the sight of the gentle hills and the open space around the inn. The sun was up by now, radiant in a glittering blue sky. Caught between the wooden struts of the verandah, the dew sparkled on a perfectly formed spider's web, with a big attentive spider at the ready to pounce on the first luckless insect that would, sooner or later, be ensnared in that beautifully crafted trap.

We were prepared for a three-to-four hour walk, depending on how many times we would have to go up before making the final descent. In the event, the few inclines were fairly gradual. Starting on a rough trail, we threaded our way upwards through a small forest, where in the spring it must have been quite lovely, full of rhododendrons and orchids; then down onto a dirt path that led across a field, and up again to enter a small village perched on the hillside.

This was a Newar village, which was made up of no more than five or six houses. The inhabitants came out to greet us, led by a gentleman who turned out to be the village elder. It was as if he hadn't seen anyone for months, so wide was his smile as he warmly shook hands with all of us in turn. He was short and thin, his wizened skin the colour of leather. He had three large brown teeth which did nothing to detract from his happy, cheerful face. He wore a white (well, I imagine it had been white at some time) pillbox cap and a faded red tie-dyed collarless shirt over a cloth wrap-around skirt, his skinny legs supported by heavy boots. He was joined by two younger men and a small horde of solemn, staring children, all in grubby vests or well-worn T-shirts, some wearing pants, some not, but all, it seemed to me, coming from one family. In spite of their varying ages, they all looked so alike with their heavy-jawed, flat-faced features.

There are many villages and hamlets scattered in and around the hills and valleys of Nepal, and in most of them, life has changed very little over the centuries. The people are still dependent on growing their own food, building their houses from local materials, relying very little on money, and they seldom see much of the world outside their own particular area. The houses here were really quite charming, built of wood and a kind of cemented mud, with grass thatched roofs. Each had an outside low wooden deck, where underneath, free-range chickens pecked at the cindered earth. I noticed a huddled figure sitting in the corner of one of these decks, wrapped in what appeared to be a big white blanket. I asked the village elder (through translation by our guide) who he was, and whether he was ill. 'He is my father and yes, he is very ill, he is dying. We leave him alone in peace to die.' By now this same gentleman had spotted my pack of Silk Cut cigarettes tucked in my shirt pocket. Would I exchange one of my cigarettes for a blow on his hookah pipe?

We were ambling towards a small field where a yak and a couple of bullocks grazed, a goat was tethered to a tree, and where more chickens scrabbled around. The children followed us and the elders followed them, to point out to us the duck pond and the fertile terraces where their food was grown. It was a very impressive sight, with potato and barley, green vegetables, corn on the cob and millet all flourishing as a result of the extremely hard task of working these unrelenting high terraced fields. It was a tiny glimpse of timeless rural reality. It brought home to me how people in the West think they know about poverty and some will even claim to be poor. They don't know the half of it. Here in the hill districts of Nepal, half of all the farming families suffer from chronic nutrition deficits, unable to produce enough food to last through the lean months of spring, when, if they are lucky, they may get a single, very basic meal a day.

We left these nice people to continue our journey on a hard, flinty path towards Nala and then on to Banepa, where we would pick up the bus to take us back to Kathmandu. In the meantime, we had plenty of hiking to do. Going up the hills was a strain on our thighs, calf muscles and our lungs – although still bursting with a sense of adventure, we were not a young and lusty group, though we had optimistically assumed we were fit enough to tackle this comparatively short trek. Descending the trail was another matter: it was more precipitous, more difficult to negotiate without slipping and sliding on the loose surface, and very hard on the knees and lower back. We took it slowly, with Valerie and Percy taking the lead, holding hands and looking decidedly moony.

Suddenly there was a chilling screech from the front. 'Come, come quickly, Percy is *injured*!' Valerie was screaming like a demented banshee as she stooped over his prostrate body lying stretched out on the path. The rest of us slithered down to see him. 'Oh, *do* help him,' she implored, her eyes brimming with tears. Percy had obviously slipped quite heavily but was soon sitting up, brushing himself down and complaining about his ankle. 'Don't move my darling,' she cried, 'you may have done *untold* damage, we must get you to hospital *immediately*!' We all looked at each other. A hospital? Here? Immediately? Fat chance! 'Don't fret so my dear,' Percy said soothingly, 'it's only my foot, I'm sure I can manage.' Well, he couldn't. He was unable to put his foot on the ground, much less walk on this steeply descending path. 'Stay here,' said our trek guide, 'I will be back very shortly.' And he was, complete with two young men from the village, two bamboo poles and a large sack. One side of the sack was cut down, with holes made to allow Percy to poke his arms through while sitting in what was now a sling tied between the poles. No problem, the villagers carried the poles over their shoulders and we were all off again, staggering down the track with our casualty helplessly swinging backwards and forwards in his makeshift carrier. It was very hard for us not to see the funny side of the situation – poor old Reverend Percy with his arms and legs sticking out of the sack, while all the time Valerie clucked and fussed around him like an overzealous mother hen. 'I don't know what your congregation would say if they could see you now,' said Richard, trying not to laugh.

We had a quick whip-round to give money to those very kind boys from the village as we hoisted Percy, poles and all, into the transit van waiting to collect us for the return trip to the hotel. Susan immediately arranged for a doctor to attend to him, and after a thorough examination he determined that Percy had a badly sprained ankle and that he needed to rest. So did we all, except Bryan, who was the only one still hail and hearty, no blisters, and no aches and pains. 'It's because I come from good country stock,' he boasted, 'not like you weak-kneed townies' he said looking pointedly at me.

This was to be our last night in the Kathmandu hotel. The following day we hoped to do one more sightseeing tour and maybe pay a last visit to the old city before catching the evening flight back to Delhi en route to London. In the meantime, Susan had arranged a lavish farewell dinner for us.

I would probably not see any of these people again after tomorrow, but for the moment they were dear friends, bonded by mutual experience, dry humour and a total lack of pretension. Each of us, in our different ways, had shared a watershed in our lives, and we would all have a place in each other's individual memories of this trip to India and Nepal, dining together that evening was a joyous treasure for us to keep.

We had planned a full day before leaving Kathmandu. With our incredibly well-informed guide Anwar still with us, we were to visit Kirtipur for a couple of hours during the morning and then to on a proper tour of the old city of Kathmandu. None of it, we hoped, would involve too much walking!

The small fortress town of Kirtipur is strung out along a ridge only five kilometres southwest of the capital, but it still retains an unhurried, timeless air. Its impressive temples, although many now suffering from decay and mildew, nevertheless hark back to a golden age that has long since passed. In the eighteenth-century campaign to conquer the valley, Kirtipur was targeted and attacked by Prithvi Narayan Shah. After several bitter attacks and a long drawn-out siege, the king and his troops finally succeeded in capturing the town in 1766. However, incensed by the long struggle, and in revenge for the death of his brother during the resistance, the king ordered that the nose and lips of every male over 12 years old in Kirtipur should be cut off, exempting – because apparently he was a talented musician himself – only the players of wind instruments. The inhabitants of the town had paid dearly for their courageous endurance; maybe that is what accounts for the fact that to this day, they are not particularly friendly.

After this bloody episode, not surprisingly Kirtipur drifted into decline. Many of the buildings are crumbling, the streets are dirty, and a general atmosphere of seediness prevails. Some of the original temples and palaces have been turned into offices, the lovely classical gardens gone to waste, strangled by weeds and now merely a place to dump building materials. It is a crying shame that so many beautiful buildings are being left to rot or to be destroyed to make way for modern concrete structures. The rich and powerful architects of the past will be remembered for their good taste, but unfortunately, today's builders in many cases will be remembered for the lack of it. The whole place seemed a bit depressed, although signs of cottage industry were apparent in the form of dyed yarn hanging from upstairs windows and the background clatter of handlooms, where woven cloth and carpets were being crafted in people's homes. We were not sorry to leave Kirtipur, although we were glad that we had been there, if only to hear about its interesting and sometimes bizarre history from our brilliant Anwar.

We had found a gem in this man. Intelligent and well-educated, courteous and patient, he was never boring, never salacious about the more brutal aspects of his country's past, and his clearly spoken commentaries on the historical chronicles and traditional history were riveting. His own philosophical views would sometimes be revealed when, in answer to our questions, he would make thoughtful comparisons between eastern and western cultures. Responding to our appalled reaction to the barbaric treatment of the Kirtipur inhabitants all those years ago, he said, 'Barbaric behaviour has never been confined to the East, you know – one has only to think of our living memory of the Holocaust, a more subtle method of cruelty perhaps, but still a massive example of western inhumanity. It is always hoped, of course, that the peoples of the world will one day learn something from their mistakes.' Never judgmental but he always left us with something to think about. Apart from all that, he was so *dishy!*

We were driven back towards Kathmandu, where, although we had walked around the old city several times, we were anxious to learn a little more of the history surrounding the ancient buildings clustered around the majestic Durbar Square. Evidently there are more than fifty monuments around the Square, the oldest dating back to the 12th century, when the area was already an important centre at the junction of two major trade routes. Many of the temples there today are more recent, maybe three or four centuries old. Others date from the 17th and 18th centuries, and some were damaged by the great earthquake of 1934 and rebuilt, not necessarily in their original form. Durbar Square was where the city's kings were once crowned, and although no king presently lives there, it remains the traditional heart of old Kathmandu.

It is here, in the Kumari Bahal, a richly decorated, red-brick, three-storey building, that was home to the Kumari Devi, at least for the length of her reign. Built in 1757 in the style of a Buddhist monastery, it has a three-storey courtyard enclosed by magnificently carved wooden balconies and gilded windows over the entrance.

A living Goddess, the Kumari Devi, a Buddhist Newar girl, is worshipped as the incarnation of the Hindu Goddess Durga (for Taleju in Nepalist). Even the King of Nepal bows before Kathmandu's Royal Kumari because she apparently has the power to confirm his rule for the coming year. There are all sorts of legends surrounding the origins of Kumari worship, dating back at least to the 16th century, but whatever the background, in reality there are several living goddesses around the Kathmandu Valley, although none are as important as the Kumari Devi.

She is initially chosen from a high Newar caste made up of gold- and silversmiths. Five high priests conduct the search for a likely candidate, a girl child who shows promise of the '32 perfections'. These 'perfections' could be anything from the colour of her skin or her eyes, to the shape of her teeth. Her horoscope must also coincide with that of the King, to avoid future confrontation. The child will be between three and four years old and the final candidates will be tested by being left in a darkened room filled with grotesque and bloody buffalo heads, where terrifying noises are made, while men dance in horrific masks. Naturally none of this would frighten a real goddess, so the one who remains calm and collected throughout this ordeal is selected to be the new Kumari.

The successful candidate is then installed in the Taleju temple, where she is subjected to a secret ritual as the spirit of the fierce Goddess Durga slowly possesses her body. She is finally incarcerated in the Kumari Bahal, where she lives a sheltered, pampered life, cared for by doting attendants who bathe her and dress her in a red robe and ritual jewellery; her eyes are painted in black khol and the third eye is placed on her forehead. She is not allowed to play outside, for her feet must never touch the ground, though occasionally she will make an appearance at a beautifully carved wooden window, and she also makes a few ceremonial forays into the outside world each year. At her own special festival, the Kumari Jatra, she is carried by attendants to her chariot, which is then dragged through the streets of the city so that this regal little girl, enthroned on her wheeled shrine, can give her blessings to the crowds gathered in the streets.

The child's reign ends at the first sign of menstruation, when the spirit of Durga is deemed to have left her body, and her divine status is lost. The ex-Goddess is then sent back to her village to lead a normal life, uneducated and unmarriagable, with only a comparatively small stipend for her trouble.

I tell you, folks, it was hard for us westerners to take all this seriously, but when told the story by Anwar in his impartial 'once upon a time, there was a little girl . . .' way of speaking, we listened attentively, having by now learned to respect the ways and traditions of his country.

I was very, very sorry to have to say goodbye to this man, we had learned so much from him. It was not only his country we had learned to respect, he himself had gained our immense regard and admiration. Before he left us, and feeling that he might be offended with a gift of money, we all found a small way of showing our appreciation for his work. Richard gave him a fold-up umbrella; Bryan, under pressure, wrapped up his beloved Harrods tie which he had worn a few times on 'special occasions'; the Reverend Percy and Valerie gave him a little jewelled autograph book which we had all signed; and Stella and I hurriedly managed to get a photo printed of the group with Anwar standing with us, which we had fitted into a very pretty frame. We placed money in an envelope, 'donated', we told him, 'for your children', and that, complete with a big bag of sweets, was how we tried to show our thanks. He was utterly overwhelmed. He kissed us girls, shook hands with the men, and that was it; merging into the now-familiar sights and sounds, the exotic spicy smells of cumin, turmeric and cloves of the old city of Kathmandu, he was gone. A totally unforgettable character, as was Kathmandu, and as was the whole splendour of Nepal itself.

26

Who will live in our house
After we've gone?
Will they have green plastic
Instead of a lawn?

Who will live in our house
After the wars?
Will there be mutations
That crawl on all fours?

Will the shiny robot workers
Be dreaming strange new dreams?
Will the pigeons, big as turkeys
Roost on our ancient beams?

Who will use our kitchen?
What will they cook?
Who will sleep in our room
And how will they look?

Will they feel our ghosts disturbing
Their cybernetic years
With the echoes of all our laughter
And the shadow of our tears?

Will there still be lovers?
Who will sing our songs?
Who will live in our house
After we have gone?

Mary Edmonds, *Reflections 1996*

I felt as though I had been transported home on a magic carpet, as if in a dream, and brought back to where I started, where the house would be full of children, my dogs and my cats, and the garden enhanced by the colour of full-blown roses, the smell of lavender and thyme, the lawn covered with the debris of daytime activity. But it wasn't a dream, no one was there, the garden was a disorganised mess of overgrown shrubs, dandelions and daisies growing recklessly among the profusion of weeds between the flagstones and over the uncut grass. I had gone off in a hurry on my latest trip to foreign parts, leaving garden furniture and tools exposed to the elements, and all had deteriorated through being left out during persistent rain.

If I needed the immediate companionship of my family on my return, then I had picked a bad time. My daughters were abroad and my sons were working away, and there was nobody about to greet me this time. Somehow though, strangely, this time I didn't mind. Although I felt disembodied, dispersed, scattered, with my head still in those mystical places I had seen, this temporary quietude promised to give me a chance to mull over my recent personal encounters, my still-fresh memories of that other world I had so recently left, and to understand what had really happened to me as a consequence of it.

The peace was soon shattered. The telephone rang. For nearly a month I had not heard its loud, shrill tones and it made me jump. It was Stephen. 'You OK, Ma? Enjoy your holiday?' 'Yes, thank you, it was lovely.' Lovely? How inadequate was that? 'Good, see you soon. Mind how you go.' One down, three to go.

Only a short time elapsed. 'Hi Ma, you OK?' 'Yes, I am fine.' It was Nicolas. 'That's all right then, be home tomorrow, catch up with you then. Bye.' Short and sweet, that's my boys. Two down, two to go.

In no time it was Jacqui. 'You're back then – how was India?' A few years ago, barely out of her teens, she had bravely travelled the hard way, the long overland journey across Europe to reach Delhi. 'I don't think much has changed since you were there, but I found it quite exciting.' Quite exciting? I think I found it a bit more than that. 'Got to go,' she said, 'be over at the weekend. Bye.'

I had to wait a while before hearing from Fiona. 'I thought you *must* be back by now. Have a good time? Bring back a maharaja did you?' 'No dear, not for want of trying though,' I said, going along with the daft idea. 'You must be slipping. Well, take care, talk to you soon. Love you. Bye.'

It was enough for the time being; they had all touched base, and I knew they cared. I was left to resume my reveries in solitude. What I would have given just then to have had just one hour to talk with that lovely man I had lost, a thought that had occupied my mind so many times before. Now though, it was different – I found it not so difficult to realise that I could make my peace with knowing this will never happen. Instead, I remembered something that a dear friend once said to me. He said, 'You know, Mary, when people die we are supposed to assume that they go up to heaven, but I don't think that is the case. I believe they stay all around us, in the trees where the birds sing, and in the whisper of the breeze that ruffles our hair, or in the glow of a beautiful sunset, they are there, watching and guiding us and nudging us in the direction that is right for us.' I so wanted it to be true then, and now I really believed it. At that moment, I felt an overwhelming sense of gratitude; the perpetual ache had gone, my heart felt whole again, and I knew that although my life had irrevocably changed, I could create a kind happiness for myself without feeling I had torn up the roots of love.

At last I can admit that there are times when I actually enjoy my own company and not being dependent on anyone else. I can play or listen to my music, turning it up as loud as it is meant to be heard; I can read a book until the early hours; I can go to bed or get up when I like, eat when I like, go out or come in when I like, or push off altogether if I want to. Being alone is not the same as loneliness – that ghastly, desperate need for the company of others. I have rarely felt lonely, but for so long being alone meant to me a constant floundering to cope with everyday decisions, being unable to share intimate conversations with the one person whose integrity and judgement I trusted most, and having no one to hug me just because I was there.

Happiness is such a transient, fleeting state of mind; sometimes it can last for only a moment, and I had many such moments in India and Nepal. The pleasure and smiles on the faces of those little Indian village children, holding our hands whilst with such pride they showed us round their first, brand-new schoolroom, their eyes lighting up when accepting our modest gifts; the sight of that glorious, eternal monument to love, the Taj Mahal, bathed in gold at sunset; the excitement of Kathmandu, its atmosphere, its history, the dark, mysterious alleyways, the thrill of the bazaars, the strange religious sites and rituals, and the sheer beauty of its countryside. How privileged, how fortunate was I to have had the opportunity to see the Himalayas in all their splendid magnificence, to walk in the clean, unpolluted air of the foothills, to meet the friendly, unsophisticated farmers and their families, and above all, to witness the splendour of the early-morning sun rising out of that huge, endless sky, with the spectacular snow-capped mountains in the distance glinting in the light of a new day. All that, together with the delightful company of the courteous and wise Anwar, and the dry humour, banter and, ultimately, affection of my travelling companions, could do nothing other than provide me with profound moments of happiness.

At home again I can look forward to those other precious moments of joy – watching the antics of my beloved grandchildren playing happily together; sharing the pride of their parents doing their level best to take tender loving care in their upbringing; and catching up with the friends and family who love me – warts and all!

I began to unpack, sorting stuff out into piles – gifts and souvenirs, dirty washing, clothes and silly shoes I never wore. It seemed that by tidying my belongings I was tidying my mind, until finally I fished out my journal. It was not, I have to admit, a meticulous account of my journey, but I began to think it was enough to consider the prospect of realising another distant dream, long buried under a mound of excuses – I never had the time, or the space, there were too many other priorities, or too much else to think about. Now I have no such excuses. I must get on with it. Yeah, that's what I'll do, I will get on with it, I will write a book . . .